W9-BZD-549

Han Suyin is the daughter of a Belgian mother and a Chinese father who, a Mandarin and scholar entitled to enter the Imperial Academy, had chosen instead at the age of nineteen to travel on a scholarship to Europe.

She was moved by the poverty and sickness she saw around her to take up medicine. She studied Chinese classics and mathematics while waiting for a place at Yenching University. Then, after completing her pre-medical education, she travelled across Siberia to Europe on a scholarship and continued her studies at the University of Brussels. In 1938 she returned to China, married an ex-Sandhurst Chinese officer, who later became a general in Chiang Kai Shek's army, and practised midwifery in the interior during the Sino-Japanese War. From this experience she wrote her first book, *Destination Chungking*, in 1940. In 1942 she came to London, where her husband had been appointed military attaché. Three years later he returned to active service in China, leaving Han Suyin to complete her medical studies in London. After her husband was killed in 1947, she spent a year as house surgeon at the Royal Free Hospital before accepting a doctor's post in Hong Kong. There she wrote the Eurasian love story (her own) that brought her international acclaim and success as a writer. The *Sunday Times* describes *A Many-Splendoured Thing* as 'an astounding love story . . . brilliantly topical, but far more than that, for she handles an eternal theme with power, insight and unfailing artistry'.

Since that time she has written numerous books, both novels and non-fiction. Her combined autobiography and history of China in five volumes, has been hailed as an important contribution to international understanding. Bertrand Russell said of the first volume, *The Crippled Tree*, 'during the many hours I spent reading it, I learnt more about China than I did in a whole year spent in that country'.

By the same author

China: Autobiography, History

The Crippled Tree
A Mortal Flower
Birdless Summer
My House Has Two Doors

Novels

A Many-Splendoured Thing
Destination Chungking
. . . And the Rain My Drink
The Mountain is Young
Cast But One Shadow and *Winter Love*
Two Loves
The Four Faces

Non-Fiction

China in the Year 2001
Asia Today
Lhasa, The Open City
The Morning Deluge: Mao Tsetung and the Chinese Revolution 1893–1953
Wind in the Tower: Mao Tsetung and the Chinese Revolution 1949–1975

HAN SUYIN

Phoenix Harvest

Volume 2 of My House Has Two Doors

China: Autobiography, History, Book 5

TRIAD
PANTHER

Published by Triad/Granada in 1982
Reprinted 1985

Triad Paperbacks Ltd is an imprint of
Chatto, Bodley Head & Jonathan Cape Ltd and
Granada Publishing Ltd

First published in Great Britain by
Jonathan Cape Ltd 1980
Copyright © Han Suyin 1980

My House Has Two Doors was originally
published as one volume under this title.
In Triad Paperbacks it is published in
two volumes: Vol 1 *My House Has Two Doors*
                    Vol 2 *Phoenix Harvest*

ISBN 0-586-05414-6

Printed and bound in Great Britain by
Cox and Wyman Ltd, Reading

Set in Times

Contents

1966–1979

CHAPTER 1

The Lowering Sky – The Cultural Revolution: 1966

In January 1966 I went to Peking for ten days, because I had been invited to a seminar to be held on China at Chicago University. At least five such seminars were taking place in mid-western cities of the United States that year. I wanted to glean the latest thinking in Peking.

I filled a notebook with interviews on China's policies, on economics, and became thoroughly confused. I was not able to see Chou Enlai. Little did I then know that the most intense confrontation was occuring at the top, between Mao Tsetung and Liu Shaochi; no leaders were therefore available for interviews, and no interview could provide a definitive statement. I fell back on two sentences which I could relate to Premier Chou: 'The United States sooner or later will have to reappraise its foreign policy, because there is no direct conflict of interest between us,' and 'The period before us is one of crises, great upheavals and great changes and reversals. The US will have to readjust its views on its own role in the world . . .' Not very much to go on.

Kung Peng, and Tang Mingchao, who had been educated in America,* were interested by the new hesitations in America, eager to know the result of the symposia. 'It takes a long rope to catch a whale . . .' said Tang Mingchao. 'America's press seems to have much power . . . it is really a separate force,' said Kung Peng. And added, 'A tree does not grow upon bare rock.'

Mao in his interview with Edgar Snow† had been noncommittal. I had no opportunity to find out about the intense Party struggle that was going on; the pall of secrecy

---

*Later in the Secretariat at the United Nations.
†See Edgar Snow's article in the *New Republic*, February 27th, 1965: 'Interview with Mao Tsetung'.

was clamped upon all hints. Hualan, not high enough in the cadre hierarchy to know, could only say that there would be another rectification movement 'in art and literature and also in education'. The Party establishment still envisaged the Cultural Revolution as merely another political campaign, of the style so customary in China.

Hualan's sister had returned from another stint in the rural areas, of 'socialist education' and the 'four cleans' in the countryside. The skin of her face was rough and her finger joints thickened with rheumatism. 'My job was to try to break down feudal and capitalist ideas . . . I've had very little time to paint . . .' Many hundreds of thousands of cadres, intellectuals and students had 'gone down' in teams for this work. She was looking forward to teaching and painting again, 'But at the moment we are having a great many political study classes on Mao Tsetung Thought.' She added, 'We are taking the army as a model.' Hualan was full of enthusiasm. 'It is very important: we are fighting revisionism in all its forms.' The ballet, *The White-Haired Girl*, had been performed. It dated back to 1944 in Yenan, when it had been created (the music leaned heavily on Tchaikovsky). 'Our workers–peasants–soldiers don't like Western ballet, they don't understand it. They want ballet, opera, with which they can identify, such as this one.' A young man who was to dance the role of the Prince in *Swan Lake* came from a poor peasant family; he had rejected the role; he felt he was 'throwing away the face' of his family by dancing as a prince . . . 'Only after the dancers have been to the villages can they put real emotion into the scenes of our new ballets and operas,' said Hualan.

There was hushed talk among the writers of the criticism of a theatre piece by the Vice-Mayor of Peking, Wu Han. In November 1965 a literary critic from Shanghai, Yao Wenyuan, already known for his acerbic condemnations of rightists in 1957, had written a long and scathing attack against Peking Vice-Mayor Wu Han's theatre play *Hai Jui is Dismissed from Office*. Hai Jui, an honest Ming dynasty

(1368 to 1644) official, had upbraided the Emperor for not listening to the people. Now it was rumoured that his 'historical play', first shown in 1960, was a plea for the rehabilitation of Minister of Defence Peng Tehuai, who in August 1959 had openly criticized the Leap.

At dinner with some friends, the distinguished chief editor of the People's Literature Printing Press, Yen Wenching, asked me what I thought of *Hai Jui*. I replied truthfully that I had not seen the play. Historical subjects, articles about personages who had died many centuries ago, were vehicles for expressing present-day situations, events and people. This had always been done in China, and it continued to be done. But now not only Vice-Mayor Wu Han, but many other historians were being attacked and criticized as 'promoting a bourgeois line in history'.

A foreign resident in China told me that Teng To, chief editor of the monthly *Frontline* (the magazine of Peking's Party Committee), was undergoing criticism. He had written: 'Everyone must have some leisure and only eight hours of work.' 'The idea of leisure time and the idea of revolution don't go together,' said this man. Young workers in the factories had been infected by the habit of looking at the clock.

The January air was not only freezing but turgid with unvoiced apprehensions and abstruse theoretical argument. I interviewed three philosophers, who were to give me the latest 'thinking'. (I had not reckoned that the word 'thinking' would involve me in the high spheres of theoretical abstraction.) The three talked of the necessity of a cultural revolution. Only a change of thinking in the people could propel advance: a transformation of ideas and habits and behaviour *before* a change in the material conditions of living could occur. But could mankind really overleap itself in thought, overleap the environment in which it dwelt? Certainly, they replied. Had not men dreamt of flying machines before the aeroplane was invented? All progress comes from concepts, and concept strode ahead of any tangible material stimulus. The philosophers added that the theory of productive forces as the motor of progress was 'revisionist' and capitalistic, it negated the cultural revolution 'which is a fact of history'.

I was even more confused. How would I relate this to the American seminar? I seized upon my favourite topic: 'Language affects thinking; our knowledge of things *must* always be inexact and approximate since it depends on words.' I did not agree with Stalin, who pronounced language devoid of any class nature. The very shape of the Chinese ideogram was based on feudal concepts, and it had a lot to do with Chinese continued propensity to think in terms of tradition, hierarchy, precedence, with our continued literal-mindedness. 'The comrades are talking to you of Chairman Mao's Thought,' said Hsing Chiang with some asperity, reminding me that I was waffling. I thanked the philosophers and I went out and bought some very beautiful snuff bottles of agate and jade. They were cheap at the time, and looking at them eased my confusion.

The Chicago University Center for Continuing Education was an imposing pile; but access to it was through some dismal negro slums. Dirty snow piled up with the garbage in heaps, leaning against derelict clapboard bungalows. Afro-Americans walked very lightly clad. How could they endure the freezing streets in such insufficient garments?

The seminar lasted from February 8th to 12th. I was delighted to meet Harrison Salisbury of the *New York Times*; an immediate empathy developed into a valuable friendship. The organizers had provided all shades of opinion. There was Joan Robinson, an English Marxist economist; Jan Myrdal, a Swedish one; and the China experts John Lewis and Franz Schurmann. A few hawks too, like Mark Gayn and Morton Halperin. I told Schurmann (with whom I sat, for through a typical oversight my name had been listed under S instead of under H) how much I had enjoyed his book *Ideology and Organization in Communist China*. I was asked to write a piece for the *Bulletin of Atomic Scientists* by its editor, Ruth Adams. I do not think I contributed much to the seminar; but I learnt a great deal: that forces both within and outside the American administration were urging a new policy on China; that west coast businessmen and even mid-western city businessmen were overwhelmingly *for* trade relations with China.

Lectures; television appearances; many meetings . . . Joy to be in New York with Sidney and Yungmei and my grand-daughter Karen, born in November 1965. Exhilarating to meet the supple minds of erudite and self-effacing American scholars, with their immediacy of contact and total lack of jargon. Some of the more renowned 'experts', however, struck me as over-estimated. But was it not the same everywhere? Word inflation, rather than lucid thought, carried a man upwards . . . By June 1966, as a result of the intense battling of American scholars an editorial in the *New York Times* asserted that a revision of policy towards China was due.

Spyros Skouros, head of Twentieth Century-Fox, asked us to dinner. By that time it was clear that Paramount was having difficulties making *The Mountain is Young* into a film, despite several attempts. In 1959 Paramount had sent a team to Singapore. It was led by Ed Dmytrik as potential director of the picture, accompanied by his wife and by script-writer Bob Authur. Dmytrik had taken preventive antibiotics before leaving California, and the result of his overcaution was intestinally disastrous. His wife suffered from cultural shock, because the festival of Thaipusam coincided with their arrival in Singapore, and it is a rather gruesome affair. The sight of people jabbing themselves through both cheeks or through arms and legs with stilettos (no blood gushed), walking on blazing charcoal fires, or weighed down with *kavadis*, huge confections of flowers and tinsel propped upon metal spikes embedded in their ribs and back, was a little too much for her.

From Singapore the three proceeded to Nepal and to another culture shock. The festival of the goddess Durga, she who is frenzied for blood, was being celebrated, and the Gurkhas were sacrificing rows of bulls. This was a solemn diplomatic event, and the ambassadors in Kathmandu all attended. So did the Paramount team. The bulls were lined up, and a Gurkha approached, balancing his heavy, razor-honed blade. He took a running leap and with one blow struck off the bull's head. The Gurkhas shouted with appreciation as gallons of blood leapt in the air, and Mrs Dmytrik fainted. The Paramount team left Nepal the next day. I don't know whether Spyros knew the story. 'We would have made a great film of your book,' said he. And possibly he was right.

On to Paris, to see André Malraux, the famous author of *Man's Fate*, and Minister of Culture in de Gaulle's government.

André Malraux received me in his superb and airy office. We talked for nearly two hours; or rather he talked and I said a few words. Henri Hell, literary critic and literary editor, afterwards told me that Malraux was enchanted with our meeting. Malraux did invite me to return, and said he wanted to give me lunch at Versailles, and have me speak to the Quai d'Orsay people. He said, 'You have brought humanity and understanding to the Chinese scene through your books.' He was modest about his own splendid contributions. He described Mao, whom he had seen in 1964, and said he was vigorous and well, and 'among the few who have a *vision d'ensemble* of the world'. He contrasted Stalin and Mao. Stalin inspired the reverence of fear, while Mao compelled the respect of authority. Malraux had told Mao, 'Stalin hated you and would have killed you.' Mao, smoking away, had calmly replied, 'Yes, that is true.'

Malraux also spoke of President Kennedy, whom he had seen in 1962. 'He gave me a long rigmarole about preserving India from Chinese aggression,' he said. 'I warned Kennedy of the danger when a gap between the American dream and the reality of Asia would become manifest. America will not be able to stomach a defeat; it will cost her a generation span to recover.' He predicted defeat in Vietnam.

Malraux diverged, grimaced, gestured, but oh, what compelling brilliance! I listened, entranced. 'It's better than the Peking National Day fireworks.' Malraux did not like Lui Shaochi, nor for that matter Chou Enlai. Only Mao 'transcended his own present, as all great men must do'. But he deplored the crass ignorance of the Chinese interpreters and others who took him around. 'They did not know their own history . . . did not know I had been in China in the early 1920s . . . I showed them the photograph in their own museum in Kuangchow, where I am with Chinese revolutionaries. "Who is this?" I asked, pointing to myself in the photo. And they did not know.'

To London, where *The Crippled Tree* and *A Mortal Flower* were doing very well. I was finishing the third volume, *Birdless Summer*. I lectured; met many people; and we drove to Wales to call on Bertrand Russell. He was a small-boned and vivid young old man wrapped in frantic honesty and surmounted by a great shock of beautiful silver hair.

'Why did not China give a good example to the world by forswearing the atom bomb and disarming unilaterally?' he asked.

'The world is not run on good intentions alone,' I replied.

'When I think of a nuclear holocaust, I cannot sleep,' said Russell, and his light, eager voice was quavery with anguish and distress.

On to India, to call on Indira Ghandi, by the simple process of telephoning her aide in the Secretariat, my dear friend Natwar Singh, whom I had met in China in 1956. Indira looked very striking; the cares of office had not yet heavied her grace. 'I haven't changed,' she said, smiling. We talked calmly about the frontier problem and about the famine in India that year, and India's great resources and her enormous potential. 'Enmity with China is not our aim,' she said. She was, however, disturbed by the 'untoward' propaganda from Peking in favour of Pakistan (when the

1965 war between India and Pakistan had taken place).
'India needs absence of tension,' said she. And Pakistan was
a perpetual tension for India. 'It is a problem we'll have to
solve.'

In May 1966 I went back to China. She was entirely *other*
that May. Again that unpleasant throat clamp as the raucous
loudspeakers assaulted my eardrums for hours . . . how was
it possible to remain sane with the perpetual noise, the
blaring and the shouting and the screaming and the singing?
All the posters had changed. Now furious-fisted young
people squashed diminutive snakes and bull-headed figures
(imperialists and revisionists). A thousand portly, rosy-
faced Maos everywhere. The customs officials remained
calm and courteous, relaxed, impervious to the cacophony.

At the railway station no lunch was available; the
waitresses were holding a political meeting. I saw them
practising a dance in front of a large panel painted to
represent Mao. Their hands lifted imaginary hearts from
their breasts towards his smile. I listened to the loudspeakers
but there were too many of them and the sound waves
interfered with each other so that the result was a hopeless
quack.

In Hongkong the Kuomintang newspapers had predicted
a rupture between Mao Tsetung and Liu Shaochi. There had
been rumours of an assassination plot against Mao. Here
there was much talk of a 'black line' which had for the past
seventeen years infected, infested, deviated, twisted,
distorted culture and education and the arts and literature in
order to promote 'restoration of capitalism'. I groaned
inwardly. 'That's it. The intelligentsia is going to catch it
once again.' But I continued, of course, to smile and to hold
myself tightly in control. And to hope my Family would not
suffer too much – and that I would not break down.

In Kuangchow the well-cut suits of 1965 had disappeared.
Every one of the cadres greeting me wore unpressed shirts
and baggy pants and plastic sandals. There was no

brilliantine upon the hair of the men, and the women cadres all had straight short hair. No more perms.

In Peking, however, the admirable Hsing Chiang continued to wear a crisp neat blouse and skirt; until one day in July when Kung Peng would say quietly to her, 'Your clothes look a bit bourgeois.' A friendly warning.

Nowhere in China, in the next few months, was there any hint that Liu Shaochi was the target of the upheaval. In fact I would see him twice. He remained visible, making speeches, receiving guests, and the Hsinhua news agency would report on the mass rallies he held for Vietnam in July. And yet, in 1970, Edgar Snow would be told by Mao that in January 1965 Mao had already decided that Liu Shaochi must go . . .*

'We shall be going to Manchuria, as you asked,' said Hsing Chiang. We would be back in June in Peking.

Manchuria. Limitless flat plains, length to abolish the horizon; space and a clean sky that ran its blueness in echoless silence. The kind of land that makes one want to be on horseback, the sound of hooves to pound the silence into music.

I saw factories, and communes, in Shenyang and Changchun and Fushun and Anshan and Harbin; the Anshan steel works; the Fushun opencast mines (where, in 1947, nineteen years previously, Pao my husband had died). So many notes, so many people telling me of their lives. And in every factory the *tatzepao*, the wall posters, pasted upon all the walls, swinging like banners, strung across from machine to machine, almost swamping every workshop. All of them uttered dire threats against 'black liners' and 'freaks and monsters'.

On May 8th an editorial against the 'black anti-Party line' had come out. 'All those who oppose Mao Tsetung Thought must be toppled, no matter how high or how famous,' shrieked the posters. 'Down with seventeen years of black

*See Edgar Snow, *The Long Revolution* (Hutchinson, 1973).

anti-Party line' blared the radios. Occasionally I discerned names ... names of experts, engineers, factory managers, not prominent political figures; names of educators in the universities. But obviously the Party was still firmly in control, 'directing and leading' the Cultural Revolution. And so the search for 'freaks and monsters' and for 'bull-headed devils and snake spirits' was among the middle ranks, the technical experts and professors and engineers. Not a single top leader in the Party, at the time, was mentioned. The highest in rank were Party secretaries at city level and some university chancellors.

The higher Party cadres receive me and entertain me lavishly. I eat bear paws, an expensive delicacy. I am given a marvellous ginseng root worth thousands of *yuan*, which I shall give to Wanchun when I return to Peking.

After a few days of reading accusatory editorials and slogans and listening to the radio my brain goes into a stupor. I am numbed; even by imprecations. I smile and nod and because there is too much repetition I begin to speak like the people round me, and so my trip is a success as I am outstandingly docile. I read now with practised, jaded eye the posters above the machinery: 'Sung Chiming is enforcing a revisionist line in the screws and bolts third workshop!'; 'Wang Ahmeng has countered Mao Tsetung Thought for many years by saying: Too much political verbiage, not enough scientific work.' I do not know Sung and Wang; I only hope that things won't be too hard for them.

At the Shenyang machine tool plant I meet a worker who is a specialist at cutting tools through sheer application of Mao Tsetung Thought to knife-cutting edges. In almost every factory I am told how much harm the Russians have done, and of the enormous amount of meat, rare metals, oranges, textiles and shoes paid out for equipment.

At Anshan, the great steel works and China's pride, I am shown innovations attributed to Mao Tsetung Thought. In one workshop the Party man in charge introduces me to a pretty young woman worker who writes poetry. She has written decadent, bourgeois love poetry because in school her teacher was following the decadent revisionist black line and corrupting her with feudal poems. But since the intense political studies started in January she has remoulded herself and written some excellent proletarian poetry for workers–peasants–soldiers. The pretty worker begins to recite one of her old poems so that I may judge her wickedness. Then she recites a new one. 'I would like to have some of your poems,' I say, hoping she will also give me the old one she has recited. But alas, the Party cadre has seen through my bland cunning. 'Not these, not these,' he says as she riffles through her loose-leaf notebook. I get, at last, three rather tedious slogany scribbles. 'These are the latest,' says the Party cadre, beaming. He is kind, but I turn back to look at the girl and she too is watching me, and picking meditatively at her thumb. I now wonder what will happen to my dearest friend Yeh, who has printed in *Chinese Literature*, his English monthly, some of my translations of decadent feudal song-poems of the Sung dynasty (AD 960–1279).

In March, Lin Piao, designated as Mao's 'close comrade-in-arms', has issued a directive to 'put politics in command'. And production has gone up by so much and so much per cent everywhere, owing to the 'heightening of revolutionary consciousness' among the workers. Production increase is no longer ascribed to the heroic, the fantastic, the real work of the marvellous, incredibly patient and stoic people of China, but solely to the study of Mao Tsetung Thought . . . Cadres frown when I say that pump stations, canals, fertilizer factories, increase production . . . And that here in Manchuria electrification of communes started in 1948 with the Leap Forward . . .

In one commune I am shown earth mounds terraced for cultivation. This brigade has distinguished itself learning from China's model, Tachai, proclaimed by Mao in 1964 as *the* example for all China. Tachai is sited in the cratered, fissured, gullied loess region of Shansi province. There are not twenty square metres of uniform flat land in these canyons of silt. Tachai terraced its promontories and filled its gullies by hand labour. But here in Manchuria the plains are flat . . . whence, then, these earth mounds? Eleven years later I shall learn the hilarious and pitiful story: the mounds I saw were artificial; they had been raised up and fields laddered upon them to resemble Tachai. That is how 'In all things learn from Tachai' had been interpreted by the literal-minded cadres.

But the official taking me around in 1966 tells me that these terraced fields are the product of the young educated middle school students sent out to labour in the countryside. 'They built these fields with one hand while their other hand was occupied by the precious book of Chairman Mao,' he says. I write it all down.

There are no foreign travellers in Manchuria in that early June. In the hotel's empty dining room I sit at a small table covered by a white cloth. I am surrounded by white cloth screens, and they make me feel that I am dying, that I am in a hospital, and the nurses have hastily wheeled screens round my last agony. Opposite the hotel is the main city square, and a gigantic statue of Mao is being erected, seven (or is it more?) metres high. Mao is clad in a Russian-style overcoat and points the way forward with an infallible concrete hand. The square is illuminated at night because work on the statue continues throughout the twenty-four hours.

On the radio there are thunderous fulminations and denunciations of writers I have met and liked. I get stomach cramps.

In Harbin I meet seven 'outstanding activists' of the Cultural Revolution, and only years later shall I realize how important is this meeting. Two of the seven will become prominent leaders within the next decade. One of them is Li Suwen, thirty-two years old, at present a salesgirl in a food store; later she will become member of the Central Committee, a minister, almost a vice-premier . . . The other is Wen Chuming, twenty-nine, and she is a primary school teacher but she will become the vice-chairman of the revolutionary committee of Liaoning province.

Li Suwen is vibrant with energy. She talks uninterruptedly for over three hours. She describes her own life, her thinking, her emotions. She is unstoppable. I take notes, take notes . . .

'What is the meaning of life, of my life? Then I read about Dr Norman Bethune, and I read Chairman Mao's works, many times, and a window opened in my heart. Unselfishness was the key! Selfishness is revisionism, is capitalism, is imperialism!'

Li Suwen sold soya sauce and vinegar and vegetables according to Mao Tsetung Thought; going to the houses of clients with the provisions. She started cleaning their houses and washing the nappies of the babies and comforting the children, and everyone praised her. There was not a shred of reticence in Comrade Li Suwen as she recited word for word the compliments heaped upon her. 'I also innovated a system of planting vegetables for Shenyang city . . . this saved three hundred trainloads of vegetables for next winter . . . We are the beacon of revolution because we have Mao Tsetung Thought . . . we may have a few intellectuals against us, but they will disappear . . .'

My hand is numb and my brain a pulp, so I interrupt. Perhaps someone else will speak? Li Suwen subsides unwillingly. But everyone is quite upset that I should dare to interrupt her.

Even Hsing Chiang, later, tells me off. 'You should not interrupt . . . it is arrogant.'

I get angry. 'I think she was arrogant, taking up everyone's time, talking about herself.'

'But Li Suwen is a delegate to the National People's Congress; and a film will be made about her; we must all learn from her.'

Obviously she is a model in that gallery of new heroes for this new age.

In 1977, Li Suwen, who meanwhile has become an official

in Peking and has tried to take over the Ministry of Finance from that seasoned Long Marcher and veteran, Li Hsiennien, is identified with Mao's wife and her group. She is demoted and sent back to Manchuria. 'Let her continue to sell vinegar, soya sauce and vegetables,' says Marshal Yeh Chienying benignly. Marshal Yeh's role in arresting the Gang of Four and thus saving China from total disintegration, will never be told.

I liked the second woman activist, Wen Chuming. Short, snub-nosed, she too rose, 'ascending like a missile,'* and then fell; but I persist in thinking that neither she nor Li Suwen were wicked; simply women made use of and then carried away by promises of power. I think the perception of power, how it conditions minds and is instrumental in decision-making, occurs at all levels. In that frightful struggle for power which was to develop during the Cultural Revolution these two women were only cogs.

Mid-June, and back in Peking. Peking is noisy, too noisy. There are processions of lorries and trucks full of workers; long files of middle school students marching, girls in front, boys at the back, holding red flags and singing. In front of each procession are carried large portraits of Mao Tsetung.

One morning, very early, I stand on the balcony of my room and I see such a group march past, and I go down quickly and follow. The marchers go up the street which is lined with mimosa trees and halt in front of the Party headquarters of the Peking Municipality, a tall building covered in white glazed tiles, vaguely like a hospital. A small knot of people representing the Party Committee stands at the gate to receive the students. There are speeches and the young pledge their loyalty to the Party and to Mao Tsetung Thought. Throughout the day they come, from various schools, and thus 'report' to the Peking Party Committee.

---

*In China the swift ascent of such people during the Cultural Revolution was known as 'taking a helicopter', or being 'propelled to the top like a missile'.

But the Peking Party Committee has itself undergone drastic change since May. Peng Chen, the Mayor of Peking has been dismissed: 'His subordinates prevented him from entering his office and he is at home.' And Teng To, who has 'viciously attacked Chairman Mao' through a series of witty, satirical articles which had wide circulation and were reprinted in many provincial newspapers. According to Peking gossip, Teng had a large private collection of priceless classical paintings and antiques illicitly obtained from museums . . . Peng Chen owned a sumptuous villa in the Western Hills where he held large parties. Peking loves gossip and fabricates it all the time, most of it unfounded.

But an African friend, resident in China, tells me that Peng Chen defended the Vice-Mayor Wu Han and his play *Hai Jui*. Peng Chen even said, 'All men are equal before the law.'

On June 1st an editorial, 'Sweep away all monsters' calls for action against 'the black line'. On June 3rd the reorganization of the Peking Party Committee is announced as a 'victory for Mao Tsetung Thought . . .' The old Committee was 'shot through with a black anti-Party, anti-socialist line'. On June 22nd Lin Piao calls for all factories to become 'great schools of Mao Tsetung Thought'.

There is an immense stir among the young. On June 13th some middle school asks for the abolition of 'bourgeois and élitist' examinations. This is granted by the Municipality on June 18th. About half the students are from worker and peasant origin, and examinations still favour the sons and daughters of the intelligentsia and the old bourgeoisie. For how can generations of brain sharpening, a background consummately intellectual, stores of books and erudite conversation in the family not produce young students more articulate, and therefore more successful at examinations? While peasants' and workers' sons and daughters, are still crowded in small houses, do not have a table of their own to write on; often no room of their own, and certainly no store of books to browse among. Very soon the students will divide themselves by class origin: the five good, the five bad.

What is noticeable is the effervescent enthusiasm of the young. Mao has sent a circular on May 16th, 1966, following another stormy Party conference held in Peking. It directs all university teachers and students to 'thoroughly criticize all revolutionary bourgeois ideals in academic circles . . . and the representatives of the bourgeoisie who have wormed their way into the Party, the government, the army and cultural circles . . .' The young are ecstatic.

'A wave of happiness swept through us,' says the son of a friend, Jenyi, who later became a Red Guard, fought for Chiang Ching, and then began to desert her (this happened to so many millions). 'It was at first like a festival, a big fun fair of criticism . . . we felt we were no longer being treated like stupid children. We could criticize the officials and pour out our hearts.' The same tumult of spirit, the same straining impatience for total freedom came upon Jenyi and his generation as it had come ten years before in the Hundred Flowers.

'Chou Enlai had said in 1957: Unless the Party mends its bureaucratic ways we shall lose our youth.' Jenyi knew this; and being intelligent he had followed and understood Mao's preoccupation with the problem of 'revolutionary successors', of Party renewal; with his perturbation at the fact that the average age of Party cadres at grassroots level was forty . . .

In the socialist education movement, Jenyi and other youths from his class had gone to the villages. 'The idea was that the Party should recruit from among us worthy young people, tempered by this contact with China's actual condition, the reality of the rural areas.' Nearly all the third and fourth year students from the major universities had been deployed in villages during the autumn of 1965, 'and this sensitized us to the problem of Party renewal and Party purification. We saw corruption and authoritarianism and high handedness . . . we saw how the people put up with bad Party cadres. We also saw many good things, of course, but we began to question, to wonder . . .' Now they were enjoined to act, to purify the Party through their own exertions. 'The whole world was ours to change,' said Jenyi exuberantly.

Jenyi went through every step of the Cultural Revolution, and in the end he was jailed by Chiang Ching's group, which he had supported. But he found himself through this bitter ordeal. 'Now I know what being a communist means,' he says. He is one of the many millions of young people (seldom mentioned in the West) who have truly understood their own country and its problems. In people such as Jenyi resides hope for the future.

The Cultural Revolution was made under the auspices of 'vast democracy' and the 'dictatorship of the proletariat'. It was meant to involve 'the masses' ousting high Party bureaucrats who betrayed the revolutionary cause. But the Chinese Communist Party certainly meant to guide and to supervise the movements at every step. Although posters covered the university walls in May 1966, denouncing political deviations, no real political target, no tangible bureaucrat of high calibre guilty of misdeeds, was being produced. It was obvious that the first people to suffer would be the academic staff; they were at hand, and many of them were of course of 'bourgeois background'.

But the campaign turned very swiftly into an immense wrestling match for supremacy, a major struggle to capture the young. Young people under eighteen years of age must have formed at least half the population of China in 1966.

The protagonists were, on the one hand, the Party establishment; on the other, the new constellation dubbed the 'Left', whose main figures at the time were Lin Piao and Chiang Ching. Their alliance enabled Chiang Ching's rise to power.

It was Lin Piao, and not Mao, who catapulted Mao's wife, Chiang Ching, into prominence. It happened at a twenty-day symposium on art and literature, held in Shanghai in February 1966, after the final split between Liu Shaochi and

Mao Tsetung. Lin Piao nominated Chiang Ching to direct all 'art and culture' in the army. 'She is most competent . . . thoroughly understands how to apply Mao Tsetung Thought to art,' he said. This gave Chiang Ching a very formidable platform, the army. Immediately thereafter, the Ministers of Culture, of Propaganda and of Education were attacked through the pen of the vociferous Shanghai critic Yao Wenyuan while 'activists', such as I had seen in Manchuria, were being selected by army cadres, in factories, shops, administrative offices, institutes and schools. The Red Guards from a particular middle school attached to Tsinghua University in Peking were organized by the army.*

The offensive began May 25th, when a poster appeared in Peking University condemning the Chancellor, Lu Ping (who was also the Party First Secretary). This wall poster was allegedly composed by a woman, Nieh Yuantzu, together with several other minor staff lecturers. It was praised by Mao himself, who called it 'worthy of the Paris Commune of the 1870s'.

The idea of giving the Chinese people the right to total criticism and revocation of Party officials (or 'vast democracy') was borrowed from what had taken place in France, at the birth of the Paris Commune of 1870. And until 1969, echoes of the Paris Commune would haunt the Cultural Revolution. Undoubtedly it had fascinated Mao Tsetung. Mao had always been a populist, full of trust in 'the masses', always ready to 'turn Heaven upside down' in favour of the people.

But the Party machinery continued to function, and when Nieh's poster was publicized, Party work teams were sent into the universities to 'guide' the movement. The result of this guidance was the processions of young people I had seen marching to pledge loyalty before the white glazed building of the Peking Municipality.

The work teams were supposed to counter 'anarchism'.

*Or rather, that part of the Chinese army directly, or through allies, under Lin Piao's command.

'Who opposes the work teams opposes the Centre and the Party.' This saying was only imposing another kind of submission; it did not allow the young to express their own ideas. It was entirely at variance with trusting the people and letting them decide what was right or wrong.

The work teams, to protect high Party cadres, found 'freaks and demons' among academic staff. They not only allowed but also in many cases themselves inflicted humiliating physical punishment on chosen unfortunates. Unlucky professors, lecturers, even heads of universities, artists and writers, were thus sacrificed . . . It is customary to ascribe all the violence of the Cultural Revolution in Lin Piao, Chiang Ching and her acolytes, but at the beginning brutality was used by the work teams sent by the Party; and this meant Lin Shaochi.

The writer Ouyang Shan, whom I interviewed in 1978, told me that his ill-treatment had come from the work teams. He was chairman of the Kuangtung provincial federation of literary and art circles. 'It was done in order to disgust people very quickly with the Cultural Revolution' said Ouyang Shan to me. 'The Party was desirous of winding it up, to declare all demons and pests "exterminated" [of course not physically] and to get on with progress in China . . . but they had to find some demons here and there.' Ouyang Shan was one of the temporary 'demons'.

The brutalities inflicted upon hapless individuals during June and the first part of July were nothing compared to what happened when the Lin Piao–Chiang Ching alliance won the struggle in August. Neither did they succeed in stemming the Cultural Revolution. But the work teams did manage to confine the movement within the walls of the universities, offices and factories. It would not erupt on the streets until August 18th.

At the beginning of May, thousands of ordinary people had been allowed into the universities, to wander round the campuses, as curious onlookers, and to read the wall posters. 'We saw the teachers sweeping the grounds, cleaning the water closets and the kitchens. Some wore dunce's caps and others were abused as freaks and monsters.'

But in June when I returned and asked to go to Peking University to see Third Brother, I was not allowed. The students were engaged in political study, I was told, and were not to be disturbed by visitors. And the gates of the universities were closed. In Sian and other cities students were not allowed to return home . . .

The work teams now turned the students against those who had distinguished themselves, like Nieh Yuantzu, by 'rebellion'. Suddenly the activists of the Cultural Revolution found themselves held incommunicado, dragged to public criticism meetings, while the students were incited to 'struggle' against them. Wen Chuming in Manchuria told me that she had a dunce's cap put on her head and her clothes were bespattered with filth . . . she had challenged the Party and was therefore 'counter-revolutionary'.

I had prepared for Kung Peng a memorandum outlining some of the conversations at the seminar on China in Chicago, and also those I had with Malraux and Indira Gandhi.

But I did not see Kung Peng on my return from Manchuria, and when I asked whether she had seen my letter, Hsing Chiang with an uncomfortable expression told me that she had had to destroy it.

'I put it down the toilet.'

'Why?'

'I cannot tell you.'

Some weeks later in August, seeing Kung Peng again, I realized how dangerous my chatty letter had been. The Ministry of Foreign Affairs was being attacked. Kung Peng and her husband would be paraded with dunce's caps, and Chiao in the following year would be badly beaten, so badly that he was ill for a long time. The Lin Piao–Chiang Ching group was dead against America and anything to do with America or the West.

I wondered about Chou Enlai. During these baffling first months, Chou Enlai managed to keep his head and to keep China going. The government functioned as usual, despite the dislocations which occurred. The choice Chou had made, siding with Mao and for the Cultural Revolution, of course impressed and influenced me. Obviously, if Chou was for it, it *must* be all right.

I did not understand completely at the time that Chou Enlai, whose concern was China and the Chinese people, was for the motivation of the Cultural Revolution, the bold concept of mass democracy which animated it; but not for the rising constellation of potential power-holders. He acted in the subtle, long-term, masterly way which was his: the only way to prevent a total rupture in the Party, and hence a breakdown within the country itself. I confused, as so many did, the cause with the individuals who, for a while, represented this cause.

I noticed the disappearance of all musical instruments – Chinese and Western violins, pipes, guitars – from the music shop on Peking's main street; only bamboo clappers, cymbals and drums in the window. The philatelic shop which sold and exchanged stamps from all over the world was closed, its doors padlocked. Collecting stamps was a bourgeois pastime. The flower shops were suddenly flowerless . . .

Chou Yang's fall was announced. I was surprised. Chou Yang, the 'tsar of literature', was, for me, impeccable and even too orthodox a person, ardently preaching Mao Tsetung Thought, severe on writers who deviated. The opera star Chou Hsinfang was denounced; and Ho Luting, who had composed the famous guerrilla song of the Sino-Japanese war, and had organized the Chungking symphony orchestra . . .

I went to see Yeh, still accessible. We remained reticent on current events, on the people we knew. Around us our friends were pilloried or defamed . . . I could not say to Yeh,

'I hope you will be spared.' We talked of poetry, of Hakka proverbs and Szechuan metaphors. I asked Yeh whether he thought this was going to be a big mass movement and he looked at me incredulously, and laughed until he was out of breath.

'I always think of the rolling pin action of the masses, kneading the helpless dough of the person,' I said. And how terrifying, to be alone in the midst of a crowd which had turned against one . . . 'This is what bourgeois authorities dread most . . . to lose their dignity,' the newspaper had written.

'I suppose one must get used to everything,' said Yeh. 'But we have our responsibility to history. *We must endure.* I expect we shall have to fight through this like a guerrilla war.'

A guerrilla war? Attacks here and there; skirmishes; lightning raids on such and such a cultural institution, and casualties, of course. Would it remain a guerrilla war, or go on and expand? We were at the end of June . . .

When I left Yeh that night, he and his wife Yuan Yin walked with me across their courtyard to the gate. The moon was pensive in the pewter sky. The easily tired grass of summer looked like brittle silver. We stopped by the peach tree. In the previous autumn Yeh had celebrated my birthday under his peach tree, and with peaches. Alas, the peach tree would not survive the next few years. It was uprooted when the Red Guards came looking for 'concealed documents' in Yeh's house and dug up his courtyard.

Across the courtyard, greeting us, came the old eunuch who lived in two rooms in the opposite building. He was one of the last survivors of the imperial dynasty. He mentioned that his son was taking part in the Cultural Revolution. For of course the eunuch was married. A peasant boy, he had been bought by another eunuch when he was seventeen, since according to Confucius the most unfilial thing was to leave no son behind one. All eunuchs therefore 'married', and adopted sons. And now the eunuch was eighty-six and his wife was eighty-one. She was a comfortable, gentle woman, and she said, 'I've missed nothing in life, I have had food and bracelets and ornaments in my hair, a husband and a son and a house. What more is needed for happiness?'

'The eunuch used to make virility wine with herbs he grows in our common garden,' said Yeh. 'He gave me a bottle.' It had had no particular effect. And then, as if we knew it would be a long time before we would meet again, we talked of Auden and Isherwood, whom Yeh had met in England. He had loved his years in England; though I told him England had changed very much. 'Memories remain fixed, while the person or event that gave rise to them has already changed,' said Yeh quoting Proust.

'I would like to attend the Afro-Asian Writers' Emergency Meeting.' It was being held at the end of June in Peking; an excellent opportunity to meet writers suddenly turned invisible. There were 180 participants from fifty-three countries listed to attend, and I went as an 'observer'. The purpose of the meeting was to prove that China was the reliable base for world revolution; to condemn both US imperialism and USSR imperialism, to indicate support for all liberation movements and especially for the heroic struggle in Vietnam.

A car was obtained for me since I could not possibly walk to the Great Hall of the People, where the meeting was held. Lowly pedestrians would not be admitted. My chauffeur was extremely surly, and never on time. I was not surprised when, in 1969, I was told that he had become a member of the notorious 'May 16' storm troopers, organized by Lin Piao and Chiang Ching.

The distinguished archaeologist, writer and poet, President of the Academy of Sciences, Kuo Mojo led the Chinese participants at the Emergency Meeting: a galaxy of eminent writers, among them some I knew well. But the foreign delegations, with the exception of the Japanese and a few excellent Third World writers, were a padding of nondescript people who could never be called 'writers' by any stretch of the imagination. I missed Lao Sheh; he was in hospital, with asthma. My friend Hsieh Pinhsin, Heart of Ice, was also unwell. But Pa Chin, the grand old man of Chinese literature, had come from Shanghai to attend the meeting. He was China's most financially independent writer; and it was said that at one time he had remarked that the officials of the Ministry of Culture treated writers like monkeys who had to go through hoops. But he was honoured and had never been harassed, and Mao Tsetung had gone to Shanghai to see him in 1957. As for Lao Sheh, he was showered with honours.

I shared a car with Pa Chin once or twice, and we exchanged small talk. I lunched with the playwright Tu Hsuan, whom I liked very much. The woman writer, Yang Mo, I had already met and travelled with, and Han Peiping and Liu Paiyu and Li Chi, the poet Chu Tzechi and Yang Shuo the essayist (who would die during the Cultural Revolution) were all there, and of course sprightly Tsao Yu, full of wit and gleam. And there was also Ching Chingmai, acclaimed for a recent novel, *The Song of Ouyang Hai*. This novel was held to fulfil all the canons of socialist art. It was, in fact, well written and lively. Last but not least, in fact the brightest star of this galaxy, was Hsu Kuangping, the widow of the great Lu Hsun, whose spirit and writings were for ever being invoked as truly revolutionary; whose statues and sayings dominated parks and cultural institutes.

A swinging speech by the Foreign Minister, Chen Yi, on June 27th started us off. Chen Yi looked full of spirit. His speech was long, and one section which made me sit up was when he spoke of the 'great proletarian Cultural Revolution'. It was slander to say that it was 'directed against all intellectuals', said he. Its aim was to destroy the social base of imperialism and modern revisionism, prevent a 'usurpation of power' by revisionists . . . Neither the US nor the USSR dared to launch a cultural revolution in their countries, said Chen Yi. He put a lot of vigour into his speech, and we clapped.

At the many meetings which took place during the week, most of the speeches were praise of Mao Tsetung Thought, praise of Mao, recitation of his poems, vows of hatred to imperialism and modern revisionism. Some speeches were more distinguished than others. Kuo Mojo gave a humorous talk. Certain people abroad, said he, were concerned because, in April 1966, he had been reported as declaring that his previous work was merely fit for burning. There was no need for anxiety; he planned to write much more, which would serve the people better. Some delegates managed to instil a deep tremolo in their voices and others burst into tears while speaking. All these words, words, words, where are they now?

Almost every evening there was some kind of entertainment by the art troupes of the People's Liberation Army (since all other art troupes were in abeyance, being scrutinized for political deviation): the poems of Mao, set to music, music and songs in praise of Chairman Mao.

The foreign participants did not know me. One thought I was an interpreter and called upon me for services. Another asked me to meet him in his room. 'I need a woman,' said he. 'But not a grandmother,' I replied.

I asked the writer Ching Chingmai to lunch. *The Song of Ouyang Hai* concerned a young hero of the PLA who had sacrificed his life to save his comrades. Ching was a middle school graduate and had tried to become an actor. He had written some plays. Then he went down to the communes, to manual labour, 'and there I encountered great heroes, among the common people'. He spoke of the splendour and the sacrifices of the Chinese people. Thus he had learnt of Ouyang Hai, who had given his life to save some people in danger. 'I could not forget him.' He stayed with Ouyang Hai's army company, interviewing all his friends and comrades, 'and thus I wrote the book'.

I was certain that this book would never be condemned, since Mao himself had received Ching Chingmai, and praised his work. But I was wrong. His hero had (in the first edition) seemed equally inspired by both Mao Tsetung and Liu Shaochi's writings! This was a natural in 1964 and even in 1965, when the works of both men were being recommended together to Party members. Even in June 1966, while Ching and I sat on the terrace and talked, the work teams sent by the Party to guide the Cultural Revolution among university students enjoined the recalcitrant to read Liu's book, *On Perfecting Oneself.*

Ching Chingmai would try to save himself. In November 1966, he was present at a large gathering, exalting Chiang Ching, and he spoke in praise of her. But in 1969, when I asked about him, I was told he was 'counter-revolutionary'. What kind of counter-revolutionary? Right or ultra-left counter-revolutionary? He was 'ultra-left', a May 16er.

In 1979 Ching Chingmai surfaced again. Like so many of the young and not so young who, for a while, believed in Chiang Ching and served her, he was denounced and jailed when sacrificial victims were needed; he spent years in jail, was released after Chiang Ching was arrested, and has begun to write again.

I had a very interesting meeting with Hsu Kuangping, Lu Hsun's wife, and the star of our writers' gathering. She told me heinous things about the four writers who had opposed her husband and 'the Thought of Chairman Mao'. Of the four, one was Chou Yang. Hsu Kuangping told me things against Chou Yang, and this was to make me quite prejudiced against him, a prejudice which I have since tried to correct by interviewing him twice,* in order to get to the bottom of his quarrel with Lu Hsun, and why Hsu Kuangping said these things about him. She also told me that her book and a film on Lu Hsun had been suppressed and she herself held in obscurity between 1961 and 1965. She also accused Chou Yang of 'falsifying' what Lu Hsun wrote.

*In 1978.

None of us knew then that this quarrel between Chou Yang and Lu Hsun, going back to the 1930s, was to become one of the main weapons wielded by Chiang Ching and her allies to cast down the officials of the culture and propaganda departments and ministries and seize control of the whole apparatus of culture, education and propaganda.

In 1978 Chou Yang, released after eleven years, would give me his side of the story. He had never led a 'black line' against Mao in the 1930s, since Mao's line was unknown in Shanghai in those years; the Shanghai league of left wing writers was totally cut off from any directives from the Party. 'I found a progressive magazine which urged us to a United Front. The magazine was Russian,* and I found it at the back of an obscure bookshop in the French Concession. Since there was no way of knowing what Party policy was at the time, I thought it best to adopt this line, and in fact it was approved of later.' In this way the slogan 'Literature for national defence' came about, which later was so violently attacked as 'capitulation to Chiang Kaishek'.

'Lu Hsun did not agree,' said Chou Yang. 'He was ill, and perhaps irritable. He brooked little contradiction. We went to see him, to try to argue with him.' Obviously, this had been a personal skirmish, and Chou Yang agreed that Lu Hsun had been right. 'But it was a problem of understanding, not of wilful or deliberate betrayal of the correct political line. Anyway, after 1937, I went personally to Yenan, and there I faithfully adhered to Mao Tsetung's line in art and literature.' But this old quarrel had been resurrected, said Chou Yang, and used by the Gang of Four, who turned it into a 'counter-revolutionary plot'. 'This would enable Chiang Ching to get rid of all of us older writers, and to take over the Ministry of Culture and the Ministry of Propaganda, and also Education.'

I know how writers can hate, revile, excoriate each other; how much virulence there is in their personal resentments.

---

*Chou Yang is a translator of Tolstoy and Gorky.

But I still cannot understand Hsu Kuangping's detestation of Chou Yang. 'Chou Yang was always very nice to Hsu Kuangping . . . He procured a nice house for her in which she could live and work,' said Heart of Ice to me some years later.

But that Chou Yang had been harsh, intransigent with wayward writers, he would himself acknowledge, and make a thorough self-criticism upon his return in 1977. I would ask him when I saw him in 1978, 'Mr Chou Yang, I have been told many things against you, that is why I wanted to have your own views . . . now what about Ting Ling?'

The woman writer Ting Ling had been one of those who had been pursued with great venom by Chou Yang; she had been accused, along with others, of organizing a 'clique' and trying to seize control of the Writers' Federation. And in 1978 Ting Ling, about whom I had enquired several times (notably from Yang Mo in 1961), was still an accountant in a commune in the far north of Manchuria.

Chou Yang said that there were still 'some problems to be solved' about Ting Ling. But now she too is back, after twenty-three years, and exonerated. And Chou Yang, rehabilitated, has probably learnt tolerance and gentleness towards his fellow writers, however ideologically errant they may have been.

With the works of Mao in hand, Hsing Chiang and I went to the Coal Hill Park and squatted in the summer grass, seeking coolness under the glazed pavilion roofs. We talked. The word club came up.

'It's a bad word now,' said Hsing Chiang.

'Why?'

'All clubs are bad . . . the Petofi Club . . . intellectuals always think of organizing clubs.'

I change the subject and talk of my projected book, *Phoenix Harvest*.

'Phoenix is not a good word. It's the name given to a landlord's wife.'

'It's only a bird.'

'Not a good bird.'

Obviously, I must now make a list of bad words, not-to-be-used words.

The Emergency Meeting is coming to a close and there are major receptions. The heads of delegations are received by the top leaders while we wait in a large hall. They return, and in files Liu Shaochi, the Head of State, Madame Soong Chingling, as lovely as ever, and Teng Hsiaoping, and many others. A photograph is taken.

There is another reception on July 10th. The Great Hall of the People is brightly lit. A final communiqué of the writers' meeting has supported Vietnam and condemned the United States. In the next twelve days, there will be mass rallies all over China – Liu Shaochi presiding over one held in Peking – condemning American imperialism and pledging total support to Vietnam, 'whatever the sacrifices we must make'.

On the rostrum of the Great Hall that day sat the American Sol Adler, who lives in Peking, and Rewi Alley, and Anna-Louise Strong, and Kinkazu Saionji of Japan and Djawoto of Idonesia. I am also happy to see there Lao Sheh, recovered, and Mao Tun, the Minister of Culture. Their presence comforts me. Perhaps things are getting back to normal. Chen Yi speaks of the insane adventurism of the United States in Vietnam and the shameful demeanour of the lords of the Kremlin. The wife of old Marshal Chu Teh, Kang Keching, who heads the Women's Federation, and the representative of the youth organization, Wang Chaohua, also speak.

Then another reception; in comes Chou Enlai, and with him are Kang Sheng and Chen Pota and Tao Chu. And there is a stir in my heart, because Chou is with the people who are identified with the 'Left', with Lin Piao and Mao. It was Kang Sheng who denounced Mayor Peng Chen, now dismissed. And as for Chen Pota, he is now editor of *Red Flag* and very powerful. He and Chiang Ching have gone together to speak to the university students; Chen Pota also went to Szechuan in the spring to 'stimulate' activists there against the established officials.

Chou Enlai is with them. And somehow because of Chou's presence, because I trust him, I think the others *must* be good people. I forget that Chou is consummately a statesman, that he will do anything, anything that is necessary for China.

Yet I do not like Chen Pota's face. But he is a close friend of Lin Piao and Chiang Ching. And people say that he is Mao's personal secretary; has been for many years . . .

Chou Enlai makes an able speech. Later he catches sight of me. 'Oh, you've also come here,' he says. I cannot tell whether he thinks it a good idea or not. Somehow I get the feeling he disapproves.

Some of the foreign translators living at the Friendship Hostel are having a bad time. One of them, a Frenchman, son of a prominent Party member (pro-China) says his father owns a dog. It is impossible, his Chinese comrades say, for a true Marxist-Leninist to own a dog: he is vilifying his father. 'But he does have a dog,' replies the unhappy young Frenchman, who refuses to make a self-criticism, though enjoined to do so.

All the mirrors in the rooms are covered over with portraits of Chairman Mao. The waiters and servants are so busy holding meetings, that no one cleans the rooms any longer.

One night I hear great sobs. Someone rushes into an empty hotel room, and locks himself in. Somebody else comes after him. 'Open, open, don't take it like that . . . it's only criticism . . . open . . .' There are muffled sounds, the door opens. Silence.

The Pei family have arrived, and I take them to dinner. Mr Pei and his wife are friends of mine from way back in the 1940s. They have lived a good many years in Europe, where Mr Pei worked as a scientist. Now he has decided to return to settle in China. 'I am getting old. I want to lay my bones in China. Perhaps I can do something to help.' His wife Lucy and his daughter Millie come back with him. Millie is sixteen, she glistens with youth, she has the fragrance of youth, she is like a peach, like a beautiful fruit, and her total ignorance of her beauty is compelling. She is also witty and bubbles with gaiety. The Peis have just ended a trip round China at government expense; to acquaint them with the achievements of socialism. They are enchanted. Now they will have a comfortable flat in an enclave for overseas Chinese in Peking; and Millie will attend the university. They are very happy. They know nothing about what is happening around them.

I walk back to my hotel with a poet. He does not seem unduly perturbed. 'I am not a high official,' says he; nor a Party member. We recite poetry. Poetry is a preservative and a disinfectant: it helps us to fend off the miasma of slogans and dread. A good many friends, Yeh, my late cousin Pengju, and in Hongkong Lee Tsungying, who runs *Eastern Horizon* magazine, have or had the same habit of reciting poetry to themselves. 'High hills and the moon dwindles, low tide and the rocks appear . . .'

Something is going on which I cannot grasp, however queasy it makes me. If only there were less words in the air . . . my gut feelings dissipate like smoke wisps before the immense wind of words, and the ersatz emotions they evoke replace true instinct. Almost I persuade myself that I must confess and be redeemed through a public denunciation of myself. But confess what? Chinese poetry holds out its melody and guards my spirit against relinquishment. 'China. China. She has opened the garden of love to me, and I must stay my heart with care of her until the end of time.'

CHAPTER 2

Thunder and Lightning: 1966–1967

On July 12th, 1966 the universities exploded, as the tension between the 'activists' – middle school and university students already formed into Red Guards, but not yet publicized – reached a crisis stage. Led by the lecturer Nieh Yuantzu, some forty youths denounced the 'terrorism' of the teams. During the following seven days there was total confusion in the universities.

Precisely during that week, the Afro-Asian writers left Peking, and so did I. Accompanied by writers and officials of the culture and propaganda organizations, we proceeded by train to Tientsin and on to Tangshan, to a remarkable brigade called Shashihyu (meaning sand and stone gully), formerly a haunt of beggar families. The rocky waste had been transformed into a fertile valley, nestling among hillocks now planted with thousands of fruit trees. Here soil had been brought in baskets by the inhabitants to make fields, the stones having been quarried away by hand. It had taken ten years. Two Pakistani diplomats were to write a major thesis on Shashihyu, which was published in the United States. Undoubtedly this was part of the magnificent work of China's millions, and it could not be denied that unless the Communist Party had organized these millions, and infused them with hope, this small huddle of beggar-land would not have flourished.

I lunched with a peasant family; the peasant had five children, a good house and a thriving vegetable plot, but no pig. In fact there were very few pigs at Shashihyu, 'but we plan a piggery for next year'. We returned in a bus cavalcade to Tangshan, the industrial and coal city which I knew well, for Papa had brought me here when I was a child. Tangshan supplied coal to the railway. In 1976 it would be razed in a frightful earthquake in which nearly 400,000 people died.

There were banquets and long speeches and then a shadow play, the folk tradition of the district. By that time it was midnight and most of the 'writers' simply went to bed. I felt sorry for the folk artists who had waited to show us their subtle and intricate art, which in Indonesia and Malaya is called *wayang kulit*. Figurines cut out of animal skin and painted are manipulated behind a screen, a lamp throwing their shadows on the cloth. I had become a devotee of *wayang kulit* in Malaya.

We went south, to Changsha, and there with the fatigue, the speeches, the banqueting, the heat and above all the unease, the tirades and the threats on the loudspeakers, I had an attack of hysteria. Round me at table some 'writers' had been passing odious remarks about the Chinese, while the Chinese strove to be so tremendously hospitable; and this contributed to my nausea. All I remember of this shameful exposure of mine is a foul odour, a sweat, a clamminess, a wrenching of spirit; the sweat of fear and the babble of terror from my mouth, and Hsing Chiang listening stolidly, patiently, and with love putting me to bed . . . and the Chinese cadres so kind, so self-controlled, so heroic in their fortitude, for they were under stress, every one of them, while I was safe – I would not be hit, and paraded and pummelled and reviled . . .

We went to Wuhan. The Kiang Nan Hotel was reserved for the Afro-Asian writers' delegation. The heads of delegations were given beautiful suites. As an observer, tacked on at the last minute, I shared with Hsing Chiang the smallest and most stifling room in the hotel, with the sun shining in from morning to late afternoon. It was forty-one degrees Centigrade in the shade, and the air was immobile lead. Hsing Chiang again displayed masterly calm: not a word from her. She gave me the cooler bed. We sweated, we dripped from night to morning and morning to night. I wore no nightgown and went naked in the room, and Hsing Chiang was a little shocked, but did not say anything. There was not even a fan and when we asked for one we were told none was available as they had all gone to 'important writers'.

But the Chinese writers and I had delightful cups of tea together. Cheerful Yen Wenching, tall handsome Liu Paiyu, and Li Chi, so clever and good, made special time for me (though officially they devoted themselves to the others). All three were not only good writers but also veterans of wars, of guerrilla campaigns. Yen Wenching described how he had walked all the way from Yenan to Manchuria behind a mule carrying a heavy load of weapons, and the mule had sores which stank to high heaven. Liu Paiyu had been a hero in the guerrilla war, and so had Li Chi. All three were also members of the Ministry of Culture and Federation of Writers. They remained calm, unperturbed. Their very presence somehow assured one that all was well. Yet they must have been under great strain, since the attack that July was headed straight at the Ministry of Culture, at the Federation of Writers, at the Department of Propaganda; it was certain that they would also become targets of the campaign. But what splendid unruffled urbanity, what lightness of demeanour and measure of speech – what a lesson in self-control and courtesy they gave me, when they knew themselves threatened! They fulfilled scrupulously their duty, making their guests feel important and pampered. And some of their foreign 'colleagues' took themselves very seriously. What thoughts coursed through the minds of Yen, Liu and Li in the hot restless nights when they had put their charges to bed? I do not know. Yen Wenching was to suffer almost seven years of duress, Liu Paiyu and Li Chi eleven years . . .

All three of them are alive. I have seen them again and talked with them about that time in Wuhan in July 1966. 'Did you know what to expect when you went back to Peking?'

'No. We thought it would be hard, but not that hard, not that long.'

July 16th. A suffocating day in Wuhan. Forty-two degrees Centigrade. We are taken to the monstrous Yangtze River, here over a mile from bank to bank, which rolls its glowing ochre mud to the sea. Motor launches decorated with flags are taking to the water, and there seems to be a hierarchy of launches. But all of us are on one launch, and as we clamber on board a beaming Kuo Mojo appears, surrounded by young girls and boys, swimmers, who erupt from the cabins and form squadrons soon to leap into the stream.

Four hundred thousand people cover the shores; squares of swimmers in red and blue and green suits mass along the banks with banners on poles strapped to their shoulders, and music, music, music is relayed through loudspeakers. The swimmers plunge in, squadron by squadron.

Our launch, flag-bedecked, rolls upon waves of song. There is a small breeze; and suddenly 60,000 more swimmers precipitate themselves into the water from both sides with an immense and gleeful crescendo of acclaim.

'Chairman Mao, Chairman Mao!'

'Chairman Mao is swimming in the Yangtze River . . . he is swimming,' a young interpreter, face streaming with tears is shouting. The news goes through our launch and all of us rush to the railings to see Mao. Helplessly, I take snaps, but our launch is not in front, and I can only hope that perhaps *his* head will bob up in my picture, among the many heads in the water. Our writers begin to shout and sing and wave, and some Africans begin to dance. Later they will assert that they have seen Chairman Mao. The more emotional delegates kiss each other and shout 'Long live the Revolution'. I have not quite perceived Mao's head above the water but perhaps I have, and Yen Wenching says, 'Yes, he was there.' Then I know it is so.

The next day, July 17th, we are convened to meet Chairman Mao.

It is in a large building, part residential, part hotel by the West Lake of Wuhan. We are taken there in the usual cavalcade of buses. The heads of the delegation ride in imposing cars.

We assemble in the marble-clad, air-conditioned reception hall. All is white and grey, suave stone and white curtains against the windows; an impeccable cleanliness; and the hush that surrounds greatness . . . We are moved into ranks, according to that protocol which I shall never grasp. The first row is the heads of the delegations. Observers occupy the end of not the very last row, but the one before last.

And then Mao comes into the room. He looks as usual bland, benign, with that tremendous persona, that extraordinary flat calm which flattens everything in his presence. He has an extra dimension and I think: he is man-multitude, man-ocean. He brings with him something beyond time, as the ageless rock engulfs the centuries, because it just is. And I am glad that I am not in the front row, which has to grin and cheer and clap and shake hands with Mao. Three rows behind, the effluvia reach me, and I recover from the hebetude into which noise and words, too many words, have plunged me.

Mao shakes hands. We are in a state of expectancy. For usually Mao talks, jokes, with everyone, sometimes makes a little speech. But today, not a word. We continue clapping. And then he is nudged into the centre of the first row and is photographed with us. Then he waves an urbane, casual hand at us and goes away.

He has not said a word.

It is July 17th.

We smile, smile, smile. My face hurts from smiling. We file out. Mao has not spoken to us. But everyone professes himself highly gratified, honoured. Mao has received us. We get back into the buses.

The next day, July 18th, Mao flies to Peking, and the Cultural Revolution whose fires were being dampened, erupts, an uncontrollable volcano, all over China.

The first eighteen days of July have seen muted implosions, muted in the conflict between the two forces contending for supremacy. As radio telescopes detect only after light years the fury of a nebula, only now can we see what unleashed wrath was being prepared.

During the week July 12th to 18th, 'activists' appealed above the heads of the work teams to Mao. 'They are authoritarian . . . they refuse to discuss problems . . . they do not let us out of the university, they shut the gates and tell us to study political texts . . . yet Chairman Mao has asked us to make revolution throughout the land . . .' The activists received the support of *Red Flag* and its editor, Chen Pota. Chen Pota and Chiang Ching had visited Peking University at the end of June, and officially seen Nieh Yuantzu. It is now said – on that fabulous Peking rumour-grapevine – that Chen Pota had drafted Nieh's poster, so much praised by Mao.

On July 18th Mao arrived in Peking. On the 19th and 20th Chou Enlai and Chiang Ching visited the universities together. In these visits, Chiang Ching appeared all sweetness and conciliation, eager to soothe, to unite, to reconcile; for already the students were divided into quarrelling factions. With Chou Enlai, she asked the students not to use the saying: 'Father a reactionary, son is a rotten egg. Father is a hero, son is a true revolutionary.'*

Chiang Ching was not the only top leader's wife visiting the universities. Wang Kuangmei – Liu Shaochi's wife – had been doing so since June, speaking to the students. The majority of the young were still indecisive; they did not know whom to follow.

On July 24th and 25th, the work teams were withdrawn not only from the universities but from all other units as well, after a severe admonition by Mao Tsetung.

Liu Shaochi continued to appear. He was Head of State,

*The evidence for Chiang Ching's moderate stance at the time lies not only in the speeches she made, as reported, but also in a book, *Madame Mao*, published by the Union Research Institute, Hongkong (1968). The Institute benefits from the learned advice of the Jesuit eminence, Father Ladany, and cannot therefore be considered biased in favour of the Cultural Revolution.

and Ho Chih Minh had written to him from Hanoi, appealing for China's support in the Vietnam war. Rallies were organized. Were these rallies, at which Liu appeared prominently, intended to redirect the Cultural Revolution? Were they designed to get the army prepared for confrontation with the United States on behalf of Vietnam? This is a hypothesis for which I have no definite answer. It was put to me by a very good friend of China, and it is not absurd speculation. But it remains speculation.

To make the situation even more confused, peasant delegations, workers' trade union delegations, mixed with the students in a display of massive popular support at the rallies against the war in Vietnam.

Anna-Louise Strong, who became an honorary Red Guard on September 12th, tells the story of the birth of the Red Guards in her 'Letter from China' Number 50, sent to many Americans.

> They began as a movement of left-wing students to protect themselves against reactionary school authorities. The first organization is that of the middle school attached to Tsinghua University. It began at the end of May, but was 'under cover' until the new Peking Municipal party committee sent a work team to the school . . . The Red Guards came out in the open on June 6.

'Who prepared them?' I asked Anna-Louise.

'I think it was Lin Piao's army units,' she replied.

By July 15th, the garrison troops in Peking had been replaced by battalions loyal to Lin Piao. From my hotel balcony I saw their olive green trucks parked in quiet alleyways and courtyards around the Forbidden City. I had not seen so many army trucks before. Later they would be used to convey the Red Guards in their millions to parade before Mao Tsetung.

All was geared to a showdown, but Mao would not proceed without another meeting of the Central Committee. He would strive once again to unite his old comrades, to win them for what he felt was most imperative: a great 'rectification' of top leaders in the Party, a change of consciousness among the masses, creating a mass movement which would be anti-revisionist, purifying the Party and renewing it with youth and revolutionary ardour . . .

I was back in Peking on August 1st. At the airport I would see a great many high officials, members of the Central Committee, arriving. They came from the provinces. The Party was holding an enlarged Eleventh Plenary Session, which began that day. But the Central Committee members were outweighed, as the communiqué made clear, by members of the 'Directorate of the Cultural Revolution', a group now nineteen strong with Chen Pota and Chiang Ching in command and with 'representatives of revolutionary workers and students', that is, the Red Guards. The 'Directorate' would soon become an extremely powerful group, replacing both the Central Committee and its Executive Secretariat.

Between July 17th, when I saw Mao, and August 1st when I returned to Peking, I tried to go to Tibet. I had received permission from Chou Enlai through Kung Peng, and since the way to Lhasa was through Chengtu, I would see Third Uncle.

I had vainly attempted, in Wuhan, to visit my protégé Ying Hsiung, a young man from Malaya who worked for my clinic in Johore Bahru and who went to China to escape being jailed. He now taught English in a middle school in Wuhan. I used to drop in to see him, but in 1966 this was not allowed. 'The school is busy with political study.' I could only leave a message for him.

But first, because it was suggested to me as the thing to do, I went from Wuhan to Chairman Mao's birthplace, Shaoshan. Shaoshan was crowded with endless files of pilgrims, including many Uighurs from Sinkiang. A large building was being put up; a museum to house relics of Mao's life. In the farmhouse, sacerdotal and full of reverence, the guides indicated a rough comb for animals which had been used by Mao. I dared to finger it, an amulet of luck. I ventured to say, at one moment, that Mao Tsetung did not get on with his father, and the heavens almost fell upon me. 'This is slander . . . Chairman Mao's family has been full of virtue from generation to generation . . . at most, his father was *occasionally* irritable . . .' There could be no flaw in any of Mao's relatives; no reprehensible distant cousin in the whole Mao clan . . . and to hint at Mao's own revelations, made to Edgar Snow, was sacrilege . . . which I committed. Afterwards I was asked to write my valuable views. Of course they were to be in praise of Mao.

There is, in the district of Shaoshan, a mountain called Phoenix Mountain, where legend says the birds of the air assembled to pay homage to the great sages of antiquity, Yao and Shun. My effusion was interlarded with references to phoenixes. Using the word phoenix was a small act of defiance; since in Peking at the time the word phoenix was such a bad word.

In that atmosphere of religious exaltation, any small reproof took on phantasmagoric proportions. Thus already the titles of my books, *The Crippled Tree, A Mortal Flower*, had been denounced as 'derogatory to China'. How could China be likened to a crippled tree? I explained it really meant that the withered tree revives with the spring. As for 'mortal flower', it meant that flowers die but new flowers take their place. Agility of mind is essential in a universe of slogans. There was, among some bureaucrats, a virulent criticism of these two books, but dear Hsing Chiang carried them around with her courageously. She would turn to the photograph of Mao inside *A Mortal Flower*, to show that my heart was red-sun inclined. But here too there was a hitch. The photograph taken by Edgar Snow, showed a young Mao in Yenan, wearing patched trousers. Was there not, in the patches, an intention to deride Mao? Hsing Chiang said forcefully that it only showed how modest, frugal, heart-linked with the common people was Mao. Another mental world, a universe of symbols . . . I became so careful that I began to mutter to myself. As film after film I had liked, book after book I had read, thought good and radical and not badly written, would become 'poisonous weeds' and part of the 'counter-revolutionary conspiracy' against Mao Tsetung Thought, I began to wonder whether I should not accuse myself of counter-revolutionary intent? My intestines failed me, as usual. Hsing Chiang strove to protect me. I must be *careful* in my language. 'Luckily you dress very simply.' She was under immense strain all the time. She knew that, as soon as I had gone, she would go into the rectification machine and be examined, scrutinized, criticized. And then there were her sons in school; she worried about them. 'The young don't listen to anything any more . . .'

We flew to Chengtu and there were large posters on all the avenues; posters of sturdy young men and women spearing bullheaded freaks and serpent monsters. Not as much noise as in Peking. The university was now out of bounds to me: 'Busy with political study'.

The hotel in Chengtu was totally empty. I was the only 'outsider'. In the street there were occasional processions, factory workers with posters banging drums. But a soldier was at the hotel gates and when I neared them, three men erupted from the gatekeeper's lodge. We went to the theatre, and it was all changed; no more 'feudal' plays (so beloved by me!) but a repertoire of songs, of music and dancing, consisting of two or three people at a time eulogizing Mao or impaling 'freaks and monsters' with furious gestures. And much shrieking. It was so bad that Hsing Chiang made due criticism to the director, who nodded briskly. 'It's too exaggerated,' said she. Now was this deliberate sabotage, to make the Cultural Revolution activists ridiculous to the ever-humorous, quick-witted people of Szechuan? I learnt about the two – or multiple – faces and interpretations of every so-called fact in that year.

We settled down to wait for the aeroplane to Tibet. I asked timidly to see Third Uncle. The cadres I had met on previous visits were no longer there. One of the new comrades in charge had a face which spelt 'vigilant', like a Chinese opera mask. To this category of cadres promotion comes with their zeal at discovering freaks, monsters, and hidden secret agents . . .

It was suggested that I go again to Tayee, where I had been in 1964, to the landlord Liu Wentsai's mansion. But this time there were no exhibits of socialist education; and the clay figures of the previous years had been rearranged, given expressions not of weariness, misery and despair, but of fierceness, fury, revolt. 'It was wrong to depict the people in these passive moods . . . it was revisionist,' I was told; (the artists who designed the first batches of figures must have been undergoing criticism . . .). Now every little baby, in its mother's arms, looked with rage at landlord Liu Wentsai.

I went to see Third Uncle and Third Aunt. A cadre and Hsing Chiang came with me. It would not be possible to be alone that day, but again heroic Hsing Chiang exerted herself mightily, and in the next days I saw them alone. The neighbourhood atmosphere had changed – it was hostile. And always in the common courtyard there would be one or other member of the street committee watching us. Of course we did not get angry or even make a remark. We simply ignored the surveillance. I knew better than to become irate and bring trouble upon Third Uncle and Third Aunt. This would be unfilial. I realize now that, perhaps after I had left, Third Uncle's rooms might have been searched, in case I had left guns, gold, or secret counter-revolutionary documents with him.

Third Uncle sat in a frightening calm, his body all gathered together, coiled upon the fear at its core. Fear that he did not voice, of course. Third Aunt sat by him, her face smooth. They endured. We sipped tea. We talked of the weather and of my going to Tibet. This was an 'exceptional honour', said Third Uncle. 'Of course we *know* you will praise the socialist achievements in Tibet,' he said, 'and also the Great Proletarian Cultural Revolution.' Having seen him the previous time almost break down at the thought of his body going into a common cemetery, in a common coffin, I knew he must be agonizing within his soul. For he never pretended to be brave; he had too much sensitiveness and imagination to pretend.

I asked after Sixth Brother, his son. 'Your Sixth Brother is very busy. He is in his organization. It is the Cultural Revolution. *Of course* we rejoice that such a great event has come; we heartily support it,' said Third Uncle. I asked to see Sixth Brother, but he was too busy. 'Political study?' 'Yes.' Third Uncle's hands played on the table, with his black fan. Never had his voice been so thready. It was extremely painful to hear him inhale, need air, between each sentence. And yet he would not falter or break down.

I unpacked the things I had brought for them. I saw by Third Uncle's face that they were not welcome. He was afraid to receive anything new, from outside, foreign. There was warm underwear, but it was of various colours, and that was bad. I gave him money. He took it without a word, holding the crisp new hundred-dollar notes in his hands, then he folded them and put them back in the envelope and left them on the table.

Every morning, for the next seven days, we went to the airport, Hsing Chiang and I, to wait for the aeroplane to Lhasa. The Ilyushin revved and whirred and strolled a bit up and down the tarmac. The very nice Szechuanese cadre in charge of security at the airport sat with us. Comrade Hu was a soldier of the PLA and had been four years in Tibet. 'Many of our Szechuan people have gone there to open farms and build roads,' said he. Hu liked the Tibetans. 'They are very sincere, they like to sing and dance. They have their own wisdom.' Hu did not have a Han superiority complex. 'I wouldn't have minded staying there for ever.'

The aeroplane to Lhasa did not leave that day, or the next, or the next . . . Every day Comrade Hu sat companionably with us, and we played rummy waiting for the meteorological report. By ten in the morning Comrade Hu would say cheerfully, 'Time for lunch'. By noon, it would be too late to fly. 'Tomorrow perhaps.' The pilot would get out of the cockpit and come to us with a broad, happy smile saying, 'The storm over the mountains has not abated.' We would go back to the hotel and in the afternoon I would go to see Third Uncle and Third Aunt. 'Perhaps you will leave tomorrow,' Third Uncle would say. He was less distressed now than on the first day. And so we sat and looked at each other with our great love masked by a careless grin, and Third Aunt would grip my hand and we would walk a little in the courtyard, up and down, and she never stumbled though her bound feet were so small.

The teahouses of Chengtu were closed that year. The streets were curiously full of silent people, just walking. Unlike Peking, there seemed to be few processions – until suddenly one day there was an immense rally, and great crowds assembled in the stadium, and through the streets poured serried ranks of workers with flags and drums and cymbals.

I suggested to Third Uncle and Third Aunt that I should take a photograph of them. Anything to prolong our time together. Third Uncle acquiesced. Third Aunt asked the relative who stayed with them, and who was the old concubine of Third Granduncle,* to call the barber. The barber came and he cut Third Uncle's hair before the photographer came. The old concubine knew her place as a half servant and went on faithfully serving Third Aunt, but Third Aunt always refused to be photographed with her, so she could not appear in the picture that was taken.

Third Aunt attended classes in political study run by the

*See *The Crippled Tree*.

street committee. 'She is most diligent in her attendance,' the street committee man said. Third Uncle could only walk with great difficulty, so was excused attendance. After almost a week of daily visits the street committee man was reassured about me and left us alone, loudly shooing away schoolchildren and women and men crowding round to catch a glimpse of the 'outsider'.

Third Uncle now did some calligraphy, which indicated that he felt better.

> A myriad families plunged into sworrow;
> Men perish amid brambles and weeds.
> Could their grief and laments but shake the earth.
> Thoughts roam wide, stretch over the wilderness.
> In the silence I hear the rumble of thunder.

I went to an exhibition and was briefed on Tibet by a supercilious cadre, who told me incredible and inaccurate stories. He spoke of Princess Wen Cheng of the Tang dynasty who had married the Tibetan King. He said that union between Tibet and China had then taken place. He was wrong; the fusion came five centuries later at the time of Kublai Khan, grandson of Genghis Khan and Emperor of China.* I said flippantly that the King of Bhutan had recently married an American girl, but that did not make Bhutan part of America. (Alas for my rashness of tongue! The cadre turned a raging pea-green and poor Hsing Chiang again rushed to shield me.)

By the seventh day I knew that, even if I waited another month, I would not be able to go to Tibet. That immovable storm over the Himalayas would not budge, the weather reports would continue to be bad. Although Chou Enlai had given me permission, no one at local level would take the responsibility of conveying me to Tibet – it might one day, turn out to have been a mistake, a 'pandering to foreigners', a 'letting out of state secrets'. Who knows?

---

*The founder of the Yuan dynasty (AD 1271–1368).

I said goodbye to Third Uncle and Third Aunt. 'Please tell Sixth Brother I hope to see him next year.' Third Uncle nodded. His eyes were upon me, and oh, the unspoken grief in them. This was the last time I would see Third Uncle. He would die in 1968. Third Aunt is still alive, and I go to see her every year.

The tiger heat of August in Peking drove all the bound-foot grandmothers out of doors; they sat on small stools, and fanned, and watched the rare passers-by in the small dusty *hutungs* where the children played. Hsing Chiang went home. 'I must put my affairs in order.' I merely walked around, but it was too hot, and everything was a blur.

Hualan sat in her living room hacking off the heels of her new shoes, shoes I gave her in May, from Hong Kong. They were walking shoes, but they had a slight heel.

'It will spoil the shoes, Hualan.'

'Well, my dear, I still think the heels are too high . . . it's a sign of bourgeois behaviour, high heels.' There was about her the same intense inner preoccupation which I had noticed in others. Suddenly she said, 'My dear, those dresses you've given me . . . can you take them back?'

'But I don't want them back.'

'We may be searched.'

I stared at her.

'House searches,' she said. 'In the movement.'

'All right, I'll take them back.' But I left her a black silk dress.

She frowned at it. 'I'll have to cut off the hem.' The hem had some gold embroidery. 'I'll have to burn some of the other clothes.'

Her sister's oil paintings had been taken off the walls. Only portraits of Chairman Mao were pinned up. I went with her into her bedroom. Her brother was prizing away, one by one, the figurines of bright stone decorating her black lacquer chest. They represented women in flowing robes and with fans, a beribboned scholar, all very feudal, and suddenly nostalgically beautiful. On the veranda all the flower pots had disappeared.

Hualan walked out into the street with me. We walked slowly. Two children were playing at the street corner. One, an urchin of six or seven, shouted 'Foreign devil!' at Hualan and me.

'I haven't heard that for a long time,' I said.

'I haven't heard it for sixteen years,' said Hualan, 'but the kids now learn it from their grandmothers.'

She was wrong. It was not only from the grandmothers.

The year 1966 was the centenary of the birth of the great Sun Yatsen, who made the 1911 Revolution which ended Imperial China, and installed a Republic, and started the convulsions of China's entry into the modern age.

I went to interview Madame Soong Chingling, Sun Yatsen's widow. She lived in a large mansion which had belonged to the Manchu imperial family. She was eternally youthful and glowing, with that lustre of skin and hair, that lovely voice, and always the will of steel beneath the dazzling soft beauty. Her house was air-conditioned, but she complained of arthritis in the knees, due to the air-conditioning. She had fractured a wrist, which made writing difficult for her. 'This is the mansion where Puyi, the last Emperor, was born,' she told me. There was a large portrait in oils of her husband on the wall. The carpets were cool and sea-green, the living room austere.

'You still have not returned to live in China?' she said. Did the gracious lady ever forget anything?

'I think I can be of service even abroad,' I replied.

She then launched into the interview. 'What Dr Sun Yatsen had begun is now being accomplished. We must study the historical context when we want to judge a man. Dr Sun was not a communist but at the end of his life he was very near to the Party. Things were very difficult in those early years. I remember the last time Dr Sun returned from Japan to China. We stayed in the garret of a French newspaperman's house in the French Concession in Shanghai; we disguised ourselves when we went out, and we went out in the daytime.

'I love the American people. I consider America my second home. I have no doubt the American people will do something about the war in Vietnam before too many of their boys are killed.'

I asked what she thought of the Cultural Revolution.

'It is of vital importance; for nothing is inevitable about a new order; it must be fought for, it must be defended; a restoration of the past is always possible; it must not find a rank-and-file mentality ready to accept it . . . *We must arm ourselves against ourselves*, bring in *consciously* the new order . . .'

In that autumn some Red Guards would deface a shrine erected to Sun Yatsen in his native province. Sun had made a 'bourgeois' revolution, they said, and all 'bourgeois' relics, monuments, shrines of the past had to vanish. Chou Enlai promptly put an end to this vandalism, and ceremonies to commemorate Sun Yatsen were publicly held in November in Peking and other cities.

Madame Ho Hsiangning sat on her bed, dressed in black silk, her daughter by her side. She was five months away from ninety in that July of 1966. She remembered entertaining me at dinner in 1956. Age had shrunk her, the bones were minuscule, but her spirit soared and her face was fine ivory. She still painted, muscular and sinewy tigers of beauty and power, rampaging in luminous forests. She had a strong brush stroke, and used high colour, in the Japanese manner of the Ganku school. 'I doubt that I shall reach a hundred, though I would like to see the changes wrought by this mighty Cultural Revolution of ours.' She discussed her death without a tremor, her sprightly eyes picking out every detail of my face and dress. 'This body of mine has gone through nearly a century of history; perhaps it is enough.' She spoke of her youth, studying painting together with her husband Liao Chungkai in Japan. 'But he was too busy with the Revolution to continue painting. We loved painting together, it was such happiness.' And she showed me with a youthful gesture, as if a young girl again, a composition: 'My husband painted that figure waiting under the tree.' She had painted the tree.

In 1904, as a student in Tokyo, she heard Sun Yatsen lecture and went up to offer him her services; and joined his association. Liao Chungkai became Sun Yatsen's devoted helper, and he would be murdered in August 1925, by order of Chiang Kaishek.

'Sixty years ago, Sun Yatsen made a revolution; today it is Chairman Mao Tsetung . . .' She had taught her son Liao Chengchih, and her daughter Liao Menghsin to do manual labour. 'Revolution is our family tradition.' She hoped her grandchildren would continue China's long revolution. I said she would live to be at least 120 and she laughed cheerfully and gave me replicas of two of her paintings.

Many people explained the Cultural Revolution to me; each in his own way. Rewi Alley and Ma Haiteh in unemphatic speculation; Israel Epstein, reputed a Marxist theoretician, in high-flown style.

I filled a great many pages of my notebooks with observations, theory, data . . . But truth is never merely an accumulation of facts. Facts do not correspond to events, the outcome of a situation does not depend entirely on what one has put into it. Always there is the perverse, intangible unknown, unexpected, the gone away . . . The logic of verity is its illogic. I sculpt out of the unresolved a purposeful recital; imprint upon the shapeless a continuity, merely by writing it down. But reality always escapes; no computer fetters it into order. It remains the unbound mystery which animates all things and men.

As I stared at the ceiling in my usual thinking-horizontal, it seemed to me that the Cultural Revolution corresponded to that streak of anti-bureaucratism so forceful in Mao when he was young. How he detested bureaucrats! Yet by 1966, the revolutionaries of the Long March had all turned, willy nilly, into greying bureaucrats. How else could a country be run, except by an organization, an Establishment wielding power? But something in Mao, wistful and perhaps childish, always hungered for revolt; the revolt against tutelage, paternalism, against obvious authority, and now, in his old age, Mao was revolting against this bureaucratic greyness and its attempts to systematize everything.

Bureaucracy. Twenty-eight ranks for cadres, four lower non-cadre ranks for service personnel, eight grades for engineers, five grades of technicians, four grades of assistant technicians, eight grades of workers. In this staircase universe, every rank stuck to itself, frequented only its equals, dared not 'intrude' upon higher ranks save through monstrously slow paperwork. And yet there was very little economic difference. The difference was in 'power wielding'; whose word counted. No lower rank dared take responsibility for any decision, so that the final three upper ranks were weighed down with decisions about the paltry trivia of regulations. So often, referring cases of abuse or malpractice to the Establishment (mostly complaints from overseas Chinese), I found that nothing could be done at lower level; even a simple bureaucratic muddle would have to go right up to Chou Enlai.

Paradoxically, this general shirking of responsibility was accompanied by the 'feudal practice of arbitrary dictation'* and against these fiats nothing could be done. This too Mao was trying to uproot. But there was more to the Cultural Revolution. Now that the Soviet Party had become 'revisionist'; was once again a Tsarist state, the duty of upholding revolutionary example had fallen upon China. She was now fortress, vanguard, solid base of all liberation . . . Suddenly China had become the base of world revolution. It was not easy to see the present events in

*Mao's words.

the context of this grandiose vision.

Dostoevsky makes one of his characters say 'Starting from unlimited freedom, I end with limitless despotism.' Mao, in an attempt to accelerate political emancipation among his people, 'took the lid off' (as everyone was saying in July and August 1966); attempted to break the clamped control of the Establishment upon the masses. 'Mass democracy' was the herald call of the Cultural Revolution. One editorial would even suggest a universal vote. It was this exalting vision of freedom, release from all control, which had captivated the young, but which would also victimize them in the end.

From August 1st to 10th, the Eleventh Plenary Session of the Party Central Committee (enlarged) was held in Peking. Out of it came the decisions on the Cultural Revolution; a framework of official approval, called the Sixteen Regulations of the Cultural Revolution. This document declared open hunting upon 'those within the Party *who are in authority* and taking the capitalist road'. On August 15th, in the middle of the proceedings, Mao Tsetung himself had written a wall poster, condemning the 'fifty days of white terror' of the work teams.* And Lin Piao, in a major speech at the Plenary Session, asked for a general purge of all those in the Party 'who oppose Mao Tsetung Thought'.

The executive of the Central Committee were in the hands of Liu Shaochi, and its secretariat under Teng Hsiaoping, were now totally paralysed. They were replaced by the nineteen-member Directorate in charge of the Cultural Revolution, headed by Chen Pota and Chiang Ching.

On August 18th, a one-million-strong rally of Red Guards from seven cities was received by Mao.

Almost one-third of middle school and university students in Peking would become Red Guards. Within ten days the movement spread to all cities. Although the Sixteen

*June 1st to July 20th.

Regulations specifically forbade violence and 'physical struggle', this was the hallmark of the next two months. By the end of September fear reigned in many cities, where gangs of youths, invading every street where there were 'bourgeois' or intellectuals living, committed brutalities upon unfortunates. Yet contradictory reports came out: 'Remarkably little violence,' said some; 'A reign of gratuitous terror – horrifying,' said others. In every city and quarter it was different: from harassment to murder, from endless interrogation to beating to death.

By October, in Peking alone, 86,000 'counter-revolutionaries' had been discovered. In Shanghai 400,000 'bourgeois and capitalists' were removed from their houses.

An overseas Chinese girl, Alice, told me in 1975, 'I was looking through my window, and I saw them come for me. I was paralysed . . . I could do nothing but open the door for them. For six weeks they stayed with me in relays, group after group, questioning me; night and day and day and night . . . I slept no more than two or three hours a night because they woke me up to question me. They went through all my books, my letters . . . why had I so many Western friends? Why did I not confess that I was a spy, had come back to China not to serve China, but to spy for America? I had to translate every word of all my letters from my friends abroad . . . Finally they let me go, but for six months I had to clean the school lavatories, sweep the courtyards . . . then I went into a study period for six months. I was kept in the school, not allowed to go home, and then I went to a May 7 cadre school for a year.'*

Utterly strange to relate, this same Alice, on her return, would be changed, so changed as to believe in Chiang Ching and her group, and adhere to her although it was because of the Chiang Ching-organized Red Guards that she had suffered this harassment!

Another witness: 'Ho and I worked in the same office in

*For May 7 cadre schools, see footnote p. 101.

the Foreign Language Press. We even shared the same lamp. The Red Guards from the Foreign Language Institute and the aviation school (they were among the worst of the lot) came to get him. They took turns beating him in the courtyard. He kept on shouting "Long live Chairman Mao". Then they took him away in a truck to the Western Hills where they kept their prisoners. I never saw him again. I don't know why they singled him out. Sometimes it was all so capricious.' He adds: 'None of us moved.'

From Uncle and Aunt Ting, who lived in one of Papa's houses: 'Band after band of Red Guards came down our street. Many of them were from other cities. They obtained from the street committees and the public security bureau the names and addresses of "bourgeois families" living in the quarter. But sometimes a person with a grudge invented a story. Our daughter had bought a bag in Shanghai. It was prettier than the Peking ones, and a neighbour coveted it. She told the Red Guards that we had foreign goods, and they turned up everything in our house, dug up the floors and the garden, chipped the plaster off the walls to uncover gold pieces or documents. They took away books, pictures, vases, anything "old" or "foreign", and also a table and a cupboard.'

Uncle Ting's house was searched, and by night he and his family left the city. They lived in a ramshackle hut in the suburbs; but they returned in 1968. Many other families of 'bourgeois origin' were compelled to go away, and their houses were occupied by workers. Papa's houses were all thus occupied. But then I had already given them up formally, writing official letters to that effect in 1965 and again in 1966. However, they were returned to me in 1972. But I never went near them until 1978, when the matter of 'compensating' me for them came up.

As for the Peis, of course a team of Red Guards came to investigate them. They found that their clothes were all wrong. They did not understand why the Peis had lived abroad; why they had decided to return to China. Mr Pei was arrested and detained for three months for having 'illicit relations with foreign countries'. His wife and daughter were held incommunicado for weeks, at home. Two youths kept constant guard in their flat; even to go to the toilet they had a girl Red Guard with them.

'I nearly went through the window,' said Mrs Pei when at last she talked to me, in 1975. 'I begged them to let me die. What did they want, what did they want? Why were we treated in this way when we loved China, and wanted to come back to live here? But they did not believe us; they said we had returned to spy.'

In the end the Peis would remain in China, and be honoured, and given jobs. 'But it has taken ten years out of our lives,' says Mrs Pei.

'You may not think it can be true, but it also took ten years out of my life,' I say to her, and we both laugh.

Mr Pei, who is a perennial optimist, fared well in jail. He was not isolated, and he made many friends. After three months he was released. 'Of course due to Premier Chou Enlai,' he says.

My friends the Yangs also went to jail. 'Almost everyone I knew and respected was in jail with me. The jailers were very pleased to have important people to look after,' says Yang Hsienyi. He met there several former ministers, and also some petty thieves. 'Now the ministers are back in important positions, and they say, "Old chap, anything you have to say, come and tell us." As for the petty thieves, they will never steal anything from me.'

There were many absurd and ugly things being done, like the trials in Shanghai of cadres supposed to have committed adultery, who were beaten on the buttocks by self-appointed youthful judges. The Red Guards changed the names of streets and of shops, until the Post Office complained that they could no longer deliver letters, 'since every street and every shop has the same name'. There were good and bad Red Guards. The good ones – among them the children of my friends – helped the peasants with the harvest, and protected people and state property. But the worst not only burnt books and destroyed historic monuments; they also killed and tortured. Chou Enlai could not shield all, protect everything, everywhere. Although he tried. He protected, at least, the top scientists and artists, and many museums and monuments. But sometimes he was too late. The harm was done.

There were the parades. My revered friend, Dr Lin Chiaochih, an eminent gynaecologist trained in America, and a great-grandmother, was paraded as a 'bourgeois authority' with a dunce's cap on her head. She told me so herself, laughingly, in 1969. And immediately after the parade (which lasted seven hours) she went straight back to the hospital and started operating on her cases for the day.

Thousands of 'bourgeois authorities', doctors and scientists, diplomats and professors, went on working, despite the harassment, the humiliations, despite being made to stand many hours in uncomfortable positions, wearing dunces' caps and labels round their necks, and having their hair pulled and their faces slapped.

'The Red Guards who beat my husband were *directed* by Lin Piao and Chiang Ching,' says Lao Sheh's wife, the painter Hu Tsietsing, to me.

Directed violence, as distinct from spontaneous brutality, would become more obvious after November 1966, when the Directorate conducted its first attempt at seizing power in all the cities, ousting all the old cadres.

But in that August the targets were the Ministry of Culture, of Propaganda, and the educational institutions. Thus not only Lao Sheh, but many other writers were 'all being beaten while in front of them burnt a huge bonfire, a great pile of theatre props, of costumes used for the Chinese opera and the stage, and musical instruments. Lao Sheh could not understand . . . that he, so honoured for seventeen years, should suddenly be so treated.'* When his corpse was

*From an eye-witness, the writer Yang Mo.

found in the Lake of Peace, he had clutched to his heart the writings of Chairman Mao, as if he had searched in them for an answer to what had befallen him.

I have now been to see so many of the survivors, one by one, interviewing them as soon as they could or would talk (for even the Westernized Peis would not say a word until 1975). They all say the same thing. 'At first it seemed awful . . . we wondered if we could bear it . . . but as the days went by, and *all* of us, all the people we knew, all the old veterans, anyone of some stature or merit, were reviled or harassed, or beaten or jailed, suddenly it became nothing . . . we were all in it together – a new fraternity. It became shameful not to be harassed, to be left free.'

And so many, almost two out of three of these writers, artists, literary critics, musicians, singers, actors I talk with add this: 'We had faith. We knew it could not last.'

'Because we trusted the Party – and the Chinese people.'

In October of 1966 I flew to a Toronto University teach-in on China. David Crooke came from Peking on purpose to deliver a speech, and Felix Greene came from England. But the whole exercise was fairly futile; all communication was actually broken. And the next year David Crooke and his wife, both staunchly communist, were to be jailed in Peking for some three years, on totally fabricated charges.

I did not write to Kung Peng about Toronto. Her husband Chiao was being treated in a most cruel way, condemned to sell newspapers on the streets. 'Please let me sell them on the back alleys,' he pleaded. 'On the main streets I might meet foreigners, and they know my face . . .'

I attended at that year's end a meeting of the World Family Planning Organization, in New York, and on this occasion met McGeorge Bundy and Margaret Mead, who refused to shake hands with me.

I went to India and Ceylon, and there I met again Theja Gunawardhana. An Asian economic seminar had been held in Peking at the time of our Afro-Asian writers' meeting.

Theja Gunawardhana, an economist, had attended. At first she was suspicious of me, but later we became friends and I went to see her in Colombo. She seemed to have 'inside news' because two of her sons were studying in China.

Theja spoke darkly to me of plots and conspiracies. 'I have written a letter to Lin Piao,' she said firmly. Her sons were very critical of the foreigners (American and British) living in China, and of their role. 'Do you know that it is an American, Sidney Rittenberg, who is almost in total control of all China's radio broadcasting?' said she in outraged tones. I have since often wondered, when in the following year some of the foreigners resident in China were arrested, whether Theja had not been influenced through her sons by the spy mania prevalent in China then. Theja was a fiery and fascinating woman, but very idealistic and intransigent . . . She was also – total contradiction – a devout Roman Catholic as well as a Marxist revolutionary.

I was back in Hong Kong in December. My friend Tsungying had returned from a trip to Kuangchow. His eyes shone more than usual, and he exhibited signs of thyroid trouble. His family in China was under great duress. In 1957 his brother and sister-in-law had been dubbed rightists, and now what would happen to them? Noble Tsungying, not a word of complaint from him for twenty years. He told me the Red Guards he had seen 'talk philosophy better than I do'. He praised their discipline, eulogized their sense of responsibility. Nothing about his own worry, his fears. And so, lulled by ignorance, I felt more reassured.

But another Chinese journalist, on his return from yet another excursion, went over to the Americans. He described corpses hanging from the trees in the parks of Kuangchow, talked of the beating to death of Nan Hanchen, Director of the Bank of China, an economist, in charge of China's economic relations abroad. Nan Hanchen, a devoted patriot, was now described as a 'counter-revolutionary'.

When I went to the American Consulate in Hong Kong for my visa, because I was scheduled to do yet another lecture tour in 1967, the visa officer said to me, 'In view of what's happening in China, will you perhaps just say that you've changed your mind? Then we'll dispense with all this waiver business . . . we'll just clear you.'

But I could not. 'I have not changed my mind,' I said.

He sighed. 'I thought you'd say that. Well, we'll just have to go through the usual business.'

By that time, so I learnt from a friendly State Department official, it took five hours to go through the files on me. I felt flattered. So much paperwork for nothing.

CHAPTER 3

The Storm: 1967-1968

In January 1967 Shanghai was captured by the 'Left'* in an assault upon the Party offices by a million Red Guards and workers. The leaders were Wang Hungwen, a worker at the Seventeenth Textile Mill, and the writers Chang Chunchiao and Yao Wenyuan, the collaborators of Mao's wife. These three men and Chiang Ching would form the notorious Shanghai Group, later dubbed by Mao himself, in 1974, the 'Gang of Four'. The Mayor, Vice-Mayor and Party officials of Shanghai were hauled to criticism meetings, paraded through the city, accused of 'towering crimes' and of restoring capitalism. The Lin Piao–Chiang Ching alliance pressed on. A public exhibition was held in Peking. Peng Chen, the ex-Mayor, Chou Yang, Yang Shangkuen, head of the Party school, and Lo Juiching, former Chief of Staff, were shown, with large placards round their necks, to a crowd of five thousand – among them some Westerners resident in China. All over China such displays took place, designed to strike terror among older cadres in high positions. The writer Chao Shouli was taken from village to village through the north-west he had described so well in his books. He died of the ordeal.

Now the 'Left' proceeded to seize power in all the cities of China. They hoped, in the vacuum of authority, to establish themselves, but this was not easy. The veteran cadres fought back; so did the workers' and peasants' unions who detested the bullying Red Guards. The latter, split into many factions, were fighting each other.

---

*As the Lin Piao–Chiang Ching alliance was called. It is now called 'ultra-left' and 'counter-revolutionary'.

In the havoc lay purpose. Lin Piao wanted to consolidate his hold. The attacks against Lo Juiching, Chu Teh, and other Long Marchers of the army such as Ho Lung, were planned. Power could only be seized by placing Lin Piao's own men in their key positions. Lo Juiching was Chief of Staff, General Secretary of the Military Council, and the former head of the Public Security Bureau. He was apprehended in September 1966. In the ensuing 'investigation sessions' he was pushed – so it is alleged – through a window, and his leg was broken. He received no medical care for this injury. He was carried to his public humiliation in January 1967, in a large basket, and had to crawl on the floor, dragging his broken leg behind him. At the place of his public trial he was supplied with a chair, because there were 'outsiders' present.

Ho Lung was Vice-Chairman of the Military Council, in charge of the executive. He was an egregious man, a popular commander. He had been with Lo Juiching and Chou Enlai at the Nanchang uprising on August 1st, 1927 as had Chu Teh and Chen Yi (and Lin Piao himself, though in a subaltern position). And this memorable episode, which was the beginning of the Red Army, had forged strong bonds of friendship among these men. In fact, some Western 'experts' said Lin Piao was a 'protégé' of Chou Enlai!

The 'Left' had to break up this solid nucleus. For many months, Mao Tsetung would not agree to Ho Lung being 'investigated'. Chou Enlai would personally protect him, giving him asylum in his own house. But after months of shielding Ho Lung, Chou had to relinquish him. Mao had finally allowed an 'investigation'. Ho Lung was treated most savagely. He was diabetic, and was refused medical care. He was beaten regularly, being first wrapped in a blanket so that the welts would not show. He was allowed only three *fen* a day for food. Ho Lung believed in Mao to the end of his life. 'If Chairman Mao only knew what is happening to me.' But his petitions went unheard. They were not relayed to Mao. All this was not known – it could not be known – since Ho

Lung was held in top security conditions until his death in 1969.* Mao cannot have known what was happening, for he sent a message to Ho Lung – but Ho was already dying when he received Mao's message.

In 1973, Chou held a ceremony in Ho Lung's memory, attended by more than 2,000 people. Not a word appeared about it in the press. In 1974, I would see the small casket containing Ho Lung's ashes in the building where the ashes of Party members were kept – but Ho Lung's photograph was so small that I nearly missed it. 'He died of natural causes. He was seventy-six years old,' said the keeper.

Besides these two men, the Lin Piao–Chiang Ching group would endeavour to discredit or to paralyse Chu Teh, Yeh Chienying, and Nieh Jungchen, who was in charge of the atomic power programme. Chu Teh was ignobly reviled, but such was his prestige that no one dared to drag him to jail. Yeh Chienying was so respected and popular in the army that it was impossible to mount a campaign against him – but his son, son-in-law, daughter and other members of his family were imprisoned for five to seven years. Yeh Chienying's son-in-law was none other than Liu Shikun, one of China's greatest pianists. China's other renowned pianist, Ying Shengtsung (Felix Greene made a beautiful film about him in 1960), went over to serve Chiang Ching. I would read an article by Ying in the newspaper, describing how he had been saved by her from his 'bourgeois upbringing' and ideas. This article was to serve artists as a 'model' of conversion to her and her group.

Marshal Yeh Chienying kept silent during all those years. He had saved Mao's life during the Long March, hence it was difficult to shake Mao's faith in him. But he would never mention to anyone, and does not seem to have even hinted to Mao of the treatment that his family was enduring. His long patience was not due to fear or passivity. All China knows

_____
*The family of Ho Lung did not speak about his martyrdom until 1977.

what she owes to old Marshal Yeh Chienying, who waited until the time had come to act.

On the civilian side, getting rid of Liu Shaochi and Teng Hsiaoping did not solve the problem of toppling the Establishment. There was one formidable obstacle, and that was of course Chou Enlai. Chou's strength lay not only in his total indispensability, but in the fact that after Mao he was the only man in China whom all the people knew by name and loved, the old as well as the young. 'No one will believe anything against Chou, not even the Old Man,'* Chen Pota is alleged to have remarked one day. Chen Pota had been entrusted by Lin Piao and Chiang Ching with the formidable task of 'getting rid of Chou'. Chou was to be denounced, at first indirectly, by innuendo, as the 'great protector' of top officials and 'capitalist roaders' in the Party, 'the mandarin who shields the imperial dynasty', to revert to the feudal phraseology with which even present-day political articles in China are so copiously riddled.

Throughout the months since that fateful August of 1966 Chou had striven to minimize disruption. He had forbidden the interference of the Red Guards with communes and with factories. 'Workers and peasants make revolution at their place of work . . . revolution must stimulate production, not destroy it.' But in November, he seems to have lost out on this point to the Directorate. Chou had shielded not only Marshal Ho Lung but so many other useful and valuable people; he had recommended 'moderation' in attacks against the cadres and gone against physical violence. He had succeeded in protecting many scientists, especially in the atomic and nuclear installations, so that a clause in the Sixteen Regulations specially mentioned them.

One way to topple a man, according to the traditional Chinese art of war is to 'remove those by his side'. Attacks against Li Fuchun and Chen Yun, the economists and planners, and above all against Chen Yi, Foreign Minister,

*Mao.

all of them Chou Enlai's helpers, advisers, friends, colleagues, were designed to weaken Chou. 'Let Chou do all his own work, let him have no rest, no sleep, harass him until he dies of strain . . .' This was the intention of the Directorate. And indeed, by August 1967, Chou would exhibit cardiac stress.

Chen Yi was attacked from February 1967 onwards, repeatedly, for many months; not only Chou stood by him but of all the ministries, the Foreign Ministry proved the toughest, refusing to yield hostages, and ninety members of the diplomatic service put up a poster in defence of Chen Yi. The ebullient Chen Yi fought every inch of the way, got angry with the Red Guards, called them 'ignorant children', shouted back at them when he was shouted at. In between sessions of 'criticism' (and physical abuse of him and his wife, the beautiful Chang Tsien) Chen Yi would go home, wash his face, change his clothes and attend a diplomatic reception or receive a foreign embassy with unruffled countenance and humour. For they all went on working, these extraordinary men; Li Hsiennien, the Finance Minister, coming back from hours of being grilled, would preside over a meeting of the Finance Committee. As for Chou Enlai, he was everywhere, did everything – attending Red Guard rallies and lecturing them, presiding over high-level meetings on industry, electric power, finance, transport, flying here and there to the provinces to put a stop to armed conflicts, managing all China, and trying to keep food flowing into the cities.

'Chou is more dangerous than Liu and Teng.' Long before Mao had emerged as leader in 1935, Chou had already established the Communist Party organizations. He was both an intellectual and a military commander, he had created the key network of insurrection in Shanghai in the 1920s, and he was the head of the State Council, the huge government machinery which made China function. He had conciliated Chiang Kaishek in a 'United Front' in 1937, and he was the architect of Peking's foreign policy.

I am still amazed by the strength of mind, the foresight, the superb bravery of Chou Enlai in these crucial years. How he manoeuvred! How he was able to tell truths within untruths! It was supreme statesmanship, the art of arts. He played not for himself, but to save China. But how did he do it? Some parts of the immense task he undertook with such boldness and prudence are unfathomed. If ever there was a book worth a lifetime of effort, it is a book about Chou Enlai, and what he did from 1966 until the time he died of cancer, ten years later, in January 1976.

Perhaps because of this consummate, single-minded, ability to see further than others, to utilize skilfully even reverses, and press on to his goal, Chou Enlai was for many years attacked, reviled, vilified, by Western writers, as a 'turncoat'. He was said to 'change sides', to be a 'coward' (when he was utterly brave) and to have no integrity. He was, they said, a man for all seasons, always ready to bow to the prevailing wind.*

Yet when he died, all the world mourned him.

It must have been, for Chou, a difficult decision to make, in 1965, to side with the alleged 'Left' against the Establishment which he, too, had created. But it was a decision guided by something more profound than simple loyalty to Mao or blind faith. I think it was a total realization of all the elements, contradictions, conflicts in China at the time.

He was always the great 'readjuster', the man who, when a situation appeared frozen and desperate, managed somehow to unfreeze it; to find that scarcely perceptible detail which would provide a new start; Chou Enlai, siding apparently with Lin Piao and Chiang Ching, made it extremely difficult to remove him . . . What he would do, in the end, would be to shield and protect Mao Tsetung from his 'friends' and from his wife.

*Simon Leys wrote that people in China 'hated and resented Chou Enlai . . .' He could not have been more wrong.

Throughout 1966, Chou Enlai had spent himself as only he could do, scarcely sleeping, always available, doing everything, including offering to polish the shoes of foreign guests at the hotels when the waiters declared they would no longer clean shoes, answer bells or serve meals. He kept the government departments working while all the administrative and technical staff running China, from coal mines to banks, from steel plants to foreign affairs, were systematically paralysed by the removal of all the senior experienced personnel, to be criticized, humiliated, beaten or jailed. Out of 70,000 people employed in the State Council under Chou, by 1970 only 10,000 or less remained. 'I have no one left to help me except Li Hsiennien,' Chou said to Edgar Snow.

The strategy of 'outwardly knock down Liu Shaochi and Teng Hsiaoping, actually destroy Chou Enlai' was started by Chen Pota in October 1966. 'Everyone can be criticized, except Chairman Mao, Lin Piao and Chiang Ching,' said he. And this meant, of course, 'Criticize Chou Enlai'.

The first poster against Chou Enlai went up on January 15th, 1967. It was, however, taken down the next day, by order of Mao Tsetung.

The Party now fought back. In February, at a high level meeting presided over by Chou Enlai, Marshal Yeh Chienying and other veterans of the Long March protested at the shambles being created. 'Too many of the old cadres are ill-treated, and without any reason at all. Most of the accusations against them are unfounded and unproved. This is illegal.' 'Will your fifteen-year-olds run the army?' shouted Marshal Yeh, who is said to have struck the table with such force that he fractured a bone in his hand.

'The affairs of the country cannot be carried out. Is the Party still necessary or do you wish to do away with it? At present it can no longer function, and the stability of the army is also imperilled . . . are we old cadres still needed, or do we all have to die to satisfy you?' said the veterans of the Long March.

By then almost all the ministers in charge of production were being denounced or hauled away to kangaroo courts held by Red Guards. The Coal Minister would die of a heart attack under the verbal abuse he endured.

'You are using the mass movement as an excuse to attain your own ambitions,' said Long Marcher Tan Chenlin, a Vice-Premier.

'Every day you say: Let the masses liberate themselves. But it is not the masses you want to liberate. You want to topple the Party,' said Yeh Chienying. 'How will you run the country then?'

To which it is said that Chen Pota, who was present, talked about 'vast democracy' and 'the masses running themselves . . . all power to the masses', and the Paris Commune.

Now the Paris Commune idea had received a major setback from Mao himself. When Chang and Yao, the Shanghai allies of Chiang Ching, both in the Directorate, proposed to set up a Shanghai commune, Mao refused. 'Such an organization is too loose and too weak . . . it leads to anarchy.' A Shanghai commune was not set up, nor a Peking commune despite his wife's appeal to the Red Guards: 'We don't need any State Council or ministers . . . there should be a Peking commune.'

But the idea of a 'vast democracy' to be run by the 'masses' suited the 'Left' too well to be abandoned. Chen Pota called a mass meeting of twenty thousand, and denounced 'the evil wind of February' which sought to 'reverse the Cultural Revolution'. Meeting after meeting would be held, for over a year, against 'the pernicious black wind of February'. It was in these circumstances that Chiang Ching would play a major role. 'Tan Chenlin is a renegade,' she would shout (he had called her 'a new empress') and this launched the 'masses' against Tan.* 'Ho Lung is a traitor,' she screamed, without any evidence. He had called her 'a second rate actress' in Yenan, thirty years previously.

*He is of course rehabilitated, alive and well.

The Directorate now tried to operate power seizures on the model of Shanghai in several provinces; but most of the revolutionary committees formed were unstable. The army had received from Mao a general mandate: 'Support the Left', but this proved extremely dilatory. When was a left a true left or a false left? The local commanders would interpret 'left' any way they wished. Lin Piao's commanders camouflaged their own consolidation of power under Red Guard and mass demonstrations. This led to a strife of much complexity and such baffling confusion that no one knew, at any time, who was 'left' or who was 'right', or who supported whom, or how it had all come about. Chou Enlai, as usual called in to arbitrate, to expostulate, to stop Red Guard internecine fighting, would have to contradict himself twice on what was 'left'.

But by April it was clear that the Red Guard movement was spent, split into a thousand factions, and that restoration of order was in the hands of the army. The work of appealing to the young to unite, to stop fighting, to operate alliances, and to return to studies, fell upon Chou Enlai.

Many youngsters, disgusted with the violence, gave up. But it was not easy for a few hundred thousand of them,* having tasted the frenzy of destruction, having tasted power in raw, brutal form, to return to normality. 'What, go back to study? Then what is the Cultural Revolution for?' they demanded.

And until September 1967, some groups were kept on a war footing, deliberately, as 'storm troopers', by the Directorate. Among them was the notorious 'May 16' group.

The May 16ers originated in a faction from Peking's two major universities, Tsinghua and Peking Universities, favoured by the Directorate. Recruits would accompany Chiang Ching in her jaunts through China and lead the chorus of praise at her speeches. 'Whoever attacks Comrade

*There were around 30 to 40 million Red Guards.

Chiang Ching attacks the Party, attacks Chairman Mao . . . Defend Chiang Ching to the death!'

Chen Pota and other members of the Directorate organized the May 16 storm troopers into battalions, assigning them a special task, which was to topple Chou Enlai.

'We were told to discover incriminating material against the greatest mandarin of them all,' said one Red Guard, who subsequently turned against Chiang Ching. 'The Directorate would provide us with documents, or we would look for them. These were Chou Enlai's speeches, talks, interviews. We pored over each word. Each action of Chou's was scrutinized by us. In June 1961 Chou had said, in a talk on literature, "There is an evil phenomenon extant among us . . . a lack of democracy . . . many people do not dare to think, to speak, to act . . ." Was this bourgeois liberalism? We decided it was. He had also said, "Chairman Mao has corrected his own writings . . . great artists correct their own works . . . great men acknowledge their errors and mistakes . . ." Could this be finding fault with the invincible Thought of Chairman Mao? We coupled stray sentences here and there, from many of his talks, took them out of context and convinced ourselves that Chou Enlai must be toppled.'

Many of the recruits of the May 16ers were found among students of the Foreign Language School; the Aviation School of Peking produced another group called the June 16ers. These were devoted to Lin Piao and controlled by Lin Piao's son, Lin Likuo, who was a commander in the air force.

In the general disruption of order the cities' jails were opened and criminals released. 'We considered they had suffered from the bourgeois line of the capitalist roaders in the Party,' said a young Red Guard from Szechuan who, ten years later, excoriated Chiang Ching and Lin Piao. 'They did terrible things . . . if some of us learnt to torture people and to rape, it was they who incited us to do it.'

Despite the havoc, Chou's unceasing efforts to restore

unity, to get the young back to school, seemed to have partly succeeded by May 1967. Mao was quoted as saying he wanted to unite 'the left and the centre', meaning the new constellation of power and the old cadres, whom he had proclaimed 'in the vast majority good or relatively good'. Thus the much abused Chen Yi, and Tan Chenlin, and Chu Teh, and Yeh Chienying took their place with him on Tienanmen gate on May 1st. This was, in a way, a defeat for the Lin Piao–Chiang Ching alliance. And it enhanced Chou's stature. He told the Red Guards bluntly to moderate their attacks, even on Liu Shaochi and Teng Hsiaoping; and directives for 'severe punishment' for murder, arson, plunder were posted up. Nevertheless the Directorate pressed on.

In June and July 1967 Chiang Ching, who was then at the height of her popularity, made many speeches, some of them highly emotional, to the Red Guards throughout China.

Chiang Ching had been catapulted into prominence by Lin Piao's nomination of her to direct culture in the army. Her close friendship with Yeh Chun, Lin Piao's wife, was also a feature of the alliance. They were called 'two roses on a single stem' because wherever one went there was the other, directing the applause and shouting the slogans: 'Learn from Comrade Chiang Ching', 'Swear to die to protect Chiang Ching, the standard bearer of the Cultural Revolution!'

But Chiang Ching's emergence as a political star came in November 1966, at a rally of some twenty thousand writers, painters and musicians held in Peking in the Great Hall of the People. All the speakers present, among them Chen Pota, Kang Sheng, Ching Chingmai, Kuo Mojo praised her in varying degrees. So did Chou Enlai, after a fashion. 'The achievements of the Cultural Revolution in literature and art mentioned just now . . . are inseparable from the guidance given by Comrade Chiang Ching,' said he. Everyone clapped. But was it eulogy?

Chiang Ching addressed the delirious audience. Besides

the official version of her speech, there is a non-official version, only obtainable many years later, in which she reviled some old cadres by name, referred to attacks against herself, and started weeping. 'Some people try to harm me, gather black material against me,' she said. These outbursts would become increasingly frequent, and at the end, she would turn in fury upon people, in a manner which strongly suggests mental derangement.

But this was 1966, and no one at the time thought her mad. However, something possessed her. What was it?

I have sifted all the material, talking to dozens of people who encountered her through the decades, to those upon whom she wreaked her fury as well as to those devoted to her. I believe she dreaded that some episodes in her past should be made known to the general public. For even then she aimed for nothing less than supreme power, the leadership of the Party, at Mao's demise. She would say to her biographer, Roxane Witke, 'Sex and love are only for a time, but power is decisive, and is most satisfying.'*

Why was Chiang Ching so frightened? Because of sex and love.

In Shanghai, as an actress, Chiang Ching had had liaisons. Even before that – here rumour, gossip, and truth cannot be disentangled – it is said that as a poor young girl she was sold, as concubine, to a wealthy landlord who turned out to be a relative of Kang Sheng, that rigid Party member, head of the Public Security Bureau in the Red base of Yenan, and one of the 'Twenty-eight Bolsheviks' picked by Stalin to direct the Communist Party of China.†

In avant garde circles of Shanghai of the 1930s, there was more freedom in sexual matters than anywhere else in China.

Comrade Chiang Ch'ing (Little, Brown and Company, New York, 1977): a biography reposing chiefly on Chiang Ching's own testimony about herself. The words above are recounted slightly differently by Miss Witke; I have the Chinese version, from a witness present at the interviews between Miss Witke and Chiang Ching in 1972.
†See *The Morning Deluge*.

Sexual freedom was considered by Chiang Kaishek 'communist immorality', and lurid tales of young girls inveigled into promiscuity by communists were printed every Saturday in the newspaper which my husband Pao gave me to read, while I was in Chungking. Pao thought it would infuse in me horror of communism. He was infusing me with horror of sex.

But sexual freedom did not exist in Communist rural bases, where, on the contrary, the peasant guerrilla army, 'an army of virgin soldiers' as Snow would describe them, had brought the purity and strict morality of China's villages with them.

'The Shanghai leftist intellectuals thought free love progressive, a defiance of old feudal mores . . . but they got a shock when they went to Yenan,' Rewi Alley said to me.

In Yenan, Mao fell in love with Chiang Ching and she promptly moved into his cave and became pregnant. Mao then sought to divorce his wife Ho Tzuchen and to marry Chiang Ching. There was opposition in the Party; and many 'facts' – and also unfacts – must have circulated about her at the time, gossip going from cave to cave. Chiang Ching was called all sorts of names, from 'a worn slipper' (which means a prostitute) to 'a dirty woman'.

Chiang Ching did nothing to make things easier. 'She was not wicked then,' says S., an actress who knew Chiang Ching and stayed with her for a while in the same cave. 'But she was impossibly vain; she would always have to be different, would not join with other women to talk, or go for a walk . . . she wore a great cape and rode a white horse . . . always she would try to attract attention . . .'

Chiang Ching would never forgive those who derided her. She brooded on this, it festered and poisoned her. Twice, in 1950–1 and again in the early 1960s, she tried to work in films in China, but each time she came up against opposition.

Hsia Yen* was to tell me so himself. 'I was in charge of

*The Vice-Minister of Culture at the time. He has been rehabilitated and has resumed his functions.

film editing. She was mean-spirited. She always wanted to dominate. I could not entrust her with any responsible job because she was excessive in everything; excessive criticism or excessive laudation . . . I rejected her point of view about some scripts for films and she never forgave me . . . Hence I was singled out for physical abuse.' Hsia Yen was beaten, his leg broken, and he was refused medical care.

Hsia Yen is not the only one who ascribes his ill-treatment to Chiang Ching's insatiable vindictiveness. Chou Yang had arguments with her in Shanghai; he was to be treated most cruelly. 'She was revengeful to an extreme degree . . . she had delusions . . . she suffered from persecution mania and she was terrified that the Chinese people would know of her past.' Chiang Ching knew – as every woman in China knows – that the Chinese masses are still extremely 'feudal' in matters of sex. How could she become a top leader if tales of her youthful levity circulated among the people, in a land where sexual freedom is still today considered the equivalent to promiscuity and prostitution?

A tale (which some Shanghai officials aver is true) is told of an operation mounted in Shanghai in October and November 1967 to remove from libraries, newspaper archives and private houses all films, photographs, newspaper clippings, letters, which contained any reference to Chiang Ching's previous life and career. This removal was made possible through the collaboration of Chiang Ching's Shanghai supporters, Chang Chunchiao and Yao Wenyuan, the Red Guards, and Lin Piao's son, Lin Likuo.

The Red Guards of the Aviation Ministry (directed by Lin Likuo) were detailed to conduct searches among the people whom Chiang Ching had known in her youth. They were arrested, their houses ransacked; they were interrogated and also their friends and distant relatives were searched. Almost all those who had known her as the actress Lan Ping* were incarcerated for various 'crimes'. The prominent and very

---

*The name Chiang Ching gave herself in her young acting days in Shanghai.

popular actress Pei Yang was accused of being an American
spy. Film directors, scriptwriters, even an old servant of Lan
Ping, went to jail. A few of them died there.

All the material recuperated was handed over to Chiang
Ching. However, her feeling of insecurity was not allayed,
and in November 1966 she seems to have begun that
incoherent public babble, interspersed with weeping fits,
which would increase through the years and become at last
uncontrollable.

As a doctor, I feel immensely sorry for her. I understand
the terror in her heart, because I suffered in a similar way. I
understand that she had begun to hate the good and virtuous
women, the stolid and uncomplaining guerrilla women who
had frowned upon her conduct. And I understand too how
these women, who had suffered and endured so much, even
losing their children during the Long March, must have
viewed this newcomer, with her Shanghai manners, and her
arrogance, and especially her use of sexual attractiveness.

Mao's wife, Ho Tzuchen, whom he had married in the
early 1930s, had borne him children; three of them were lost
during the Long March. Ho Tzuchen was one of that small
band of women – there were about thirty of them – who
survived the Long March; everyone respected their heroism,
and called them 'elder sisters'. This was a term of love and
respect, and they lived up to it. But it is certain that they did
not see with a joyful eye Mao divorce his courageous wife
and marry Chiang Ching.

In later years, therefore, Chiang Ching sought revenge on
all the Long Marchers. 'Whenever she saw one of the elder
sisters she used to sneer,' her doctor recalled, when I
interviewed him (of course many years later; he would not
have opened his mouth when she was in power).

'What was she really like?' When people could safely talk,
after 1976, I would go round asking those who had known
her. One of the film directors of the 1930s whom she sought
to kill with ill-treatment (he had apparently refused her a
major role she had coveted in a picture) was back after eleven

years in jail. His health was shattered but his spirit was intact, and he was now rebuilding the film industry. 'She was beautiful and vivacious, but if there was a mirror anywhere, she looked at herself in it. She was always somehow acting a role, she lived in a make-believe world of her own, she was *inventing* her life as she lived it.' 'If she came to dinner,' says an artist who knew her then, 'one found oneself quarrelling with one's wife when she had left.' 'Her thirst for revenge was insatiable,' recalls another. 'This was her great weakness. She could not bear not to dominate. She would never be crossed, and anyone who did not agree with her was an enemy. She was small-minded, imagining slights where none were intended.'

Of course, it may be said that all this is criticism 'after the event'. But there is no doubt in my mind that Chiang Ching was suffering from paranoia. However, this kind of paranoia also induces devotion and fascination, a kind of *folie à deux*, and undoubtedly Chiang Ching also had charm, a certain charisma and vivacity. She would attract powerfully young girls in search of an idol, and frustrated women who saw in her a 'revenge against the tyranny of men'. She certainly convinced her biographer, Roxane Witke, that she was 'outstanding'.*

I would encounter Chiang Ching too; I would very gradually begin to realize that she was dangerous for China. But it takes years to check fully all that is said, especially in feudal Asian countries, where the gap between fact and fiction, truth and lies, is so very small.

The second assault on the Establishment began in summer 1967. One hundred thousand Red Guards quartered in front of the Chungnanhai, where the leaders of China lived. Here they set up loudspeakers, blaring night and day; Lui Shaochi must be delivered into their hands. Among them were the May 16 squads, whose tents were pitched nearest to the

---

*As said to the author by Miss Witke in New York on April 19th, 1973.

South Gate, because they were sure that Chou Enlai would come out to speak to them.* 'He will come out with Liu Shaochi, and you can kidnap him,' the young were told. Then perhaps they would do to him what they had done to other chosen victims, take him to one of the chalets in the Western Hills, built for writers to retire to, but now in the hands of Red Guards. Among those lovely hills, some terrible things were done. Chou refused to yield Liu Shaochi; and after almost three weeks of great noise, the Red Guards withdrew.

In July and August the Foreign Ministry was attacked. Red Guards swarmed in, encouraged by the presence of a 'revolutionary' diplomat, Yao Tengshan, the newest recruit of the 'Left'.

Yao had been Chargé d'Affaires in Indonesia, and in April 1967 the Chinese Embassy in Djakarta was involved in a scuffle with Indonesian troops. Yao was declared persona non grata. He came back as a hero and was photographed linking arms with Mao and Chiang Ching. He declared that the foreign policy which Chou Enlai and Chen Yi had practised was 'revisionist'. Bands of May 16ers pillaged the ministry, took files and documents away, while Chen Yi was brought to lengthy meetings to be reviled, and hit. Chou was besieged in his office by Red Guards for twenty-eight hours on end; he could not eat or drink or rest. He spoke with band after band of them, and such was his unflagging courage that they withdrew. 'Then we loved and respected Chou Enlai for his bravery. He made us ashamed of ourselves . . . and we began to suspect Chiang Ching,' says one of the ex-Red Guards whom I would meet.

Meanwhile Yao Tengshan took over the ransacked Foreign Ministry. For almost two weeks he ruled, sending cables to all the ambassadors to return to Peking, announcing that 'the whole world has now entered the era of Mao Tsetung'. Many diplomats returned, but Huang Hua in

*Chou Enlai, being Premier, would use the South or main gate.

Cairo stuck fast, an act of great courage which would cost him three and a half years of labour in a commune. Meanwhile, xenophobia was used by Yao, assaults on foreign diplomats multiplied, culminating in the burning of the British Chancery office on August 22nd. The embassies of Third World countries were not spared.

This was August 1967. Three weeks later, in September, everything changed.

Mao Tsetung had been on a tour of the provinces in July and August, returning to Peking in early September. It is probable that in this tour he met many of the regional army commanders and realized that they were not at all happy at the disruption and chaos caused by the seizure of power by the Red Guards. These seasoned fighters saw beyond the ostensible 'vast democracy of the masses'. They realized that it was a move to oust them. Earlier that year the Directorate had launched a forceful propaganda: 'Seize the capitalist roaders in the army'. It meant that the Lin Piao–Chiang Ching alliance was now out for the only power that is, in the end, decisive: the gun.* The commanders were besieged by frenzied Red Guards, their reputations ruined by spurious accusations, while Lin Piao would place his men in control of more army units.

In July, a commander of the Wuhan garrison, Chen Tsaitao, refused to abide by the orders of the Directorate and detained two of its representatives when they came to Wuhan to tell him to support the 'Left' Red Guard organization. Chou Enlai flew to Wuhan to solve the problem, and the most curious scenario took place. Chen Tsaitao made a self-criticism, and agreed to come to Peking. But he pointedly said that he did not know that the Directorate 'had replaced the Party or the Party Secretariat'. Nothing happened to him, and Lin Piao backed down, called a meeting of regional commanders, and made conciliatory

*'Power grows out of the barrel of a gun.' Mao.

noises. Chen Tsaitao today is not only a member of the Central Committee but has been admitted to the Politburo.*

Chiang Ching always swore that she had had nothing to do with the fury of August. She could prove that the Directorate had indeed telephoned the Red Guard leaders, forbidding them to burn down the British Chancery on August 22nd. But it could also be said that on July 22nd she had told the Red Guards not to give up their badges and their weapons, contradicting Mao's orders that they return to their place of study and cease from violence. She had then used a phrase which would prove a nefarious influence – so it is now said – in the subsequent general strife which erupted through the provinces and the cities: 'ATTACK BY REASON, DEFEND BY FORCE'. This was the green light for continued violence, at a time when the Red Guards were attacking army garrisons and raiding arsenals. Even trains to Vietnam were looted for weaponry.

But there are, of course, many ways of explaining events; and the defenders of the Gang of Four contend that this phrase had nothing to do with the violence which already existed.

Mao severely condemned the July and August violence as 'ultra-left' and the slogan against the army as counter-revolutionary. He said the young had shown themselves petty bourgeois radicals, not true revolutionaries; and now they must learn to integrate with workers and peasants.

'On a retreat, the general lightens his chariot,' says the Chinese art of war; which means that subalterns must be cast aside and sacrificed, to save the leaders. Chen Pota, Lin Piao and Chiang Ching condemned the May 16 groups, and four or five members of the Directorate were arrested as the main instigators of that crazy summer, as was Yao Tengshan. From that time on, the Directorate, based on the Lin Piao–Chiang Ching alliance, began to crumble.

On September 6th, Chou Enlai made a speech, with

*As of May 1979.

clearly marked points. There must now be unity; the young must return to their schools, production must go on; the army must remain stable. He refused to revenge himself. Let the young, said he, learn by experience . . . Chiang Ching was also called upon to make a speech. She was obviously disconcerted; but she had to denounce the May 16 groups as 'counter-revolutionary' and castigate those who attacked the army. 'Who dares to slander our beloved Premier Chou Enlai?' she would exclaim. Then she disappeared for three months; 'wearied by her labours,' said Chou Enlai blandly.

Among the Westerners living in Peking, strange things had taken place. A 'Norman Bethune' group of foreign residents, who wanted to participate in the Cultural Revolution, had been formed. They turned their suddenly discovered revolutionary ardour upon tried men, noble men, who had worked for decades in China, such as Rewi Alley and Ma Haiteh. They accused Rewi of being a 'traitor', of having 'clandestine' relations with the Kuomintang. Rewi was 'investigated' and it was found that he had written favourably on Marshal Ho Lung, and there was even a photograph of him with Ho Lung. Rewi was no longer visited by friends, except Ma Haiteh, and another doctor, Hans Miller, who stuck to him through every conceivable distress. The foreigners held a 'struggle-meeting', Chinese-style, against Rewi. Later some of his books were to be destroyed.

The viciousness – there is no other word for it – exhibited by these Westerners, including Americans, is a frightening instance of mass psychosis. 'You should have seen them,' said Rewi to me years later, laughing gently. 'They were trying to do exactly like the silly kids. Their eyes popped out and they spouted fire and they thought they were the tops in revolution-making.'

In September 1967 some of these 300 per centers* were jailed. However, innocent foreigners who had not run amok

*The name was given by Neale Hunter, an Australian writer, to the foreigners in China who demonstrated this excessive revolutionary ardour.

were also jailed. The general accusation was 'espionage'.

The May 16 groups, abandoned by their sponsors, and dubbed 'counter-revolutionary', were now hunted down. They scattered through the provinces and some reached Hong Kong. But their leaders were told to 'lie low – wait for another opportunity'.

In January 1967 I went back to the United States for another lecture tour.

I was extremely nervous, and suffered from fits of depression because of the Cultural Revolution, and exhaustion. In Hong Kong the *Takungpao* and its able director, Mr Fei Yiming, were having a hard time. The Hong Kong 'troubles' and riots would occur in that spring. Fei would be called 'Red fat cat' by foreign correspondents, and at the same time was threatened as a 'capitalist roader' by young activists sent from Kuangchow to 'strengthen' and 'revolutionize' the pro-communist press in Hong Kong. *Takungpao* was identified with Chou Enlai, with moderation – attacks against Chou Enlai were then being launched in China, and the Hong Kong 'troubles' were part of this campaign to discredit Chou's foreign policy.

America was also seething with violence that year. We went to Harlem. The angry ooze of the air, the song-talk of those clarinet and tuba African voices with the soar and growl of syllables ... At the time the Black Panthers were still about, and Anna-Louise Strong had pinned great faith upon them. But they would be systematically shot down by 'law and order' forces, at three or four in the morning, and they disappeared by dint of assassination, and drugs, and their own betrayals. Their leaders, Huey Newton and Eldridge Cleaver – the latter I was to interview in Algeria in 1971 – and Stokely Carmichael (who was on television with me on a Susskind show), went into religion, or respectability, or perhaps even some money. Malcolm X had been killed, and Martin Luther King even though not a Black Panther, would also be murdered.

America was, I felt then, burdened with a splendid and treacherous technology, which substituted whirrs and clicks for her existence's heartbeats, and bright dancing riffles of programmed action for her soul's humanity. The Vietnam war was now focusing both that monstrous beauty of power which had overawed Vincent and me, and its helplessness, its terror content. The trust in machines to win at every turn was ebbing, and Americans were at grips with their own conscience; very few, in 1967, still felt that the Vietnam war was a good thing. But the voices promising victory continued loud and shrill.

It was in that year, talking in San Diego College on family planning in China to an almost empty sports stadium (the student committee in charge of arrangements had resigned, and forgotten my lecture) that, from among the six people who attended the lecture walked towards me a woman, tall, auburn-haired and with beautiful grey-green eyes. 'I'm Shirley MacLaine,' said she.

This was the beginning of yet another precious friendship. Shirley MacLaine has never let her film-star success devour her other selves; her capacity for initiative and innovation remained whole, as did her refusal to set limits to her integrity. To have come in a storm, to a lecture on family planning in China – I've never quite got over thinking how much independence it took. China was not exactly a Hollywood topic at the time.

Felix Greene had been abused by the Hsinhua news agency in a report about his activities in Vietnam (he was immensely busy speaking in America against the Vietnam war). 'I'll just drop China for a bit,' said he. Mutely I wished I too could 'drop China' like that. I could not. I would be a prisoner of the Cultural Revolution for ten long years. I remembered Malraux saying of it: 'We shall see an experiment, which will both dazzle and fragment the soul of man.' It certainly almost broke me.

I had hoped to go back to China that summer of 1967.

Meanwhile, Vincent and I took a tour through France, its blessed, civilized beauty; there is no country like it in the world for making one aware of life's graces. We were accompanied by Cécile Verdurand, the representative of my French publishers. She brought her wit and robust sense, laughter and talk, and gaiety, and I would discover that intelligent, vivacious, indispensable being; the French-woman. I would have many French women friends from then onwards, and find with them an immediacy of understanding of great value to me.

By April I had finished *Birdless Summer*, and also a small book called *China in the Year 2001*, requested by C. H. Watts, the publishers in England. I sent some proof copies of the latter book to Kung Peng.

A telegram came through Hong Kong. Kung Peng advised me to make changes in the book. To begin with, the preface was all wrong. Secondly, there were quotations from Liu Shaochi and from Marshal Lo Juiching in my book. They *must* come out. I looked at the preface. It certainly was all wrong, but I could not recover the original, which I had done hastily, scribbling it because I had no typewriter available. And I had not reread it before sending it to the printer! My carelessness was due to fatigue, a dazed exhaustion, and worry over events in China played no small part in this physical depression. But other major snags were the quotes from Liu and Lo. The Liu quote was, to my mind, inoffensive; it could easily be left out because it was not important. As for Lo Juiching, I had been impressed by the clarity of his pamphlet of 1965. I knew Lo was in trouble, but was that any reason for not quoting him? However, perhaps there were many things I did not know. Kung Peng would never have advised me to do this unless it was important; for she had never previously insisted on any change. And so I took the quotes out, a matter of some ten lines, which did not make much difference to the book. Or so I thought, until I realized that the effect would be to leave Lin Piao the sole expounder of the *military* point of view of Mao.

Kung Peng was doing this for my sake. She must have known that I was being attacked in China, something I would only learn a few months later: in those wall posters in Shanghai, condemning Pearl Buck and myself as agents of American imperialism.

Another message came from Kung Peng. It was not advisable for me to come to China that year. Neither would it be advisable in 1968.

Those two years were to be among the most draining of my life. I felt desiccated, cut off from China, for how long I did not know. Suppose I could never return . . . what about Third Uncle and Third Aunt and Third, Fourth and Sixth Brothers and their wives and their children? What about all my friends?

I cannot help it if I react as a Chinese, thinking of the Family, thinking of how to protect them. Thinking: 'Never do anything to imperil another human life.' Words and notions and convictions come and go; but a human life is not to be endangered lightly.

I watched with pangs other people go to China: French and British and other 'friends of China'. But Edgar Snow and I met with refusal. Ed could not understand why. He armed himself with fortitude. However, I would often break down and weep. I would wake up in the morning with streaming eyes, and Vincent would take me in his arms, his arms my shelter against all storms, and rock me like a child, and utter cooing sounds. I regressed into a total baby. I had terrible tantrums for nothing.

'It will pass, it will pass,' said Vincent, cradling me.

Ed told me how, in his last visit at the end of 1964, he had asked to interview Liu Shaochi. 'Chou Enlai did not appear too keen. He was protecting me, I think. "Now why do you want to see Liu Shaochi?" he asked me. And then he arranged that I should be at a general reception where all the leaders of China were present. There were Mao and Liu, and Liu's wife, Wang Kuangmei, sitting side by side with Mao's wife, Chiang Ching; and they all looked serene, and no one would have guessed anything was amiss. And then Chou, with that wonderful impish smile of his, said, "Well now you've seen everybody, haven't you?"' Ed shook his head. 'I've made a lot of mistakes,' he said.

'But everybody does, Ed; and I don't think the Chinese themselves know what is going to happen . . . there will be many more mistakes, but they won't be our mistakes.'

I think that when history goes as fast as it does in China, with so many sudden capsizings and reversals, the word 'mistake' is inappropriate.

In July and August 1967, everything seemed to go crazy in China. 'You're going to have a nervous breakdown. I'm taking you to India,' said Vincent, and started packing our suitcases. Vincent always does the packing. Whenever we have moved house, or country, Vincent has done the packing. Usually, when packing starts, I shirk by becoming ill.

. But then came a message from Prince Sihanouk's secretary, Charles Meyer. Would I come to Phnom Penh? A short time before that message Charles had written to me, 'What is going on in China? It is unbelievable . . . xenophobia . . . barbarism . . . this is not the China of Chou Enlai.'

Prince Norodom Sihanouk was, understandably, angry. Some of the China Friendship Associations abroad, on orders from Peking, had behaved outrageously. They had been ordered to remove the portraits of the heads of state hanging beside the portrait of Mao; and the Cambodia–China Friendship Association had duly taken down Sihanouk's picture. In Nepal as well the King's effigy had been removed.

Sihanouk was also worried about the fate of Chou Enlai. In his last trip to China with his wife, Princess Monique, in 1964, he had been very happy. With Chou he had gone to Szechuan, and through the Yangtze Gorges in a brand new steamer, sketching and painting and making music all the way. He had composed a song about friendship with China, a song which Chou Enlai had learnt by heart, and hummed to himself.

Now we felt that Chou Enlai was in peril, and that the era of the warlords would return, for Lin Piao did not command the loyalty of all the military units in China. 'All this is very bad for China, and for Asia,' said the forthright Prince.

'Your wisdom, Monseigneur, will overcome this transient episode,' I said feebly, smiling hard to mask my desolation.

I wrote to Chou Enlai. I forget the exact words, but it was to tell him that I was devoted to him. I thought: If he is destroyed I shall have to give up going back to China.

Three weeks in India with Vincent's family dulled but did not cure my distress. Vincent's father was particularly kind, asking pertinent, shrewd questions about the Cultural Revolution, but not probing where it hurt.

In September all was changed. The downfall of several rabid 'revolutionaries', members of the Directorate in charge of the Cultural Revolution, indicated a major turnabout. And then, a little later, I learnt that my friends the Yangs were jailed . . . what had they done?

In January 1968 the film director Fred Zinnemann and I met at lunch at the Algonquin in New York. Fred had in hand a major project, a picture based on André Malraux's book, *Man's Fate*. Three writers had tried, without success, to write a film script. 'They all sounded like the "Internationale",' said Fred. Then his wife, Reneé, had suggested me. I agreed to write the script. Work was an opiate, tranquillizer, since I could not go to China that year.

Fred and his crew and I went to Hong Kong, to Malaya (where I was happy to see Tunku Abdul Rahman again) and to Singapore, for locations. But most of the work was done in London. Fred was entrancing to work with: relentless as a diamond drill. No slipshod word got past him. We fought all the way through the script, we fought on the colour of clothes, on everything. I think that writing the script saved my sanity. Fred Zinnemann even went to Calcutta's railway station to get the 'feel' of misery, of hopelessness.

In late March I attended a symposium on China at North Carolina University, together with Edgar Snow and other distinguished American experts on China, including Alexander Eckstein. The symposium was marked by a major event: President Johnson's television speech in which he announced that he would not seek re-election. The implication was an admission that America's Far Eastern policies would need a major overhaul.

In May 1968 we went for a few days to Paris, just long enough to catch a glimpse of the student leader, Cohn Bendit, and his supporters marching, marching along the Boulevard St Michel. The walls of Paris blossomed with words, and here too there was hope, exaltation of purpose . . . but also the acrid smell of tear gas and panic. Some timorous wealthy families were running away to Switzerland, taking with them refrigerators and television sets, all the encumbrances of non-living. The spectre of the Cultural Revolution in China haunted certain minds.

But in May 1968 in China the PLA had been empowered to shoot down those who refused to relinquish their weapons, who raided and killed and burned. From May to July, grim and bloody battles were fought; battles which took place primarily between factions of Red Guards, with the army trying to intervene to keep the peace, and suffering casualties. Some commanders, however, did not exhibit much tender care for the young. The mopping up operations they undertook, while they heartened the population, were certainly tough upon errant Red Guards.

The university sector of Peking was transformed into a battlefield wherein two Red Guard factions, barricading themselves in, launched assaults on 'enemies' with everything at hand, including roof tiles, bricks, mortars and machine guns. After about a hundred days of this murderous game* and repeated calls to the Red Guard leaders, Mao Tsetung ordered teams of Peking factory workers backed by army regiments to clean up the battle areas. He then saw the faction leaders and spoke to them for some hours. 'You have resisted the workers . . . you have killed and wounded workers,' said he.

Now the 'integration of youth with workers and peasants' proceeded. From September onwards millions of young people would depart for villages and state farms and army resettlement farms, in order to learn how to serve the people.

'Nothing has changed.' In January 1968 twenty factions of discontented Red Guards had published an essay, 'Whither China', concluding that the pendulum had swung back. 'The old Party committee and the old military district have now become the revolutionary committee,' they wrote; but 'nothing has changed; all is exactly as before.'

'Back to normalcy?' In Hong Kong and abroad the China watchers and the newspapers surmised and speculated. In autumn 1968 Liu Shaochi was expelled from the Party as a 'traitor, renegade and scab'. And preparations to hold a Party Congress, and to fashion a new constitution, were well advanced. All over China there was haste to set up the new organs of power, revolutionary committees, to be composed of 'the masses', Party cadres, and army men. The preponderance in positions of leadership of army men was noteworthy. Since the Party organization had been badly weakened, only the army could maintain control.

I felt slightly relieved, especially when, in early 1969, I received an indirect message from Kung Peng. In October 1968, I had been invited to McGill University in Montreal to deliver three lectures on the Cultural Revolution. I realize now that some of the statements I made were excessive, in fact, 'ultra-left', and 'petty-bourgeois radical'. Chou Enlai would surely have said so had he heard them. He did when he

---

*See *The Hundred Days War* by William Hinton, Monthly Review Press, New York, 1974.

read them. But I suffered from euphoria; for now all seemed to go gradually back to normal; Chou Enlai was strong, and even non-communist newspapers wrote optimistically of China. True, there were bad things; but it was impossible at the time (and would be impossible for some years, in fact until the end of 1976) to obtain definite, hard-core information on what had happened, although I did my best. And so many people, respected scholars, wrote books praising the phenomenon of the Cultural Revolution . . . I too wanted to believe that at last the enormous problems confronting China were going to find a solution.

By May 1969 I had five hundred pages of draft for *The Morning Deluge*, the first part of my book on Mao Tsetung and the Chinese Revolution. I had become absorbed, fascinated by the personality of Mao, his vision and the impact he had had on China and on the history of the world in consequence. I was determined to understand him, to understand what had happened.

It was impossible for me, during those Cultural Revolution years, to get away from this obsession. As my writer friends in China were stuck, unable to write, so was I blocked, unable to write of love, or romance, or to imagine anything light and pleasant – all that dredged up was China, China, and the Revolution in China. I had to write it down *to get rid of it*. Everything else somehow appeared mediocre, second rate, a narrow squint of half-life compared to the tremendous convulsions which agitated the world of China.

Only after 1976, when Chiang Ching and her gang fell, did I feel liberated. And now I think that if I had been able to detach myself, to abandon China mentally, to write of romance while my writer friends were cleaning lavatories and being abused, I would despise myself very much today.

Before I left for Peking in the summer of 1969 I met again Charles Meyer and his wife Sika. They were on holiday in Switzerland. I spent two delightful days with them at Zermatt.

Charles had greatly changed. He fulminated, vociferated, against Sihanouk. 'He is awful,' said Charles. 'He does terrible things. He must be got rid of . . . we shall be getting rid of him . . . he cannot last another year . . . just wait and see . . .' Charles seemed very sure that Sihanouk would be overthrown. What has got into him? I wondered.

I received my visa in Paris, from the chubby, gifted Ambassador, Huang Chen, a Long Marcher, and an artist of talent.* 'Your friends are waiting for you in Peking,' said he. In the hot July of France, he opened his grey tunic and fanned his undershirt, in the best guerrilla manner, oblivious of decorum. But he had so much personality, so much glamour, that he could carry off anything, and the French loved him.

*Now Minister of Culture.

CHAPTER 4

The Nourishing Tree of Truth: 1969

In Kuangchow none of the thorny xenophobia apparent in 1966 remained; no one shouted 'foreign devil'. The rice was short and very green in the fields; it was the typhoon-proof kind; and the sugar cane grew tall.

Everyone had Mao badges pinned on them; some the size of small saucers. The Love the Masses Hotel was no longer available; and Ram City Hotel was now renamed The East is Red. Every shop's name was also The East is Red.

But the apparent peace was not more than glance-deep; the peace of China is that of the Pacific Ocean which brews its own cyclones. When I went for a walk, Miss H of the Friendship Association stuck close to me. I was whisked away from a street corner where I stopped to read the posted notice calling for an immediate surrender of all weaponry and intimating death penalties to people who committed murder, raided arsenals, or set fire to state property. 'Struggle-criticism-transformation is still going on,' said Miss H, who suggested it was far too hot to walk. Why not ride in the car instead? At night, I heard gunshots and the whistle of bullets.

All the cadres I met told me how beneficial the Cultural Revolution had been for them. They admitted they had been 'shocked and shaken', but prided themselves on the manual labour they had performed. They certainly looked healthy, if dark-skinned. One of them told me how many kilogrammes of grain he could now carry: 'almost as much as a commune member.'

This would be the theme – unending, continuous, repetitious – of all the people I met that year. University professors, medical consultants from hospitals, engineers and experts, Party cadres and non-Party cadres – they all said almost the same thing. I do not think that the eighty-nine professors, doctors, lecturers whom I would meet that year (there was a singular absence of writers – I was unable to meet even one) lied to me, I think it is true that they reckoned that their experience, however unpleasant, had 'cleansed' them. 'We did believe at the time, that we had indeed been arrogant and élitist . . . and we were ready to reform ourselves.' This is what they say now. And I say to them, 'Of the dozens of your confessions which I took down, I have not published a single one. Other "outsiders", honoured guests, foreign friends, have written some very large books on what you said to them at the time. I have refrained. And now many of those who simply took down your words as truth feel angry; some feel cheated. But I know you have not lied. The human capacity for self-persuasion is infinite. The human soul is an assembly of contradictions. And therefore both your versions, the one of those years, and the one you give today, are correct.'

There had been great turmoil in the factories of Kuangtung province. 'Workers were fighting each other . . . but Chairman Mao said: No division in the working class, so we promoted a grand alliance in September 1967', said the workers I interviewed. But not all the factories were working, and in those I saw, about one-third of the machinery was idle. When I pointed to the empty benches, I was told that the workers were 'resting' or that 'we have fulfilled our quotas for the month', which meant that the workers had not turned up, or that raw material for processing had run out, or that the machines needed repairing.

'Many activists from the working class have come up through the Cultural Revolution. It is important to rejuvenate the Party'. This meant that young workers were becoming Party members by the million. In fact, the Party would double its numbers from 1965 to 1975.

I was not impressed by the young workers. They dawdled

and smoked in small groups in workshops; they played basketball in the courtyards; they loafed on the streets. Only the older workers seemed to work – and how they worked! As if they had to make up for the sloth of the young.

A cut-down in the plethora of 'administrators' had occurred; everywhere their numbers had been reduced; and the remaining ones were supposed to do manual labour at least part of the week. This was the superficial pattern exhibited all over China's factories in 1969. However, there was a new kind of overstaffing. In a commune, I found that three hundred young Red Guards from middle school were assigned to look after two thousand apple trees – which makes less than seven trees per person. Did they have other chores? No, the apple orchard only . . . They told me that they were educated youths of the working class who had decided to remain peasants all their lives. But they were only ten kilometres from the city, they all had bicycles, and they earned full salaries as commune members. 'The working class must lead in everything,' they said again and again; which meant that they probably were members of the commune revolutionary committee, and did very little labour. They were an added load on the back of the peasantry.

Primary schools had reopened nearly all over China, including Yunnan province, which had been badly battered by the Cultural Revolution. The middle schools were in the process of reopening, but the universities were still in 'struggle-criticism-transformation'. This in Chinese is tow,pee,gay, and pretty soon it became for me a verb to be conjugated: 'Have you been *tobegayed* yet?' 'They are *tobegaying*.'*

I saw a number of primary schools in seven provinces. In many instances the teachers were not willing to teach; they had been too humiliated. The admission age was raised to

*A joke shared with the American-Chinese doctor, Ma Haiteh.

seven, and as a result everywhere in the lanes of the nine cities I visited that year there were children, children, playing under the eyes of bound-footed old grandmothers, waiting for the schools to admit them.

Soldiers were in charge in every school. In March 1967 Mao had given a directive that 'the army should give political and military training in the universities, middle schools and the higher classes of primary schools'. Often the army man was a retired veteran; he turned the school into a small military camp. The classes were called platoons, and they marched in step. They sang and they studied the little red book, which was everywhere. We all had it. We carried it as a talisman, waving it at each other in greeting; and as if they had just been interrupted in a fascinating, absorbed reading of it, some cadres kept a finger in its pages at all times.

One night, returning very late along an airport road, I watched a middle school being assembled; it was going down to the countryside where there was a drought, in order to help the peasants to water their fields. The soldiers ran along the huddled youngsters shouting orders. Then, to the regular sound of whistles, they marched off. The youngsters would form long chains, passing pails of water from hand to hand, for a kilometre or perhaps two or three, to reach those parched fields away from the canal or the river.

I thought that was good.

On the aeroplane to Peking the hostesses entertain us with songs about Mao. At the airport there is Hsing Chiang, resilient and neat; she does not adopt the scruffy, unkempt style (unpressed shirt, worn-out and patched trousers) some cadres do to show how 'revolutionary' they are. I admire Hsing Chiang because she is always plainly *herself*. She tells me that she too has been 'shocked and splashed', the butt of criticism and attacks.

I see Kung Peng the next afternoon. Oh, how awful she looks! So thin, so thin, almost skeletal, pale and ravaged, and her walk is unsteady. She has constant headaches, but she smiles that wonderful smile of hers, and I remember her great beauty; it comes back when she smiles.

'Yes, I've changed, but do not worry,' she says. 'Believe me, it was all most necessary.'

I do not reply, because I feel shocked. Calvary was also necessary, I suppose . . . shall man only be redeemed through agony?

Kung Peng will not tell me what she has endured. But others do, bits here and there . . . how she had to kneel for hours, submit to abuse . . . how she has been for a year in a May 7 cadre school (which some people are calling 'cattle sheds' because Mao has said it),* and laboured planting rice . . . how Chou Enlai, who meanwhile has been deprived of almost all his ministers and their staff, and his own staff, recalled her, for he has no one to help him.

With her came Hsiung, once Chargé d'Affaires in England. He had been attacked, during that mad summer of 1967, by some British 300 per centers. For both in China and abroad Western 'friends of China' – fortunately a minority – also went berserk. 'The situation is excellent,' they kept on repeating, having read it in the *Peking Review*. They wore enormous Mao badges, and in London they wrote posters against Hsiung as a 'revisionist' (or was it 'capitalist roader'?). The person who indulged most in these antics, however, is still going to China and is an 'expert' much valued in some circles. Hsiung brushed aside the whole matter. 'A communist must be able to endure any hardship . . . He must never exact personal revenge. He must ignore the small things . . . what are these trials compared to humanity's sufferings through the ages?' I have great affection for Hsiung. Under a cold exterior, he has a warm heart and a good brain.

The Temple of Heaven was being cleaned by schoolchildren; Peking's railway station too. Large posters announced that old monuments must be respected.

*Labour camps for cadres, to reform them through work and study.

Vandalized shrines and parks were being repaired and protected by Red Guards. 'We are taking youth in hand.' The most common sight that summer was the busloads of youngsters of about seventeen or eighteen, with red flags and drums, being taken away to the countryside. With them were cadres and of course army men. Two hundred thousand youths would leave Peking that year for state farms, communes and the new army resettlement farms sited in thinly populated regions such as Sinkiang and North Manchuria.

'We are still unmasking hidden class enemies,' says Hsing Chiang, 'counter-revolutionaries.' But now the term, from being so constantly used, has lost all meaning. I ask about Pa Chin, the writer. 'He's been labelled counter-revolutionary.' So has Lao Sheh . . . so has . . . oh, so many of the writers I know.

There are two kinds of 'counter'. The ones who are 'straight counter' and the others, who 'wave the red flag to knock down the red flag', a tortuous phrase which means that they are the ultra-left, and have been, in the name of Mao and the Revolution, killing people and raiding arsenals for weapons. 'Chairman Mao ordered a thorough investigation into the May 16 groups.' But members of May 16 contingents have run away, to Szechuan, and also to Hong Kong. The hunt against them is conducted by the very same people who brought them into being. As a result, people who are *not* May 16ers are being arrested by genuine but unknown May 16ers! My Mongol cousin by marriage, he of the splendid voice – a voice which shook the window panes of the room where we sat in 1964 – becomes a victim of this deadly masquerade, and will spend three years in jail, where he will catch tuberculosis. He will be rescued in 1972 by Chou Enlai. But it will be 1977 before he will tell me what has happened to him. I meet the son of my dear friend Yeh in front of the Western District supermarket.

'How are your father and mother?'

'They are well.'

'Give them my regards.'

I stride quickly away. I do not want him to be interrogated: 'Why were you talking to this outsider? Who is she?' Neither do I go to see Yeh and Yuan Yin, his wife, although I love them well.

Yeh would thank me for my discretion when in 1971 I make bold to go to his house. But it was not before the end of 1976, when the Gang of Four were brought down, that Yeh would tell me of his ordeal, and with so much laughter and mimicry of his tormentors that we all roared and had an excellent evening.

Yeh was not 'counter-revolutionary' but he was a 'bourgeois', had 'followed the black line', so he was 'struggled against' in his own office by young Red Guards and his own subalterns. He had to stand in the corridor leading to his office for hours, clean toilets and run errands, and always be available for 'criticism sessions'.

Yet since no one else in the office was competent enough to edit the English language magazine, *Chinese Literature*, the better translators being under duress, Yeh still had to do the work on his small typewriter: translating, editing, putting the magazine together, in between bouts of being abused, having to clean the toilets, and performing other menial tasks. For almost five years, Yeh smiled, and endured, and put out the magazine, competently, on time.

'They would find fault with everything, but finally they would print it.'

'Did they beat you?'

Yeh laughs, looks at his wife, and I guess he had not told her everything. 'Only a few slaps here and there,' says he, 'and of course pulling my hair. They loved pulling people's hair.'

'Every night I went to the bus stop to wait for him,' says Yuan Yin. 'I never knew whether, one night, he would not be on any bus. Sometimes he would only manage the last bus, after midnight.'

But as soon as he was home Yeh would shake his shoulders, laugh a little and say, 'Just another day.' After some food he would settle down and write. His major novel, written in those nights, was published in China in 1979.

'You know,' Yeh says to me, 'I did not hate these childish people. I pitied them. They were so helpless. While they shouted at me, sometimes I could not stop laughing, and it made them angry.' We laugh, we are hilarious, but in our hearts is sadness. Not for us, but for the young who have become a lost generation.

Treading softly, I trod into the panorama of China in 1969; fearful of bringing trouble and sorrow to my friends and my Family. I could not go to Szechuan that year. It was 'inconvenient'. I guessed that sporadic fighting or at least some turmoil must still be going on.

A film on the Ninth Congress of April 1969, when Lin Piao was officially designated Mao's heir, is shown. I see Chen Yi among the delegates. Mao insisted that he be there; Chen Yi is so thin, so thin . . . already he is suffering from the cancer which will kill him. Chou Enlai too is thin; his face is undecipherable. I will learn (rumour?) that when the new constitution which proclaims Lin Piao as Mao's heir was taken for general discussion at all levels, Chou Enlai recommended, 'Do not discuss it too much; let it pass . . .' Why did he give this advice (if it is true that he did)? I think that Chou wanted an end to the chaos and dislocation harming China. Perhaps he felt he could work out something with Lin Piao. The key to Chou's immortality is that he was able to work even with the devil, and extract some good out of him . . . He never lost sight of the main goal: China and the Chinese people.

The Directorate under Chiang Ching and Chen Pota, which had seemingly become the supreme command in 1967, has evanesced, it is no longer mentioned. It never recovered from the blow Mao gave it in September 1967 when five of its eighteen or nineteen members were arrested as 'ultra-leftists'. And now there is a new Central Committee and a new Politburo. The Central Committee is heavily loaded with peasants and workers, and also army men. Three of the four of the future Gang of Four, Chiang Ching, Chang and Yao, are on the Central Committee and in the Politburo. And so is Yeh Chun, Lin Piao's wife. But Mao has also brought back the old Long Marchers, Chu Teh, and Yeh Chienying and Li Hsiennien, and in the Military Affairs' Commission, three old stalwarts to 'balance' Lin Piao and his forceful commander in the south, Huang Yungsheng. Lin Piao's ascendancy, the fact that his men are everywhere, is obvious. But rumour notices that Yeh Chun and Chiang Ching are not as friendly as they used to be.

The *People's Daily* carries a portrait of Mao on its front page every day, and a quotation from the little red book. As a result, it is quite impossible to throw away or to tear up a newspaper without being disrespectful. All stamps carry his head too. I affix a stamp askew and am told off by the post office comrade. 'The stamp is crooked,' she says. Her mind, trained to symbolism, may see in this a deliberate insult to Mao. And perhaps Freud would agree with her. Actually I am so dizzy with the constant propaganda that I become absent-minded and my eyes do not focus well. In the hotel post office an army man sits. He will examine every letter posted at the end of the day. To make his work easier, I only write postcards.

I visit the six Peking factories specially mentioned for their excellent revolutionary behaviour. Many of their workers, both men and women, are delegates or members of revolutionary committees in the capital. Some have become members of the Central Committee. One of these factories is the Hsinhua News Agency Printing Press. I spend some hours there; the workers talk very well; they give me a full account of how, on July 27th, 1968, they invested Tsinghua University to stop the Red Guard factions entrenched there from battering each other to death. 'Some workers were killed, although they carried no weapons . . . There were corpses in the dormitories.'

For their success, they have received a mango from Chairman Mao (who had been given mangoes by the Pakistan government). The mango is enthroned upon a table in preserving liquid, in a beribboned glass tank. I would visit several other factories in China honoured with a mango.

Everywhere Liu Shaochi was excoriated for 'seventeen years of a black revisionist line'. But surely not everything had been badly done in the seventeen years from 1949 to 1966? How otherwise justify the Revolution and its achievements? 'But the bourgeois line was dominant' is the reply. It was not so. But it is impossible to argue without being accused of 'defending the capitalist roaders'.

'The renegade and scab Liu Shaochi pushed material incentives in all our factories.' There is great reprobation of material incentives, but in the twenty-five factories I visit that year, I find that the question of salaries and wages is *not* settled; that remuneration 'to each according to his work', with better workers receiving more; is still being made. 'The wage scale here varies from 40 to 170 dollars,' say the Hsinhua Printing Press workers. They add, 'But what we must fight for is not money, but power. The working class must lead in everything.' This last phrase is the title of an article written by Yao Wenyuan. It has become a major study pamphlet for the whole Party. After 1976 the pamphlet will be denounced as part of the conspiracy of the Gang of Four to seize power, by organizing in factories and among workers nuclei of their own supporters.

Dinner with Kung Peng and her husband Chiao, and Hsiung, his wife and daughter. The daughter, who is sixteen, is a very charming girl. She has been a year at a state farm in Heilungkiang province. Her middle school had volunteered to 'go down' to serve the people, and she and a few other girls, refused because of their youth, had written petitions in blood, obtained by nicking their little fingers. They were allowed to go. This practice is traditional; petitions to authority written in blood indicate their seriousness. The young girl entertains us with stories of her resettlement farm. She describes a bear hunt. 'In Europe and America, do people my age do manual labour?' she asks.

'We have to sacrifice ourselves for the next generation.' Chiao looks worn out, gaunt, his jaw juts, his hands shake. He was so badly beaten that he vomited blood (he has an old tuberculous lesion). Everyone praises his fortitude, and courage.

'The young are showing excellent spirit,' says Kung Peng. Her son and her daughter are labouring in communes. None of the children of higher ranking officials that year are in universities or high schools. Only after 1972 would some of them be able to return to study.

When I left, I felt that I had been in an after-hurricane stillness, in the exhalation of air emptied at last of fury. The survivors had calmly contemplated the hurricane's work, and now there was the rebuilding to do.

When I went to Hualan's house, the whole street turned out to watch me ring her bell. This had not happened before.

Hualan's nephew and niece were in communes. Her nephew guarded walnut trees in a production team. Had he belonged to the village, which of course was a clan village (as 95 per cent of China's villages are), he would not have had this job. 'Because he is not a clan member he can refuse to give the walnuts to the peasants who ask for them.' Otherwise, he could not have refused anyone, not even a child.

'Six to eight educated youths is all a production team can bear. More are not wanted. They have to share the workpoints, and the peasants don't like it.' All youngsters received from the government some 30 *yuan* to start them off; but many of them were unable to make enough workpoints through labour to feed themselves.

Hualan seemed distracted; her eyes unfocused, her fingers brown with smoking. There were many things she would not tell me. 'I cannot . . . I cannot.' We went for walks because her neighbour, who lived in the same courtyard, a man in his forties, had taken it upon himself to come into the living room and stand there watching us and listening. I would not have minded it, had it not been that, owing to the heat, he was in his underpants. 'It's mutual supervision,' said Hualan calmly, and of course we showed no concern. We simply ignored his standing two feet away from me. On one occasion when we went for a walk, since he was in his underwear, he could not follow. He gave up trying after that.

'If I told you everything and you let slip something, I would be in much trouble,' said Hualan.

'I never betray . . . I'm like a clam.'

But Hualan was not reassured.

Hualan's brother was in charge of aeroplane engines at the airport. He had been *tobegayed* so much, dragged to so many meetings, that for a while he exhibited signs of mental imbalance. But he went on with his work, for aeroplanes had to be kept flying. For some years I would supply him with needed medicine. Thus he endured; and now he is well, completely normal, and talks with gusto and triumph of the painful years, as if they had been his private conquest, a victory. 'Now I shall never be afraid of anything, or anyone,' says he. And so many, so many people, young, middle-aged, and old, will say the same thing to me in the years to come.

But other relatives of Hualan have died; two of them, husband and wife, committing suicide. They were called traitors; accused of 'collusion with the outside', beaten . . . It is quite a miracle that Hualan was not ill-treated because of me. 'But I was asked about you and I said, "She loves China, as I do". And Premier Chou Enlai protected me because of my father. So I was only criticized.' And her mother was never persecuted at all. The old lady became gently senile. She never left the house, and blissfully did not know what was happening.

I walked the small lanes of Peking, with their many odours and their blind grey look and that seeping wonderful silver dust, and the all-seeing eyes behind their walls. I tried not to look inquisitive. But in every street, immediately, children ran to announce my coming to the street committee, and people came to stare at me. Spy mania. I walked purposefully, looking straight ahead.

I did manage to see my sister-in-law Jui. Her hands shook. Soon her hair would start to drop. Third Brother, her husband, had been sent to a 'branch' of Peking University in Hanchung district, on the borders of the Shensi, Szechuan and Kansu provinces.

Every university had established branches, or teaching points, in rural areas. This was a very good idea; but they were also accessory relegation sites, where the staff were to 'study' and to reform themselves. In Hanchung, Third Brother, for the space of three years, was employed as a cook's helper. With good grace he fetched and carried water in pails from the distant well. He stoked up the fire, he kept it going with a primitive wind blower; he set the tables (a canteen for three hundred), cleaned and swept the mess hall, washed the crockery. He also had to revise some physics textbooks. But the students of Hanchung would not study. 'To study is too dangerous . . . you get into trouble if you are learned,' they said, having seen what had happened to the intelligentsia.

Third Brother is himself a good cook. Like my father, he has a light, deft hand with dishes.

'Please, please,' said Jui and her children – my three nieces and my nephew, all back from the communes – 'Please, Auntie, please bring our father back to us.'

But I knew that it was impossible to bring him back immediately. I must be circumspect. I must sense the time when it would be possible for him to return. Jui had always been incapable of understanding politics. 'I will do something as soon as possible,' I said. Finally it was out of my hands, but Third Brother was back by 1970 . . .

The eminent physicist, Chou Peiyuan, trained in America, received me in his house. He was co-operating gracefully with the workers and the army Mao Tsetung Thought team which had taken over Peking University in July 1968. Bloody war between Red Guard factions, as in Tsinghua University, had happened there. He agreed with a great deal of what the Cultural Revolution had done, but he stood adamant on fundamental research. 'We must go on with it,' said he. This was a point which Chou Enlai had also constantly supported, as he supported so many progressive and at the time unpopular issues (including mixed marriages, which still today provoke reactions from many cadres of the Party).

But the so-called 'Left', that is, Lin Piao and later the Gang of Four, were opposed to fundamental research, dubbing it 'metaphysical, abstract', which in the Marxist vocabulary is heinous condemnation. In 1958 the Leap had also derided research scientists 'who count the dots on the wing of a fly instead of doing something useful for the country'. It was extremely difficult to explain, especially because the Chinese language is so poor in *abstract* terms, that research unrelated to any obvious, immediate need was important; that the greatest discoveries had been due to hazard, accidents of man's inquisitiveness; that the process of experimentation with no immediate gain in view, only to satisfy a thirst for enquiry, could not be denied.

Peking University was preparing its new intake for 1970. According to Chou Peiyuan, it would be mostly from the worker–peasant–soldier background; selected not by examinations but by merit, the approval of the masses.

This seemed a good idea, promoting progress at grassroots level. But alas, like so many other excellent ideas of the Cultural Revolution it went awry in performance. Doing away with past injustice, that is, favouring the offspring of the intelligentsia and higher cadres through examinations, only created another injustice of a different kind, because of China's peculiar, all-encompassing, feudalism. Pretty soon, only the sons and daughters of *new* cadres – those who had taken the place of the old officials now relegated to inactivity or to the May 7 cadre schools –

would be admitted to the universities; because 'the masses', whose 'approval' was paramount, would not dare to disapprove the selection of the children of new cadres.

> When there's any problem, pass the matter
>   up and up to your superior,
> In any circumstance, see how the wind blows,
> And never, never stick your neck out.

The old adage, the old doggerel, still held in China. I don't know where I got it from; but it's in my notes of that year.

I went to see Rewi Alley. He had a tail.

A security policeman, nice and young, was with him all day and every day, wherever he went. And at night he slept in Rewi's apartment.

'Oh, Rewi.' We three sat in the living room. The security chap sat some distance away, discreet and courteous.

Rewi told me that he had been accused of all sorts of things. 'Not by the Chinese, Suyin, but by my so-called friends.' The 300 per centers. Had this been done by the Chinese, it would be understandable. But what insanity befell the Westerners who thus ill-treated one of the greatest, staunchest and most useful men in China?

'Not one of my friends except Ma Haiteh and Hans Miller comes to see me now,' said Rewi, quickly wiping away a tear on his sleeve. He was shunned. He had not been allowed for some months to go to the hospital to have his skin looked at (he suffered from skin lesions), until Chou Enlai heard of the ignoble ill-treatment meted out to Rewi and ordered that he go to the hospital.

'Rewi, come and have dinner with me at the Peking Hotel.'

I could not think of anything else I could do for him; except to be with him – and his tail of course – in a public restaurant.

After dinner we walked arm in arm. He missed not being able to travel. Usually he spent August at the seaside in

Peitaiho. But that year – and until 1972 – he would not be allowed to go to Peitaiho.

'There's been a good deal of suffering . . . there always is in a revolution . . . now the emphasis must be on discipline. It's difficult to get people to work with each other again after they've shouted and hurled accusations at each other, and made up stories about each other.'

Rewi would not tell me until some years later that his two adopted sons had been badly mistreated. One of them was cruelly beaten: he endured eighty separate beating sessions. Rewi tried hard not to cry. 'Well, one thing can be said: Where there's life there's hope.' Survival. All China believes in survival . . .

Of course, Rewi made me promise not to say a word about his tail. 'It won't do any good, lass. Only sensationalism for the Western press . . . Chinese problems have to be settled in China by the Chinese themselves.'

The Cultural Revolution had also done a great deal of good, said Rewi. The school and the hospital had definitely been brought to the countryside now. There was an outburst of 'mind's beginning to function'. People discussed and there was a feeling that 'government was now down among the grassroots'. There was enthusiasm and energy and audacity.

I concurred. I had felt it. Whatever the misuse of 'mass democracy', there was a stir, a vibration palpable among ordinary people, beyond the pretences and the propaganda. Something alive. 'It is not possible to create such an upheaval, an explosion of *all* accepted ways, and not finally to shake up, to wake up, a good many people, out of passivity,' said Rewi.

'Do go to see Anna-Louise. She's a bit upset,' he added as we parted.

'Can you tell me what really happened during the Cultural Revolution?' said Anna-Louise to me.

She was not the only person to ask me what was happening. Until 1975 there would be people living in China who would ask me to explain events to them. I am not surprised. Americans in America do not necessarily know how their country's actions are viewed abroad, what is the impact of what they are doing. Witness the Vietnam war. And I believe the German people when they say that they were not informed about the death camps for the Jews. It is entirely possible that many knew nothing about it. 'Beans sizzling in the frying pan do not see the fire that makes them jump,' says a Chinese proverb.

Anna-Louise was upset; not only because Sidney Rittenberg, an American resident in China who had taken her up and down China with him to meet 'revolutionary Red Guards' and to promote Chiang Ching and her acolytes, was now in jail, but also because Nieh Yuantzu, the lecturer who had started the Cultural Revolution in Peking University, was now under arrest for corruption, appropriation of state funds and inciting violence. How could Anna-Louise explain this sudden reversal of roles and reputations to American readers of her 'Letter from China'?

Something else troubled her. Her brother had not been allowed to come to China to visit her. 'I don't understand. I'm not all that young . . . I haven't seen my brother for years. If only I could see Mao and explain it to him.' Anna-Louise's faith, her reputation, were based on the interviews and meetings she had had with Mao so freely for so many years.

But Anna-Louise was a great American. She straightened her shoulders, and there were no tears in her eyes, only in her voice. 'Well, no use moaning. I suppose that's that, we've all got to make some sacrifices for a good cause.'

I stayed a long time with her, many hours, and she told me a great deal about her life, which I shall not relate.

'I'll go crazy if I see one more Mao religious service,' said Richard Hung to me.

Richard Hung was an overseas Chinese who had given up everything, a wealthy family, a brilliant career, to return to

China. He had laboured in the communes for two years during the socialist education movement. To keep fit he jogged a mile or two in the early morning, and thus had come upon a dawn ceremony – a courtyard full of people swinging their bodies in ecstasy in front of a large portrait of Mao Tsetung.

This was the morning invocation, asking Chairman Mao for directives: rocking of the body, chanting, dancing with 'offer hearts' gestures, calling upon Mao in litany of praise ('great, great, great') for his orders for the day. Then there was the opening of the little red book, and the quotation on the page fallen upon was *the* answer. Every night, they assembled again to 'report to Chairman Mao' on their day, their work, their thoughts.

'It's like the Holy Rollers and consulting the Bible for answers and the Moral Rearmament People who speak to God,' said Richard. He did not think he could put up with it any longer. However, being Chinese, he had a long fuse, and waited, patient and enduring. And by the end of 1971, no more such 'services' were being held.

By some feat of magic, I have acquired an interdicted item, Lin Piao's own little red book, quotations of the Crown Prince's imperishable 'thoughts'. It is only circulated among higher cadres; but somehow I have purloined one. It is not very interesting or revealing, and I wonder why it is a state secret. I open it. 'In all things obey orders. I obey Chairman Mao, whether I understand him or not.'

I return it to the person I stole it from, who never noticed its absence, or its return.

There are two 'voices' in the newspapers. Sometimes a burst of articles and editorials: 'Down with foreign slave study . . . criticize foreign slavishness', and a recrudescence of criticism of unfortunates such as Chou Yang, and scholars and professors; and then another voice: 'There must be reasonable rules and regulations in running industries', 'Too much anarchism is bad for the revolution.' The strongest plea of all in 1969 is for the return of intellectuals and old cadres to responsible positions. Already in September 1967 Mao had emphasized that the majority of intellectuals 'can be re-educated . . . and should be welcomed. . .' but the last phrase, 'should be welcomed', has been strangely left out in the *People's Daily*. Why? Also Mao's view that 90 per cent of the cadres are good is left out . . . Why?

Articles about the squandering and the outrageous privileges arbitrarily seized by the 'revolutionaries' have appeared. There are cases of their taking their families and friends on great jaunts, at government expense, to Shanghai to have a good time. Some have occupied not only the mansions of former national-capitalists, but also state buildings and schools . . . it will take years before they are dislodged.

Ma Haiteh tells me that everything in the rural areas is in a state of flux; all relations between the production team, brigade and commune are being reassessed; the book-keeping method of reckoning workpoints, and remunerations. But old marriage habits and funeral habits have returned. 'Once control is loosened, the past returns damn quick.' There is already usury, and bartering of brides. And by 1975 I shall find that infanticide of female children has returned in some areas.

'The old officials may have had defects, but they were competent,' says Ma. 'Everyone is hoping that they will soon return . . . but how will they work, cheek by jowl, with their persecutors, the new cadres? The latter will certainly glue themselves to their new desks, their easy chairs . . . after all, it is a matter of the rice bowl.' The result will be an even larger inflation of the ranks of administrative cadres.

The Peis, my overseas Chinese friends who came back at the wrong time, have a very nice flat. But Mr Pei and his daughter Millie have no work to do (Mr Pei is, however, paid a salary by the government). Hsing Chiang, always kind, exerts herself and within a year something is found for Millie. Her father gets a job in 1971.

The Peis praise the 8341 army division, the one which guards the top leaders in Peking. In 1968, the 8341 began to 'clean up' the ultra-left and the May 16 storm troopers. 'A very nice young soldier came to us and asked us what were our grievances. We told him, and he wrote it all down. He was a country lad, and so pure! He even had the windows fixed for us, and he came regularly, to ask what we needed.' The Peis were gradually soothed; their anxiety left them. But when I said that Millie should keep a diary of these extraordinary days, the three looked at me as if I were mad. 'You could hide it,' I suggested. 'There is no way one can hide anything,' said Millie.

In Tientsin, in a dozen factories the Cultural Revolution has promoted women – many women workers, women in the revolutionary committees: 20 to 28 per cent. There is great praise of Chiang Ching, who has called for at least 30 per cent of women in administrative roles. My heart warms to her.

But when I go back to Tientsin in late 1974, my impression will be somewhat different from that of 1969. I shall then realize that Tientsin is one of the 'bases' of the Gang of Four, and especially of Madame Mao, and that women are being used to hoist her to power.

At the Tientsin watch factory the workers say that 'to hold power there must be rigorous self-discipline, frugality, sacrifice . . .' Where the scheme fails is that the young workers do not exhibit any discipline. I find dozens of them loafing about in the park with their girl friends; one is boasting loudly, 'The foreman comrade tells me: You're late. So what? I say. And I just walk out.' In one milk powder factory, my guides and I are clad in sterile white gowns and boots, but a young worker walks in without changing and spits on the floor, and no one says a word.

The Tientsin Third Wool Mill used to belong to the Sun

family, capitalists who left China in 1953. It is the mill where Liu Shaochi perpetrated his 'treachery'. Old workers tell me about it; they witnessed the scene. In 1950 Liu toured the mill and encouraged the owner, saying, 'You have opened factories for the good of the workers . . . capitalism is good . . . exploitation is not a bad thing . . . I hope you exploit a bit more . . .'

I can scarcely believe this, but letters from Liu to Sun, encouraging him to go on producing, are exhibited. In Liu's defence, it could be said that at the time it was Party policy to go slow, to allow, under strict control, capitalism, in order to keep industry going. After all, in that same year, 1950, Mao had approved the 'rich peasant' policy. But this is not the point. The workers are indignant that Liu was so deferential, so obsequious to the capitalist owner. Perhaps Liu as a Marxist theoretician felt that China could not leap from her semi-feudal state to socialism with a transition period of controlled capitalism. But I agree with Mao, and disagree with Liu. Once launched into capitalism, no one could govern China's future, and there would be no relief, only redoubled misery and horror, for China's majority population: the peasantry. China had to go crashing forward, stumbling and experimenting and suffering, but not giving up her attempt to accelerate historical progress. China could not give up her socialist revolution, or the inspiration of a better world of equality and justice, for then all the downtrodden people in the world would be compromised.

'We found a traitor here,' say the workers of a tool plant. 'He entered the Communist Party in 1945 and joined the Kuomintang in 1946.' The Tientsin bicycle factory has discovered so many 'Kuomintang agents' among its top echelons that it is baffling how it could have been so successful. Tientsin bicycles are in large demand all over north China.

A play is shown in Tientsin; a young girl, paralysed for

eighteen years, is now able to walk after acupuncture treatment by the PLA doctors. 'For seventeen years the bourgeois line in medicine did nothing for me.' This is the punch line: nothing was done in China about health until the Cultural Revolution! It is patently untrue. I know that great epidemics have been quelled; that venereal disease has been eradicated, that schistosomiasis has been tackled (Mao even wrote a poem praising the work done on schistosomiasis in 1956). On the contrary, after 1974, and owing to the dislocation in control, medical statistics show that malaria has returned, that tuberculosis figures are climbing, that schistosomiasis is also beginning to spread extensively.

Acupuncture is certainly in fashion, used intensively by army medical personnel. In Tientsin, Shanghai, Harbin, I visit deaf and dumb schools. All claim that 'cure' or at least improvement for deafness is due to acupuncture treatment. The man in charge of the Tientsin school is thirty and deaf; his tongue was stuck down with non-use, and the army doctor 'cut the bond which held down my tongue'. He speaks in the loud uninflected voice of the deaf.

The school has its workshops; the deaf make musical instruments. 'We also give open-air concerts, singing and dancing recitals; people like it.' The deaf and dumb sing and dance for me and I am moved to tears, for they are joyful, glowing with the quiet pride of achievement. 'We are no longer handicapped. Thanks to Chairman Mao, we are equal to those who have ears.'

The harvests are excellent (they have been superb for three years). Wang Fongchun, member of the Tientsin Municipality Revolutionary Committee, delegate to the Ninth Congress, is head of the Siyuying commune, and he tells me a curious story. 'We were in the hands of a woman named Chang. She was backed by Liu Shaochi and Chou Yang. [Why Chou Yang? He explains: Chou Yang came to do his manual labour here during the socialist education movement of 1964.] Then Comrade Chen Pota came here. He discovered that the Chang woman was a black marketeer. He could tell she was no good merely by shaking her hand. She had a soft hand, the skin velvety. "Not the hand of a true worker," warned Comrade Chen Pota. We discovered a cache of money in her house.'

Truth? Lies? There is everywhere a frothy oedema of language, overbidding, adjectival, inflated. I was so perplexed by this story that I wrote it up for *Eastern Horizon*, but only at the end of 1970. And Tsungying told me that it was not wise to print the story, because Chen Pota was now in trouble.

I think at times of the woman Chang and her soft, moist, velvety handshake. She must now be back, recognized as a true comrade, while Chen Pota (and perhaps also Wang Fongchun) are down?

Walking in a universe of slogans – 'The general situation is excellent . . . We are purifying the class ranks . . . It is a great victory for Mao Tsetung Thought' – I become impervious to the babble of tremendous conviction. Words do create a world, especially when not all the words are nonsense. Undoubtedly, good things have been done. But the mind suddenly becomes a sieve, only letting through what will please it.

In all the factories posters for discipline and quality blossom. 'Red Alert Guards', vigilante corps, appear, to see to it that work is properly done, that workers adhere to discipline: 'Too many machines broken . . . Too many young workers not observing rules . . .'

At Hopei University there were fifty-two professors and 121 lecturers, most of them 'from the old society'. Here moral decapitation has had great effect. 'The students go into the countryside to be re-educated by the peasantry, uproot their ideas of becoming wealthy and famous through education . . .' Seventeen professors and lecturers, plus the revolutionary committee (consisting of the Mao Tsetung Thought propaganda team of workers and army men) receive me. The team assures me that the policy towards intellectuals is not harshness, but 'to relieve them of their heavy load of anxiety and unease by liberating their minds of old ideas'. One by one the professors speak, uncovering their 'burden of guilt', accusing themselves of bourgeois thought, promising from henceforth zealous attention to the will of the masses.

'We inculcated in our young students ideas of fame and wealth; they had pictures of Madame Curie, Einstein and Pushkin on their walls.'

I murmur that Curie, Einstein and Pushkin were not particularly wealthy.

'I repressed young students from worker and peasant stock: From your handwriting I can tell you are stupid, I said.' This is from one eminent consultant.

I indeed know that there was favouritism in the universities, that examinations did weigh the scales heavily against workers and peasants. For the intelligentsia, and the offspring of high cadres, have favoured backgrounds; books at home, leisure to study. Very often a worker or peasant youth did not even have a table of his own to write on, and certainly no room or even a bed of his own. 'We sometimes deliberately created handicaps for the workers' and peasants' children.' The intake of the latter in universities, which had risen to 70 per cent in 1960, had fallen back to 38 per cent by 1963.

A grudge of the young lecturers comes out: 'An old professor could never be moved . . . there was no place for the young. No one dared to contradict an old teacher . . . there was never any argument or debate.'

Now the handicaps which fettered worker–peasant–soldier offspring must be rectifed. Special preparatory classes will be set up in every university to prepare 'the next intake', so that they will be able to follow the courses.

I visit Manchuria again. In Shenyang, the capital city of Liaoning province, the walls of factories are pock-marked with traces of bullets. Gaunt roofless structures reach upward, as after a bombing. There is litter, and cinders;

burnt-down plants. Here many 'foreign' things (which also means industrial) have suffered attempted destruction; and the army has been busy rounding up malefactors.

The revolutionary committee of a large plant has discovered 'Kuomintang spies and agents' among the managerial staff. Since most of the managers and chief technicians in Manchuria date back to pre-Liberation days, this is not surprising. 'Some of them are patriots. They could have run away but they did not,' I venture to say. 'We have evidence. They were spies,' is the reply.

Throughout my Manchurian travels I was not left alone, except at night in my bedroom. Even if I went to the toilet, in some factories and communes, a girl worker would come along with me, and watch me.

Everywhere girls of twenty-two or twenty-three seem to be 'in charge'. 'Old people are all bourgeois,' they say (I am old too). Is this also a revolt against parental authority? Would psychologists one day analyse the Cultural Revolution as a catharsis, liberation from a phenomenal Oedipus complex? Crudely it is also a mighty scramble for jobs now available to the young, jobs which the old and middle-aged held to so tenaciously. The young now fill them, who otherwise would be drafted down to labour in villages. I am told that a delegate from Manchuria to the Ninth Congress was a girl nineteen years old. It becomes clear to me that Manchuria is a bastion of the 'Left'. I hear the name of Mao Yuanhsing, Mao's nephew. Trained in Harbin as an engineer and become a Red Guard faction leader, he is now vice-chairman of the Revolutionary Committee of Liaoning province. Everyone expected him to become a member of the Standing Committee of the Central Committee at the Ninth Congress, but his uncle Mao Tsetung always has refused him. (He will refuse again to back his nephew at the Tenth Congress in 1973.)

But Mao Yuanhsing is 'very close to the centre'. This phrase means that he is often in Peking, allegedly to see Mao. Everyone knows, however, in the grapevine Chinese way, that it is his aunt, Chiang Ching, whom he goes to see. He has been her 'son by affection' since 1963. But he returns to Manchuria, haloed with the name of Mao, and what he says is believed to represent Mao Tsetung Thought.

Now I understand why my meeting with 'activists' in 1966 was so significant. They represented the Lin Piao–Chiang Ching alliance.

Wen Chuming, the ex-school teacher I saw in 1966, is now high on the city's revolutionary committee. She accompanies me, a signal honour. She tells me of her suffering at the hands of the work teams of Liu Shaochi, who paraded her with a big dunce's cap and held 'struggle meetings' against her. 'But my own students lay down in front of the truck and would not let it pass.' She was jailed: 'they threw excrement on me; they would not let me wash . . .'

The story is almost the same on both sides.

Commander Liu Tetsai, the army representative in this area, is a short, bullet-headed man. He tells me of the rounding up of Red Guards 'misled' into committing 'crimes'.

I am lodged in a palatial mansion surrounded by a beautiful park. Behind us are the hills with the graves of the Manchu dynasty emperors ensconced among their folds. The bright morning sun woke me and I went running in the park, but immediately, from nowhere and everywhere, people join me and start running.

The steel plant of Anshan has been badly mauled. Large machinery sprawls in despair on the ground, surrounded by squatting workers trying to repair it. In one of the workshops grey-haired people work at lathes: previous administrators: 'All our cadres are doing manual labour to extricate their minds from the capitalist roader line.'

The facility of articulate expression among the workers (how they talked! I filled seven notebooks) was remarkable. They possessed relentless loquacity. This is a feature noticeable among many adherents of Chiang Ching and her group, both male and female.

At the Institute of Engineering a worker's son told me how corrupted he had become. 'I wanted to be a top engineer and to have a bright future. My parents wanted me to become an official.' Now he only thought of serving the people. But he was a Red Guard delegate and would certainly become a cadre. Eight hundred thousand youths had gone down to the countryside in this province alone, to 're-educate themselves with peasants in manual labour'.

At the Shenyang Medical College, almost everyone was still being re-educated. In teams, they went down to rural areas; searching for Chinese herbal remedies, they experimented upon themselves in acupuncture. 'We were arrogant . . . we had no feeling for the sick.' Now, through inflicting pain upon their own bodies, they understood how careful they must be. Having watched some heartless colleagues in many countries, I thought it a very good idea.

I interviewed a dozen impressively articulate Red Guard delegates. They had travelled to the border to comfort the militia who had fought in the Russian border invasion in January. I went to the hospital to see a wounded PLA soldier, seventeen years old, shot in the abdomen. 'The Russians fired on us . . . the tops of trees were broken by their artillery. My platoon commander brought me back . . .' He was reading a book in bed.

Educated city youths now transferred to the army resettlement camps on the borders were being trained as militia. 'They will form a solid rearguard of people for our army on the borders.'

One of the Red Guards I met was a young girl of eighteen. 'Although I am of peasant stock, my ideas had changed in the city. "Three years of manual labour and you'll be back in the city," was Liu Shaochi's promise to us, as if the villages were to remain doomed places, purgatory for ever! But we shall never advance if we don't have educated teachers, doctors, book-keepers, technicians for agricultural mechanization. Consolidation of our system must come from below.' This girl and another Red Guard present, a boy named Kao, would accompany Yao Wenyuan on a trip to Albania.

I go to the Tsienchangpu brigade, a two-day motor car trip, stopping at Penghsi, an industrial city, for a night.

Tsao Yulan, twenty-three, a delegate from the brigade to the Ninth Congress, comes to Penghsi to welcome me. Again I wonder: How many delegates 'from below', young boys and girls, were at the Ninth Congress? And was it by their votes that the Central Committee members were chosen? How did they know whom to vote for?

Accompanying me is a tall, handsome PLA commander. He tells me that the delegations from the communes and factories went to Peking under army care . . . everything is becoming clear. The youths have been selected by the army, and here it means Lin Piao.

Tsienchangpu was a backward area, very unproductive 'because Liu Shaochi's black line prevailed here'. The brigade used only to grow ginseng on the mountain slopes (I can see the paler patches where it was planted). 'We did not grow any grain. Every year the state had to supply us with grain.' Ginseng makes money, far more money than grain. 'Now we grow grain.' However, I shall not spoil the landscape with unsavoury remarks.

The brigade consists of Koreans and Han people. Manchuria has many such mixed population communes. In 1968 the army came to the brigade and started to run classes in Mao Tsetung Thought. Of course there was 'a startling change'. Now every child is at school; teams of girls work in the fields; the brigade not only grows maize and sorghum to feed itself, but also makes more money than before.

It is undoubtedly a well-off brigade. Nestled in a beautiful valley, the houses are of brick, and neat. But the valley floor which grows maize is filled with stones from the usual erupting, uncontrolled stream. The stones have to be sieved out by hand.

The most beautiful girl I have ever seen in my life lives in Tsienchangpu brigade. Her name is Sun Chinglan, Golden

Orchid, and she was in 1969 a barefoot doctor. She was seventeen years old. I inspected Sun's clinic, neat and well kept. She really knew a good deal of medicine, for I questioned her thoroughly. 'You've passed my examination,' I said. Everyone clapped. Thanks to Golden Orchid, almost 80 per cent of the village women had been taught contraception. The tall and handsome PLA commander who accompanied me was obviously head over heels in love with Golden Orchid. I think that is why he had come with me.

There is no doubt that the Cultural Revolution, in its juggernaut churning and stumbling, brought to a lot of people something different, deep and stirring and seminal. Never mind if it was also directed, mobilized, conducted; it was fraught with future potential. These people talked about themselves in ways I had not heard before. For the first time, millions were openly questioning motivations. I tried to envision the scope of this immense psychological upheaval, what it would do to the Chinese people, in the decades to come.

I slept on a *kang* that night with six other girls, a tight squeeze. About two in the morning a black frost came down, and someone knocked on the door and shouted, 'Tsao Yulan, get up! We must light the fires in the fields.' But Tsao Yulan grunted and turned over, going to sleep again. However, two other girls rose and went out. They did not return until five. The next morning, walking in the valley bottom, I would find the charred cinders of sorghum stalks; smoke from the fires prevented the black frost from settling down upon the crops.

Commander Liu Tetsai arrived from Shenyang. He was a hero here, for he had chosen this brigade as a model, and worked as an unknown sieving the valley stones and encouraging the peasants to grow sorghum and maize, in 1968. He was certainly the idol of Tsao Yulan and another girl with the ecstatic face of a saint, who grasped the little red book to her heart and vowed never to marry, for 'I want to devote myself to spreading Mao Tsetung Thought'. It was she who had tried to wake Yulan to light fires, and she had spent all night in the fields. I would see the Saint in Peking for the October 1st celebration. The village girls were uncomfortable in the city. They had never seen a lift, or a modern toilet, and Peking streets made them dizzy. 'So many cars,' they cried.

Harbin is one of China's most European cities, and a beautiful one. White Russian refugees from the Russian Revolution, refugee Jews from Nazi Germany, flocked here and prospered. It is next door to the limitless Siberian span of earth. It has culture and art; the Harbin Ballet School and Music Institute are well-known. Its population is two million. It has 520,000 youngsters in school. There are 820 factories and 400,000 workers.

The Harbin Medical College has become since 1949 a fully-fledged medical school with 52 consultants, 170 research workers, an 800-bed teaching hospital, and 700 other beds in various hospitals. It has trained 7,000 doctors from 1949 to 1966 (five-year courses). In front of me sit some of its top medical men and research scientists. Such enormous dignity and reticence is theirs as they go through the usual phraseology. Perhaps some, like Sha Tin, the Szechuan writer, and Yen Wenching, my friend, were comforted by the fact that all of them were paraded and reviled together; they met and recognized each other in prisons, in the May 7 schools, at the struggle and criticism meetings.

Sha Tin had made his audience shake with mirth when, every time he bowed his head to acknowledge his 'crimes', the dunce's cap fell off, and proceedings had to be interrupted while one of the Red Guard 'judges' had to walk down from his seat, and readjust the cap. 'The crowd took his side and said: Enough!' There was also the great comic artist who, when the Red Guards came to fetch him, was waiting for them, a very tall dunce's cap upon his head. 'I made it myself, to spare you the trouble,' he told the stern young people affably.

Solemnly, the academic staff recited their sins. 'We practised the three getaways: from labour, from the masses, from the Revolution.' I think of Galileo, who also confessed, but only told a lie in order to be more free to serve the truth. I remember how Pao used to go on, hour after hour, shouting and ranting at me, in real 'struggle session' fashion, to make me acknowledge something which was quite preposterous but which, in the end, by dint of repetition, almost convinced me of its truth. Pao had died here in Manchuria in cold October, in the open-cast coal mine of Fushun, and his last letter to me said that he had served the wrong cause, the wrong man . . .*

'We shall now select by merit, not examination. We are reducing medical studies to two years.'

I jump. 'Two years is not enough to become a doctor.'

The even flow of words has stopped; the local cadres look unhappy. But not the doctors. They gleam gently.

The army man in charge of the hospital says sourly, 'Two years is enough if we have Mao Tsetung Thought.'

'We are cutting out all pre-medical study,' explains the professor of internal medicine.

We go to look at pathology specimens, exchanging inanities.

In the Harbin 43rd Middle School one of the teachers is obviously teaching; she has not seen us because the door was half open and I merely pushed it. But when she sees us she hastily puts the text book in her desk, slaps the desk shut and starts waving the little red book and so do all the students. Teaching does still go on. Parents *must* be talking to teachers, begging them to teach their children . . . I shall capture such scenes in other schools, but one has to be able to suddenly open a door to a classroom not scheduled as part of the visitor's round. Perhaps this explains why, despite the fact that schools did not work properly for many years, there

*See *Birdless Summer*.

are some startling exceptions. How else is it understandable that a mathematics contest in 1977 could produce at least two score pupils of outstanding merit, right after the downfall of the Gang of Four? That a child of twelve, therefore born in 1966, the year the Cultural Revolution began, could play Mozart and Beethoven and Bach and Chopin, all of them proscribed 'foreign bourgeois musicians' in 1977, and win a prize? There must have been a soundproof room available to him somewhere . . . and a good teacher.

Long live fraud on behalf of education.

Six hundred thousand young people from all over China will come to the province of Heilungkiang this year. Border settlements are to be set up; the province has very few people, and now there is oil. The harvest has been spectacular, all the storage bins are full, and everyone in the city of Harbin must take in 500 catties of grain to store until new bins are provided. On the radio it is announced that all medicines and pharmaceutical products will be reduced in price by 37 per cent, all over the country.

Phenomenal innovations are announced, all proclaimed to be the result of the Cultural Revolution. But I know that a good many were started before the Cultural Revolution . . . all of them are claimed to be due to the workers' ingenuity, but I know that most of them are due to scientists. I shall not say a word. Scientists must be protected by anonymity.

I meet Pan Fushen. He is the military commander of the Heilungkiang province and heads the provincial revolutionary committee. He is the inventor of the May 7 cadre schools, and a national figure because he is one of the very few Party army high officials who has 'led the masses' against his own administration, or, in other words, joined the new power constellation.

In 1957 Pan Fushen had been labelled a 'rightist'. However, the label was withdrawn in 1960.

Pan is a small, wiry man, wrapped in a swirling black cape. He eats very little at dinner because he has ulcers. He says that he had not understood the proletarian Cultural Revolution during the first fifty days but then he read more of Mao and 'grasped' his thinking. On August 18th, while Mao was reviewing the Red Guards in Peking, the Liu representatives in Harbin were reviewing their own squads, organized to 'protect the Party' against the Red Guards.

'The battle was most acute,' says Pan (even tanks were used on the streets of Harbin). Pan joined the 'rebel revolutionaries', and they won. The first revolutionary committee to be set up in China was here in Harbin. Shanghai was to follow.

In autumn 1967 Pan started, at Willow River (Liuho) district, the first May 7 cadre school; so called because on May 7th, 1967, Chairman Mao had suggested such schools for the retooling of cadres. Now each organization ran its own May 7 school. The Foreign Ministry had theirs (Kung Peng had been in it for eighteen months), and so had the Ministry of Culture. Fourth Sister Ping would be in her organization's May 7 school for two years.

Pan talked of the border aggression by the USSR. 'The Soviet new tsars have stopped all our fishing in the Heilungkiang River; they have 130 gunboats on patrol.' Despite his amiability, a pall of silence falls upon us. I don't know why; I begin to ramble, and drink strong *maotai*. At last, whirling his cape, Pan Fushen goes.

Hsing Chiang, who has arranged the meeting at my request, is a bit aggrieved. 'You talked small talk only.' I want to tell Hsing Chiang that I am too subjective; I respond too obviously to the aroma a person engenders, an odour of the mind.

I never wrote up Pan Fushen, though it would have been interesting, for the *New York Times*; for which I did several Op Eds* in those years.

Now Pan Fushen is down. He fell when Lin Piao fell.

*Op Ed: article on the editorial page of the *New York Times*.

Some praise my foresight. But it was merely paralysis, part of that block which stopped me from writing anything except about Mao and the revolution for almost ten years.

'I could see you did not get on with Pan Fushen,' said Hsing Chiang to me recently.

'It was his black cape,' I said. 'That cape reminded me so much of Chiang Kaishek. That's what put me off.'

On to Sian, to Tachai, to Nanking, to Wusih, to Soochow, to Hangchow . . . to so many places. In Tachai I meet the eminent peasant Chen Yungkwei himself, a member of the Central Committee; who tells me about his great struggles against the Liu group. In Nanking I visit fertilizer factories and chemical plants and communes, and also the new great bridge crossing the Yangtze River. Workers on the bridge, in a lengthy interview, tell me that the engineers tried to stop them from completing it in record time . . . One of the workers has become an alternate on the Central Committee. I ask for his autograph, but he can scarcely sign his name. I meet so many other enthusiasts of the Cultural Revolution, young and old, among them Lai Keke, who is a veteran cadre. It seems some of them, by joining the 'Left', can escape all harassment.

In Soochow my guide is a happy young Red Guard who tells me, chortling, how his faction, after assaulting another faction with lances and spears 'got some machine guns, and then we had quite a show.'

Back to Peking for the October 1st celebration.

The atmosphere of the banquet is extraordinary. Usually it is solemn and sticky, with its careful hierarchy of officials and diplomats and high and not-so-high honoured guests. In this society there can be much sour envy and heartburn if one is placed lower than one expects to be at one of the 400-odd tables which fill the Great Hall; and one's distance from the main table, where the leaders sit, is the subject of much speculation by assembled diplomats.

But this year the Great Hall is crowded. There are twice as many tables as usual. At them sit peasants and workers, delegates from all the new revolutionary committees; and army men.

Previously, apart from the music and the set speeches, there was little noise; only the ritual clinking of glasses in toasts, the small murmur of polite conversation. Sometimes a whole table would spend the evening in glum silence. But this year the noise is continuous. The banquet is a rowdy clamorous assembly, with people shouting 'Long live Chairman Mao', drinking and eating and laughing and roaring their happiness.

The hotels are full of people 'from below', and the hotel managers complain that they go to sleep on top of the bedspreads in all their clothes and without taking off their shoes.

The people 'from below' who have come to Peking fill the streets. They buy everything in the shops. 'We never dreamt we would ever see Peking in our whole lifetime,' they say.

The parade on Tienanmen Square is a happy festival. I am squeezed out of place by a parcel of eager young girls, representatives from districts in Honan province. They want to catch sight of Chairman Mao, who is up there at the balcony of the gate. 'Can you see him? Can you?' They crane, and almost clamber on top of me for a glimpse.

The populace is gaudy and raucous and screaming its joy, untouched by bureaucracy, and their idol is Mao. The militia does not walk in step, the floats are haphazard; and the marchers will not move on as required, but remain turned towards Mao, acclaiming him . . . Total disarray results.

Today, knowing how badly this candid devotion was misused, I still feel the lap of that ocean of humanity surging, rising towards the balcony where Mao stood, and my heart is moved and I want to shout, 'I won't let you down!' to the people, the long-suffering ones.

Mao was a far, round face, a white moon in the distance.

He was flanked by Lin Piao and Chou Enlai, Chen Pota and Kang Sheng. Chou Enlai waved the little red book at the crowd, but in between waves he paused. Someone handed me a pair of binoculars. How tired he looked . . .

Shanghai is the power base of the new constellation: Chiang Ching, Chang, Yao and the ex-worker Wang Hungwen. All four of them travel regularly between Shanghai and Peking, but Chiang Ching has no state appointment (Mao has refused to give her one).

The Number Seventeen Textile Mill of Shanghai, where Wang Hungwen worked, is organizing 'activists' for the Communist Youth League, future cadre material. This means that Wang Hungwen may take over the now moribund Youth League; that millions of youngsters will come under his control.

Madame Wan Hsiuchen is a famous woman in Shanghai. She will be written up at length in the newspapers and in *Peking Review*, and interviewed by many foreigners in the years to come. She is one of the top members of the Shanghai Revolutionary Committee; and also a Central Committee member. She is as prolix and unquenchable as Li Suwen in Manchuria (Wang Hsiuchen also comes originally from Manchuria).

She tells me the story of the conquest of Shanghai, called 'the January Storm'. I shall find it ably written up by many foreigners; a valuable story, full of 'facts'. Today the interpretation of these 'facts' is very different from what it was then. It was then a 'model revolutionary act'. It is now a 'base counter-revolutionary plot'.

But I find in my notes something very extraordinary (I record like an automaton, and am occasionally surprised by my own scribble). Wang Hsiuchen says that an 'underground' Shanghai organization helped Wang Hungwen to mobilize the workers for the capture of the city in January 1967. She then mentions Chen Ahta, who she says is a factory worker, as one of the leaders of this 'underground'.

Chen Ahta becomes a Central Committee member. He will have a major role to play, with Wang Hungwen, in the formation of the Shanghai militia, and of groups of activists which will be sent out to many provinces between 1974 and 1976 to take over government offices, public security bureaux, factories. When the Four are toppled, Chen Ahta will be denounced as head of a mafia, a gangster; and Wang Hungwen who has meantime become Vice-Chairman of the Party will be accused of having revived Secret Society methods, having formed 'brotherhood' links, distributed Party cards to gangsters.

But the word 'underground' may have another meaning. Chou Enlai, while in Chungking, organized and trained clandestine Communist cells throughout the whole of southwest China, under Chiang Kaishek's nose. I shall meet a good many members of these units, working in government offices in Szechuan and Yunnan provinces. Liu Shaochi similarly organized clandestine cells in 'white terror' areas. Wang Hsiuchen evidently wishes me to understand the term 'underground' as clandestine Communist Party cells in Shanghai. But after Liberation, there was no further need for an underground. Why then does she talk of it as if it had been recently organized?

Wang Hsiuchen also tells me how the former Shanghai Party Secretary Chen Peihsien, tried to crush the workers, and 'committed towering crimes'. In 1977 I would meet a small-boned smiling man at the house of one of my doctor friends in Peking. It turned out to be Chen Peihsien. 'I heard much evil about you in Shanghai in 1969 from Wang Hsiuchen,' I said, and he laughed uproariously.

The Huashan hospital was started in 1907 by American missionaries. It has a particularly well-developed department of surgical neurology, and ten brain specialists. Of course the doctors castigate their previous attitudes. One-third of the staff are away, in faraway places like Sinkiang and Tibet, to train barefoot doctors and to give medical care.

When they return another third will go. They assert that formerly only Shanghai's capitalists and their wives had access to the hospital. They say that peasants were asked fabulous sums for operations, ranging from 100 to 300 *yuan*. I nearly explode. It is not true. And then I understand. This is such an exaggerated charade that I catch on. So I nod gravely when one of the doctors produces a well-worn old remedy for mycosis of the toenails and tells me that it is a new innovation due to the Cultural Revolution . . . we play a perfect deadpan comedy and our audience does not know it.

In the wards the treatment of burns has been carried out to a high degree of perfection. The doctors have finished *tobegaying* and can go on working, and they do magnificent things. If Paris was worth a mass, being able to go on working is perhaps worth a 'confession'.

I go to a photographic exhibition, 'not for foreigners'. There are many photographs, episodes of the seizure of power in Shanghai; and a picture, six foot high, of Wang Hungwen. I notice other photographs, militia men with rifles, and below them the words: 'Battalions of the ATTACK BY REASON, DEFEND BY FORCE.'

But in Shanghai, in front of these photographs, I am told that these battalions are 'an arm of security' and for peacekeeping operations; that they started on August 4th, 1967, and that they protect state property. In 1972, and again in 1975, I shall try to find out what has happened to these battalions, but at no time shall I be told that they are held responsible for violence committed.

Passing through the street, I catch sight, here and there, of barbed wire atop walls. Probably temporary prisons. Each organization, factory, university has its own detention area.

I travel down through the green lush countryside of Chekiang province, to visit the May 7 cadre school of Shanghai Municipality. It is about fifty kilometres from the city, near an arm of brackish sea, on flat plain. But there are no swamps. I see neat houses of earth and wood. No barbed wire, but a palisade. No obvious guards. (None are necessary

– where would the cadres run to?)

The cadres, 2,000 of them are here voluntarily, to remould themselves through study and labour. The first group built the houses, and now the cadres are erecting larger buildings, for meetings. The school is not far from some villages, and the peasants come and go freely, and walk into and out of school. I see ex-officials collecting vegetables for lunch from vegetable plots, others pushing manure carts. I visit the pig pens. Never have I seen such splendid-looking, healthy pigs. I congratulate the official who looks after them.

'You've got the best pigs I've seen in China.'

'Yes, the villagers all come round to see how we do it,' he says. 'I thought at one time of becoming an ambassador. Now I am content to look after pigs.'

We both laugh. Perhaps he is now an ambassador.

At first food had to be sent from the city to feed the two thousand here; much of it is now grown on the spot. There is a library and the inevitable loudspeakers. Once a month the officials return home to visit their families, that is, all those who are not labelled 'counter-revolutionary'. They receive their pay; but I know that some, the 'criminals', are given very reduced pay. Of course *tobegaying* is going on – discussions, criticism, self-criticism, probably struggle sessions, when some leading cadre is hauled out in front of everyone else. But I do not get to see the criminals.

Everyone assures me that they do not feel humiliated; that on the contrary, it is an 'honour' to remodel oneself; that manual labour is not degrading. 'We are the front-line soldiers of the Revolution,' they say. Any and every cadre will have to go to May 7 schools. It is not punishment.

What will happen, I ask, when all the fields have been laid and the houses built? Surely there will not be much manual labour left to do? Everyone laughs.

'In our May 7 school we had an excellent library,' says a friend whom I shall see some years later. 'I never had so much time to read as when I was being retooled.'

'Our place was not so good,' says Yen Wenching. 'The

Red Guards and army men in charge never gave us any peace. One day I heard I was dispensed from labour. I was happy, thinking it was a favour – until I heard my name called to be struggled against at a meeting. That was bad. They made me stand in a jetplane posture* for hours . . . they pulled my hair, jerking my head.' Yen and another writer thought up the bright idea of shaving their heads clean, so that there was no hair to pull at struggle sessions. 'But it did not help. They pulled on our ears instead, and it was more painful.'

There were also very bad May 7 schools, where cadres were bullied and badly fed, and beaten and humiliated, and denied letters and books.

Back in Peking, it is late October. Soon I shall leave. But meanwhile, I wait to see Chiang Chang. I have asked to see her.

Kuo Mojo, delightful as ever, has a talk with me. He speaks of his ten years in Japan from 1927 to 1937. 'As one progresses one understands one's errors,' he says. 'I have followed Chairman Mao; as a fly stuck on a horse is carried by the horse, so am I carried by the greatness of Chairman Mao.' Kuo Mojo has written in 1967 a poem in eulogy of Chiang Ching. Is this sycophancy? I do not think so. The old man is, at all times, sincere; it is not his fault if the object of his admiration becomes unworthy.

Kuo Mojo tells me that of all the Chinese writers who participated in the Afro-Asian writers' meeting of 1966, only three are reckoned 'not bad'. He does not tell me who they are. But he says that Hsu Kuangping, Lu Hsun's wife (who died in 1968, probably of a heart attack), was 'spotless'. That leaves only two more blameless writers, out of all those assembled that July. I am depressed. It means that so many of the people I like are now 'bad'; Liu Paiyu, Li Chi, not to mention Pa Chin, Tu Hsuan, Yen Wenching . . . so many.

---

*Half-bent, arms extended backwards.

At Tsinghua University I am greeted by Comrade Hsieh Chingyi. She is the daughter of Hsieh Fuchih, now head of the Peking Revolutionary Committee (and of Public Security). A personable, clever young woman, she is a great devotee of Chiang Ching. Of course, like all the women who follow Madame Mao, she is most articulate. The revolutionary committee of Tsinghua University was formed in January 1969; and she will control it for seven years, until October 1976.

The eminent professor, Tsien Weichang, is exhibited to me. He makes the usual confession. I shall not publish a word, although I take it all down. He will repeat his exposé to Edgar Snow the following year.

Tsien is a professor of fundamental science and physics. He wanted Tsinghua to become a 'cradle for competent engineers'. He believed in technical expertise . . . he took in students on marks, not on political acumen. Already in 1957 he was labelled a rightist . . . 'I was very obstinate . . . the Red Guards did not change me . . . only when the workers' teams entered, in July 1968, did I begin to change. The workers said to me: But what about us? Where do we fit in in your scheme of excellence? Then I was moved,' says Tsien. And I believe him.

Hsieh Chingyi is knowledgeable and well organized. She tells me of the special kindergarten and nursery schools in Peking and other cities for the children of higher officials. In 1963 an educational conference sponsored by Liu Shaochi and Teng Hsiaoping had backed a system of élite schools; 1,472 primary schools and 235 secondary schools in Peking Municipality were to be selected for the 'special training' of brighter children. 'Of course this was to prepare the return to capitalism,' says she.

But strangely, it was in one of the special schools, where the children of higher officials were most numerous – the 4th Middle School attached to Tsinghua University – that the first Red Guards had been formed.

* * *

On November 7th, in the evening, I was taken to the Great
Hall of the People to see Chiang Ching. I was told, 'You
must not publish a word.' I could not take notes.

At first Chiang Ching would have nothing to do with me,
accounting me an American agent. The first accusation had
come, in 1962, from a neurotically suspicious Japanese
writer, who had gone to Peking to denounce me. The
Chinese had smiled and said that they did not think this was
correct. However, the item had probably got into my files, and
the 'information' that I was Jewish had got into Kuomintang
files about me. Chou Enlai had persuaded Chiang Ching to
see me. 'Premier Chou went to a great deal of trouble for
you,' I was told.

Chou Enlai, Kang Sheng, and Chiang Ching sat in three
armchairs. Chiang Ching was in soldier's uniform, padded,
ungainly, but above the uncouth garments her face was
beautifully made up, with excellent cosmetics. Her black
hair was waved, and glistened. It was a good-looking face in
1969, when she was fifty-seven years old.

'You asked to see Comrade Chiang Ching,' said Chou
Enlai. He looked at ease, relaxed. I was happy to see him. It
was he I wanted to talk to. But he did not say a word while
Chiang Ching and I carried on a bafflingly unsatisfactory
conversation through the next ninety minutes.

I began by saying how I had seen the revolutionary new
operas and appreciated their relevance and importance;
which was true. I had started seeing them in 1963. I thought
they might be made accessible to a public abroad as a vehicle
to express the aims of New China. I mentioned in particular
Shachiapang, once called *A Spark Among the Reeds*. And this
was my first mistake.

Chiang Ching frowned slightly. The reason (which I only
discovered years later) was that *Shachiapang* had existed
long before she had come on the political scene. She began to
speak about two other operas, *Taking Tiger Mountain by
Strategy*, and *On the Docks*. These two she considered much
superior to the others. 'I have seen Western operas. I do not

think the West can appreciate our operas. They sing anything, like: "Do you want some tea, Yes, I'll have some tea, It is very good tea". Our Chinese opera concentrates on expressing only positive emotions, important ones . . .'

She went on giving her notions of 'purifying the opera'. I listened to her voice. She had a very beautiful, distinct voice in 1969; the voice of an actress, with carrying power. By 1971, when I saw her again, something had happened to her voice; something tight and desperate lived in it.

We talked about *The Red Regiment of Women*. I had seen the film in 1962. It had nothing to do with her at the time. Now a ballet would be made of it. The original film was never shown again.

Suddenly she told me about Mayor Peng Chen, how he had opposed her new operas, put obstacles in the way of performances . . .

I plodded on. I strove to catch hold of something coherent to say, but every ten minutes or so there was an interruption. Chiang Ching would rise and go off to the toilet. During her absences no one spoke; we sat, fixed in the aspic of wordlessness, awaiting her return. I wondered what was wrong with her bladder. Or was it her bladder?

She asked me abruptly if I knew anything about Chinese opera. 'Nothing, I just like it,' I replied. I tried to speak about Aszucena opera, but this was my second error; Chiang Ching cut me off. She had a particular aversion to provincial opera, especially that from Szechuan, possibly because Szechuan opera is redolent with anti-bureaucratic satire. The possibility of introducing, within what looks like a serious play, ironic remarks about top leaders, and jokes about them which the audience will understand immediately, is almost infinite.

'What do you really believe in?' she asked me suddenly.

'I shall strive to learn from you,' I replied politely.

She was mollified. 'I am only a small student of our great leader Chairman Mao,' she said. And off we were again on *Taking Tiger Mountain by Strategy*. Obviously she wanted

Tiger Mountain to be shown abroad. She told me that there were singing and gestures in it which had never been attempted before. 'Everytime she talked of *Tiger Mountain*, you would talk of *Shachiapang*,' Hsing Chiang reminded me in 1977, after Chiang Ching's downfall. I was not aware I had been so mulish.

We went on to music, and I committed my third *faux pas*. I said something about the scales of Western and Chinese music being so different that it was not possible to mix the piano and violin with Chinese instruments. She frowned heavily. For this was precisely the innovation she was contemplating.

We came back to denouncing Peng Chen and other officials. Every time she pronounced a name, she glanced at Chou Enlai, who remained unperturbed.

Then Chiang Ching said suddenly, 'I've had cancer, did you know?'

Had I been a trained courtier, I would have recognized the opening. I would have asked about her health, and she would have given me a blow by blow account of her life. But a perverse streak in me refused this abasement. I murmured something about hoping she was now cured. 'All she wanted was to tell you the story of her life. She was looking for someone to write her up. But you turned her down,' said Hsing Chiang later.

We floundered on. 'Can anything good be produced and created in a corrupt Western society?' asked Chiang Ching. I said that there was a great deal of vulgarity, but from time to time there were good things. I mentioned, for instance, the film *Z*, which I had seen in Paris that spring. I thought it should be shown in China, as an instance of what the West could do to criticize itself. And of course, there was a vast number of books printed, 'many thousands a year'. And new ballets. I mentioned Béjart.

Chou Enlai was impassive. 'Oh,' I thought, 'I'm letting him down. I don't know how to handle this . . . I'm doing everything wrong.'

Chiang Ching left. I rose and watched her go down the corridor, waddling in that grossly inappropriate padded uniform.

Once Chiang Ching had gone my tongue-tied stupidity vanished. I turned to Chou Enlai. I had wanted to thank him, for almost two years.

'I thank you,' I said, 'for having been so patient with me, teaching me, all through the years . . . I have been a slow and stupid person . . . you told me once I was slow . . .'

'Was I really so rude?' said Chou, his face suddenly bright and young and amused. There was someone else there. Kang Sheng.

I had never met Kang Sheng before. He was so quiet that he could be forgotten. But he was quietly dangerous. After all, he had brought Peng Chen down; he was at all the Red Guard rallies. He had never been criticized. I asked him to tell me the meaning of the 'continuing revolution'.

He did so. He talked a long time. Then he asked me why I did not go to Latin America. Apparently he was under the impression either that I was very popular in Latin America, or that revolution was imminent there.

I thought Latin America unripe for revolution because it did not have enough people. Distances, geography, size, economic resources, culture, religion, demography all play their part in whether a revolution is possible or not. 'Besides I cannot speak Spanish.'

A faint shadow of disapproval crossed his aristocratic face. 'You can learn it.' I promised to try.

It was now almost one o'clock, and certainly Chou Enlai had work to do; he always worked until five in the morning, or even later. I left.

So this was Chiang Ching, or rather one fragment of her. Poor woman, she must have suffered . . . that is why she was so bizarre, so dislocated. I was filled with compassion for her, even though her waspishness when she talked about Peng Chen grated. She was under stress and that bladder of hers: perhaps a medical case, with no final cure . . .

CHAPTER 5

The Death of Kung Peng: 1970

In mid October, 1969, while I was still in China, a message came for me from Samdech Norodom Sihanouk,* inviting me to preside over an Asian film festival in Phnom Penh at the end of November. An invitation from Chino Roces, the owner of the *Manila Times*, to lecture in the Philippines came at the same time.

I told Kung Peng what Charles Meyer had said in Zermatt that spring: that there would be a coup against Sihanouk, that he would be 'got rid of', and 'before the summer of 1970'. Kung Peng assured me that this was idle talk. No such news or rumour had filtered through to the Chinese from diplomatic sources. And yet, in March 1970 – Meyer was correct almost to the month – there was a coup in Phnom Penh, and Sihanouk was driven into exile.

Meyer was to write me a jubilant letter when Sihanouk was deposed by the Lon Nol regime. He seemed to have great confidence in Lon Nol, but Lon Nol did not give him a job. Charles Meyer and his wife Sika returned to France, and Charles has since become an eminent Sinologist.

As president of the Asian film festival I was most royally treated. We had a magnificent apartment in the Palace; an enormous Rolls-Royce to take us to the hall where the films were viewed. I was kept extremely busy, but could not fail to notice that there was an economic crisis in Cambodia, and that Sihanouk was hard-pressed. He had given 'sanctuary' to Vietnamese troops on the border, and this was resented by Lon Nol and others in his government. 'I don't know how long I can keep my country at peace and free from invasion,' said Sihanouk.

Samdech: head of state.

The *Manila Times* was an independent newspaper (it has since been liquidated by President Marcos). Chino Roces, its tiny, compact, energetic owner, had the courage to make an opening to China at a time when it was almost a crime in his country.

Our suite was the best at the best hotel in Manila. A burly bodyguard, bristling with pistols, lay across the corridor at night. When we went out, bodyguards squeezed in on either side of me in the car. It is very difficult to view the landscape through two hundred pounds of brawny bodyguard knobbly with weaponry. Chino Roces had a walkie-talkie set with him, to report exactly where we were, in case of kidnapping. One afternoon I became weary of so much care and crept out while Vincent was having his noonday siesta, to wander by myself. Chino was most upset.

The Philippines are a world of seven thousand islands, and there is such great inequality and social injustice that revolution seems always just round the corner. But this is Asia, and the tropics. A revolution was almost impossible here precisely because there were seven thousand islands, absolutely disconnected, and hundreds of ethnic groups and dozens of languages.

I met some of the revolutionaries from the Philippino Communist Party who had recently surrendered to Marcos. The trouble was that they could not employ – as in China – that large web of villages to sustain a guerrilla war, and any enterprise on the Chinese model was doomed. 'Too few people,' I said to them. There was much resemblance between the Philippines and Latin America.

Some of the women wore rivulets of diamonds round their necks and one asked me, clasping her three-strand blue diamond necklace, 'Will the communists take this from me?' Just outside the walled-in enclaves where the rich dwelt was great hunger and squalor, and the stifling malodorous stink which is misery and its unwashed anger, and uncollected garbage. Contrasts so appalling that even Vincent, nurtured in India where inequalities tear one's eyes out, was shattered by the scene in Manila.

I gave a few lectures; met many people, most wealthy families living in fairylike palaces in the enclave of Makati.

President Marcos and his wife Imelda received me with pleasant informality. Marcos was resourceful, suave, steeped in knowledge of his own people; he would be able to stifle revolt against his rule for a considerable length of time. And in 1974 Imelda Marcos would go to Peking, and there be royally entertained by Chiang Ching.

Marcos was no stooge; he had brains and decision. He knew that precarious economics makes for uncertain political power, and he was not embarrassed by scruples. Much time and effort would be spent by the Third World nations before the hold of the industrialized and affluent nations on their resources and markets could be shaken off. 'They talk of freedom all the time; but they deny us the basic freedom from want that we need,' he remarked. And any one of us, Asians and Africans, would agree with him there.

While we talked, Marcos was awaiting a telephone call from Washington. He had asked for another loan. 'Seventeen million dollars only, just chicken feed for them,' said one of his aides to me.

Kung Peng and I had had long talks, and leisurely ones, in Peking. We had discussed America, Europe, all the more since we had not done so for many years.

Since 1968, there had been an increasing number of signals from the United States; such as allowing Americans to visit China without removing their passports, and allowing them to purchase one hundred dollars' worth of Chinese goods.

But there was hostility in China against reciprocation. Ed Snow kept on writing to Kung Peng, asking to come to China. But Ed had told me that there was no answer. I told Kung Peng and she said, frowning slightly with worry, 'In his articles he emphasizes too much Chairman Mao being old and soon to see God.' I guessed that 'some people' were opposed to a dialogue with America, and making much ado

about Ed's quotation of what Mao had told him.* I said that
articles abroad could not be written in the style of *Peking
Review*, that Ed's report about Mao's age only occupied 5
per cent of the article, that there was a problem of subtitles;
the author often had no control over titles and subtitles. I
wrote to Ed and told him where the snag lay; by then I had
become somewhat expert in creating the unlocking phrase
which led to a common meeting of the minds. My own
articles and speeches were not approved in China at the time.
They had, in fact, not been approved for many years by the
'ultras'. An acquaintance in France, connected with the
Marxist-Leninist Party of France, had told me that they had
been warned against having anything to do with me.

But still, I managed. Life had never been a smooth tarred
road, but a brusque and capricious river, and one learns
about canoeing in wayward water.

Before I left China it had been conveyed to me that if
General de Gaulle was interested, he would be welcome in
China . . . would I sound him out? By 1969 de Gaulle had
retired from official life; but he remained the only Western
statesman popular and understood in the Third World. I
said that I would try.

When I arrived in Hong Kong I found that an 'edict' had
been issued in Peking, forbidding all Chinese newsmen, or
anyone having to do with the pro-Peking newspapers in
Hong Kong, to meet, talk, or entertain any relations
whatsoever, with Americans.

Who had issued this edict? Kung Peng had not told me
about it. The dichotomy in Chinese policies, the fact that at
the time there was not one but several 'centres' issuing
contradictory orders was now clear. I was almost being
encouraged to go to the United States by Kung Peng, but all
my Hong Kong friends, Mr Fei, Lee Tsungying, were not
allowed to talk to any American.

There were other absurdities: *Eastern Horizon*, the

*See *The New Republic*, February 27th, 1965, pp. 17–23.

magazine considered entirely pro-Peking abroad, was forbidden entry in China, and accumulated dustily in the Kuangchow post office, labelled: 'Yellow revisionist material'. Yellow in Chinese means pornographic.

I ignored the edict, and that winter sought out Harrison Salisbury of the *New York Times*. Harrison had vainly searched for someone from China to talk to in Hong Kong. We met in Paris, and spoke of possibilities, and probabilities, and Harrison's judgment proved most sound. He had acumen, a steady mind, a genuine concern for good relations between China and the United States, and I trusted him.

Ed Snow and I also met several times. Ed wrote to Kung Peng, explaining his use of Mao's phrase, 'I shall soon see God'. And in 1970 he and his wife Lois received their visas and went to China. Ed would see Mao there, and Mao would say to him that 'some ultra-leftists' would not even allow him to see his good friend Edgar Snow. Who were they? And how could they impede even Mao Tsetung?

In Paris I set out to find what could be done about inviting General de Gaulle to China. I had met Couve de Murville, and Bettencourt, and other French Foreign Ministry officials in previous years. They had come to parties I had given in honour of the Chinese Ambassador, Huang Chen. But no French official could or would understand why the invitation had not come through official channels. No one was inclined to believe me. I bumped against the glazed and courteous blankness of French officialdom. Finally I went to see my friend Jacques Rueff, at his office in the French Academy. He had on his bureau a beautiful Dali timepiece. I thought, 'What I am saying must be as improbable as a limp watch.' But Jacques Rueff listened attentively. However, he too was cautious; the weeks went by, and when finally he wrote to de Gaulle, it was too late. De Gaulle died on the very day Rueff's letter should have reached him.

Fred Zinnemann was not happy. He had planned to start

filming Malraux's *Man's Fate* on December 10th, and had asked me to be present, but I could not since I was then in Phnom Penh and on the way to Manila. The very morning shooting was due to start, all cameras poised, came the dictum from the new bosses of Metro-Goldwyn-Mayer: the production was cut out. Not only *Man's Fate*, but about a dozen other films were thus liquidated in a retrenchment crisis. What a curious and subjective way to run business! How easily and swiftly some prominent president of some company or other would be kicked out, and replaced! There was something totally unreal, unsolid, in the whole edifice of those vast conglomerates, such caprice in this huge money power! Fred went skiing to recover his equanimity. I told him I would refuse to have my name associated with anyone else but him, for I had so greatly enjoyed working with Fred. He had saved my sanity, taking my mind off the Cultural Revolution when it was almost at its worst (although worse was to come some years later).

In March 1970, Anna-Louise Strong had died in Peking. To describe the spirit of that extraordinary woman needs a book on its own. She had her quirks: the whole of Peking knew that under her bed she kept a collection of Mickey Spillane and other detective fiction. She had also accumulated a considerable collection of old embroidered robes, which she wore at parties. She died without seeing her brother, and now I knew that he was refused entry to China as part of the total ban on all Americans issued by the 'Left' in 1969 and broken only in 1970 by Mao himself when Edgar Snow was allowed again into China.

Anna-Louise remained, all her life, totally innocent of the intricacies, the feudal deviousness, the tortuous course of Chinese politics. She was unable to cope with them because she was too straight, used to the notion of a world running from cause to effect, readable, explainable . . . whereas the feudal world of China is not at all like that. It is a world of hidden passion and groundless illogic, an implausible world where truth is only one's own story. It is not moulded in the realm of the discipline of the machine. Here time is vague; promises are ways of putting off problems until a movement of the heart solves them . . . Situations are not determined by computer analyses (or statistics) but another kind of understanding, which still consults entrails and moods and watches signs in Heaven (or on the face of leaders). And the power contest would increasingly become of the order of feudal palace coups . . . Anna-Louise's 'Letters from China' remain a great testimonial to the rational mind. Much of what she wrote was true; for the Chinese Revolution was a stupendous effort at reason and logic. But all the time feudalism came creeping back, polluting its nobility.

In April 1970, Vincent and I went to Australia for my first lecture tour in that continent. This coincided with the launching of China's first satellite, which went round and round the planet singing: The East is Red.

Australia was further discovery of the globe we live on; immensely empty land, a hollow land, baffling because upon its strangeness grow excrescences of little Europe – and yet Australia is geographically in Asia.

Despite adverse newspaper articles, large crowds came to my lectures and the tour was unexpectedly successful. Afterwards there were witch-hunting questions asked in Australia's parliament: Why had television and radio given me so much time and exposure? As a result, funds for a certain popular programme were drastically cut, a punishment to the producer for having given me time.

Founded on this lecture tour success, the Friendship Association before Australia and China was started, or so its sponsors were kind enough to tell me.

Summer again, and time to go to China.

'Why don't you go to China too?' said Ambassador Huang Chen to Vincent.

'Me?'

'Yes, why not?'

Vincent was delighted. We rushed to New Delhi, to find

out whether he could adjust his passport; it was, of course, invalid for China, as all Indian passports had been since 1962. But the fury of 1962 had subsided; even if automatically the hackneyed newspaper phrase 'China's brutal aggression' recurred. Vincent found New Delhi's Ministry of External Affairs sympathetic, even happy at the idea of this 'overture', for it had political significance in their eyes. Tikki Kaul came to dinner with us and we had talks on the possibility of improved relations; on the Dalai Lama, on Tibet, and many other issues.

Vincent thus unwittingly made history (or *The Guinness Book of Records*). He became the first Indian non-diplomat and ex-army officer to go to China since 1959. At no time, in many subsequent visits, would he encounter hostility, either in India or in China.

I went off first to Peking. Vincent was to come three weeks later, as he had family matters to attend to. I was looking forward to seeing Kung Peng, telling her of my excitement at discovering Australia and the crowds and the passionate interest.* I had just been invited by *Asahi Shimbun*, the prestigious Japanese newspaper, to make a lecture tour of Japan in the autumn. All this was concrete evidence that policies were shifting beyond the clouds of deception of certain newsmen intent on stereotypes.

July: the aeroplane landed at Peking airport, and I could see Hsing Chiang, in a white blouse and blue skirt, waiting for me. I carried a heavy bag full of books. The Chinese post office, in its cultural zeal to censor and to eschew, had been confiscating the books I had sent to friends, just as in Malaya and Singapore Special Branch had impounded them. Even my first editions of Dr Sun Yatsen's biographies, sent to his widow, Madame Soong Chingling, disappeared during the Cultural Revolution. And now I brought books with me to give away.

*See articles by Han Suyin in *Eastern Horizon* (1970) on the Australian lecture tour.

Hsing Chiang hugged me, and then said, 'Kung Peng is very sick, I must tell you.' Her face was grave. My arm went up, in an unconscious gesture, with the heavy bag of books upon it. It must have hurt me, though I did not feel it at the time.

Chiao, Kung Peng's husband, met me that evening. We both wept, looking at each other. He told me what had happened. It was in May, warmth seeping through the coverlets of cold, grit and wind, when Kung Peng received my first letter from Australia, and she was happy at the thought that I would come soon. And then she went to the bathroom, and suddenly fell, unable to move. She was rushed to hospital, but was not diagnosed for ten hours because the doctor in charge was not there (was he still *tobegaying*?). The specialist then returned; Kung Peng had a ruptured aneurysm of the internal artery in the brain.

All was done that could be done, said Chiao. But more was to come. Kung Peng ruptured another blood vessel in the skull, and so became decerebrate, mindless; her upper brain totally destroyed. Since May she had been in a deep coma, kept alive, as decerebrates are, with a machine to pump her lungs, and others to feed her. The body was kept alive, but that fine mind of hers was gone for ever.

I was allowed to see Kung Peng in hospital: her face above the bed coverlets, waxen; all the tubes going into her. Of course I could do nothing, and I cried and cried like a lost child.

My colitis returned; I went around with stomach cramps and attacks of giddiness, which made me stumble. My arm began to swell and to throb. At first I paid no heed. I could think only of the body I had seen, that it was no longer Kung Peng, just a body, just cells, organs without a brain. The hospital kept her 'alive'. She was already dead.

Vincent arrived in Peking. He would go on a trip to factories and communes with a marvellous man, Mr Li, an interpreter, who became a great friend. Mr Li and some other young men I met were the fine product of the Cultural

Revolution, the Red Guards who had refused to commit horrors, who risked their lives to protect people. No one talks about them, but they are there. And the future hinges upon these young people, who do not make any headlines, but who are the true successors, achievers of tomorrow.

As an engineer, knowledgeable about Indian conditions, Vincent could compare what was being done in Chinese factories in the only way Chinese industry can be compared, that is, with Indian factories. From the very start Vincent argued and inquired, and the workers responded well to him (not so well some of the more rigid cadres who were not accustomed to plain speaking). Lies were uncovered in a surprisingly short time by someone as experienced as Vincent, and he did not forbear to say that they were lies. But he also had a marvellously keen eye for the extraordinary and wonderful things that had been accomplished. Never an unconditional admirer, his judgment was all the more valuable. 'I did not believe you when you spoke of what was being done . . . but now I've seen it . . . it's great. You have a great country and a wonderful people.' And so he went on to Shanghai and Loyang and Chengchow, while I lingered in Peking because of Kung Peng. I was sleepless and my arm was now red and swollen. Hsing Chiang took me to the hospital and 'inflammation' was diagnosed by a young doctor. I was given diathermy, which made the swelling worse. Then another doctor (an older one) examined me and he looked grave. I had by then forgotten that when I arrived I had been carrying on my arm a bag full of books and that my arm had suddenly jerked upwards with the news of Kung Peng's illness. I could only say, 'It just began to swell.' The doctor took an X-ray; he suspected a swift-growing sarcoma.

Meanwhile, a most important engagement had been arranged for me. I had chosen two scripts of model operas and tried to put them into more decent English than the extant translations. The problem was that good translators and editors, such as my friend Yeh and the Yangs, were

either in jail or being criticized, or made to 'stand aside'*
while youngsters filled their jobs. Their motto was
'translation must be word for word'. The translations
became ludicrous. For instance, the Chinese metaphor for
integrity is 'A well-formed bamboo in the chest'. This was
translated exactly as it stood in Chinese!

Now a meeting with over twenty actors and actresses from
the opera groups under Chiang Ching was arranged for me,
and heading them was Yu Hueiyung, the youngish man from
the music academy of Shanghai, an *er-hu*† composer and
player. Yu would become Minister of Culture in 1975, but he
was already influential, and had earned the hatred of a good
many older musicians by his brutal treatment of them. The
music and script of two operas, *Taking Tiger Mountain by
Strategy*, and *On the Docks*, were due to him. I must confess
that I found the music of both very good, despite the fact that in
China today Yu, being a Gang of Four man, is denied any talent.

Yu Hueiyung was suave, deploying great charm as he
handed me complimentary bound copies of the new operas.
Because I could not take notes, owing to my arm, Hsing
Chiang did so for me, and the notes remain probably the
most complete exposé of Chiang Ching's activities in
recruiting opera singers and actors, and putting on the
model operas, that anyone has ever had.

The meeting began with an appraisal of my 'translations'.
Yu turned me over to two young women with desiccated,
fanatical faces. They were typical of the many I would see,
pressed into the service of Chiang Ching. All of them had
that ecstatic look.

The two ladies, Red Guards from the Foreign Language
School, were selected as 'correctors', probably because of
their political ferocity. For two hours I listened while they
criticized my version, not omitting a comma. Hsing Chiang

*This means they were suspended, under inquiry, but not actually
dismissed. They still received their salaries.
†*Er-hu*: a Chinese violin.

was irate. 'They exaggerated . . . you sat so modestly and humbly, merely listening . . . you were very patient.' I had indeed taken liberties in free interpretation; some of the 'positive' lyrics were painfully slogany, and I had altered them.

After that, one by one, the opera singers and actors told me how Chiang Ching had rescued them, saved them from playing only princesses and beautiful ladies, and what their tribulations had been at the hands of 'capitalist roaders' such as Peng Chen, the ex-Mayor of Peking, and Chou Yang.

They were candid. I am sure they believed that something new and important was being created. And I did agree (and still do) that besides the old classic operas, the plays on the past, there must be contemporary pieces on contemporary themes. In fact, one of the remarks I had made to Chiang Ching, and which perhaps did not please her entirely, was that one must not remain stuck in only anti-Japanese wartime stories. The way the Japanese visitors in Peking put up with being ridiculed in opera after opera was quite remarkable. The first two model operas, *Shachiapang*, and *The Red Lantern*, turned the Japanese into ludicrous figures.

A few years later some of the artists I saw that day would become very corrupt. They were loaded with honours, and promoted to high posts. Chiang Ching's favourites became an élite of their own, who never played for ordinary people.

After some three and a half hours of sitting with the opera stars, my arm became extremely painful; it stabbed and throbbed . . . I told Mr Hsiung, who sat with me, and he cut the meeting short and rushed me to the cancer hospital. I had told him that one of the two doctors who had examined me suspected a fast-growing cancer.

And there at the cancer hospital was my old, old friend George Wu, who had been a scholarship student in Belgium at the same time as myself, in 1936–8.* George, a Chinese from Mauritius, had also studied in London, and then

*See *A Mortal Flower*.

returned to Shanghai where he had set up China's first radium treatment institute (with radium from Belgium). At Liberation in 1949 George Wu did not leave China. He continued to work there, first in Shanghai and later in Peking. He had been extremely happy and well-treated throughout the years. Even during the first years of the Cultural Revolution, although harassed and criticized, and shoved aside, he had not been 'sent down' to the countryside to labour, or to a May 7 school, simply because he was far too valuable as China's major cancer specialist. He looked after all the Chinese leaders and was also consulted by Chiang Ching, since she had suffered from cancer of the uterus, which had been treated in the Soviet Union between 1954 and 1958.

I remembered George well from our Belgian student days and also from Joseph Hers's angry letter to me in 1959: 'George Wu has become as blind as you have . . . he thinks China is getting on famously.' Hers could not understand that George Wu was, above all, a fervent patriot; that like me it was not Paradise we sought, but just China, our root land.

George looked cheerful (he always did, even when criticized as 'unreliably bourgeois'). He had perhaps a little less hair on his head – but he moved swiftly, and his hands were skilful as he palpated my swelling.

Then Hsing Chiang remembered how I had jerked up my arm, and the strap of the heavy bag of books must have bruised the muscle. I was put in hospital to rest. The swelling did not go down. A doctor came and pushed a thick needle in it and aspirated. Nothing came out. I came out of hospital. I could not write because my arm hurt so much. Nevertheless, I went on a small round of visits to factories; and I called on Rewi and Ma Haiteh, and dropped in quietly to see George Wu.

The Premier Chou Enlai asked Vincent and myself to see him. He began by chiding me gently for getting so worried about my arm. 'It's Kung Peng who is seriously ill, not you,' said he, and fine lines of pain came into his face, for he cared deeply for all who worked with him. 'We must remain calm, be assured that the best is being done for Kung Peng.' I blinked back tears. There was nothing to be done; never would Kung Peng know anything any more. She was living corpse. He knew it too. Kung Peng's sister, Pusheng, was there, and gripped my hand. 'Turn your sorrow into strength.' She too was under great strain, because her husband, an eminent diplomat, had been labelled a counter-revolutionary and a renegade; but then almost everyone I knew was 'counter-revolutionary' in those years.

Chou Enlai spoke to Vincent about the border dispute between India and China. He named the Himalayan passes involved in it. He knew each one, their height above sea-level, where along the ridges the demarcations came between the two countries. The point he made was clear; there was not, there could never be, enmity between the two nations. There must come a time when reason would prevail. Of course, in all situations left over from the colonial epoch, there must be give and take. The problem was a complex one, but relations could be improved even if the boundary question remained unsettled for a time.

Vincent said that we would soon be going to India after passing through Japan, and we would probably be seeing Mrs Gandhi in Delhi . . . at least, we would try to see her.

Chou Enlai then inquired about my projected trip to Japan, and whether I had gathered sufficient information during my stay in China. He commented on Australia and the Philippines. 'All these countries would like better relations with us,' said Chou. I did not allude to Cambodia but Chou remembered: 'You told us about Prince Sihanouk being ousted before it happened.'

Of course I also called on Samdech Norodom Sihanouk and Princess Monique, his wife. In Peking Sihanouk resided at what had once been the French Embassy. Chou had made sure that he would truly have all the comforts of his palace in Phnom Penh. It was in exile that Sihanouk's grandeur, his fundamental steadiness of mind, became clear to me. He took personal disaster with great calm. All I could do was to say that I was certain that he would return soon to Cambodia. 'Five years, Monseigneur, five years and you will be back.' Monique smiled her very beautiful smile, and said, 'Do you really think so?' and was heartened.*

We walked about in the steamy heat of July, a heat I cannot remember because I kept on thinking of Kung Peng. But Vincent noticed many things, for to him China was new.

'Look at all the big black cars full of military men,' said he. Then the aspect of the street came into focus. On the avenues, in front of the big supermarkets were big black cars, but also jeeps, and khaki army vehicles, not for a state of siege but conveying men in uniform, and their families, to the shops.

Because there was no longer a distinctive uniform for officers, at first glance these men might all be simple soldiers – but not to Vincent or to me. Vincent could smell authority; and of course I could see it – in the leather shoes (rather than the plimsolls of the lower ranks), in the cut of the pockets, and the texture of the cloth jacket. But above all in that essential, smooth extra layer of fat on cheek and neck and the paunch waddle of authority. For in China, traditionally, health, wealth and happiness are transmuted into extra calories.

'It's becoming a military state,' said Vincent crisply.

I protested. 'No, it's just that a lot of the military are now doing their shopping in the big cities.'

In 1964 it was high Party officials and their families who had requisitioned public motor cars for their private use; but now it was high army commanders. The crowds appeared indifferent, jostling amiably on the crowded pavements. But they saw, they registered; they paused, quietly stared, and then walked away.

'Something will be done about it. Somehow, in China, someone always finally does something,' I said.

---

*Sihanouk returned in 1975. This was sheer coincidence, not crystal-gazing.

It was late August 1970. And it was precisely at that time that the downfall of Lin Piao began.

In Japan, *Asahi Shimbun* treated me with impeccable courtesy. We were magnificently entertained, lived in marvellous suites, enjoyed superb Japanese dishes. Vincent became a favourite with the Japanese newsmen. He delighted them with his open-hearted, unfeigned enjoyment of Japan.

I think that for many Japanese Vincent's appearance brought to mind those dark-faced killers of demons of their legends. A black face in their theatre, as in Chinese opera, indicates courage; and a legendary Chinese judge, whose righteousness could not be moved by bribes, was always represented with a black face. Vincent resembled the Tang dynasty statues of heroes and warriors, and also the Buddhist traveller from India, Damo, who in Japan is revered and in fact has become a toy found everywhere. Vincent totally won Japanese hearts when he fell for Japanese wrestling, *sumo*, which he did in a major way, exclaiming his delight at the skill and speed of the elephantine wrestlers. Had I listened to Vincent, we would have done nothing except watch these enormous barrelly men pummel each other among ritual courtesies.

With us on our travels through Japan was Prince Kinkazu Saionji, heir of a noble house, with the face of a samurai warrior, the manners of an English aristocrat, and a convinced Marxist. With Saionji, there was an aura of dash and adventure about our lecture tour; his spirit was still that of his ancestors, utterly fearless, even if it appeared prosaically political in our lack-lustre days.

The lectures were very well attended; thousands of questions were asked. I would meet businessmen and scholars, among them Mr Kakuei Tanaka, later to become the Japanese Prime Minister, and Mr Ohira, today's Prime Minister. They came to inform themselves about China. The *Asahi Shimbun* director, a most able gentleman whose suits

were superbly Savile Row, reflected, however, a contrary
opinion. He told me that normal diplomatic relations
between Japan and China would not be established 'for
another ten years at least'. 'I am sorry to disagree with you,
but I think they will start much sooner,' I had to reply. This
was October 1970, and in 1972 Japan would indeed establish
diplomatic relations with China, and Premier Tanaka would
go to Peking.

It was at the Tokyo Foreign Correspondents' Club, where
I delivered a lecture, that I first heard the rumour that Teng
Hsiaoping might be rehabilitated. He and Liu Shaochi had
together been dubbed by Lin Piao and Chiang Ching 'chief
capitalist roaders', but Mao had always made a distinction
between them. Everyone knew that Teng had requested hard
labour for himself in a commune sited near Inner Mongolia.
In 1970 Mao Tsetung was calling for the urgent return of old
and competent cadres.

I wrote to Chiao Kuanhua about the result of my Japanese
tour, and added the stray rumour about Teng Hsiaoping.
But I never received a reply.

It was in that September–October, at the second session of
the Ninth Congress of the Party, that Mao began to suspect
his heir, Lin Piao. Not before. I had wrongly conjectured*
that Mao had begun to suspect Lin right after the first
session because of the hunt for the 'ultra-left' and the May
16ers, but I was to be told categorically, in 1977, that this was
not so.

At the second session, Chou Enlai, following Mao's
instructions, was urging the rebuilding of the Party committees at every level, and emphasizing that the Party
committee decisions should not have to be ratified by army
committees set up by Lin Piao. Mao concurred, for he had
never meant China to become a military dictatorship. The
army, having restored order, must now back down – it was as

*See *Wind in the Tower.*

Party member, not as military commander, that Mao had selected Lin Piao to succeed him. 'The Party must command the gun, the gun must never command the Party.'

In 1969 Mao had repeatedly demanded the return of old, competent cadres. 'I have faith in my old comrades.' He had wanted to administer a lesson to the bureaucracy, but it did not mean casting the seasoned officials into oblivion. Chou was now carrying out Mao's purpose, but under enormous difficulties; for at all times rehabilitation of a cadre might be condemned as 'reversing the edicts of the Cultural Revolution'.

The rumour of Teng Hsiaoping's rehabilitation in Tokyo must have been based, however wispily, on a demand for Teng's return at the time.

But the rebuilding of the Party, the return of the old cadres, all this was an immense threat to Lin Piao. Heir or not, his contemporaries, his own companions of the Long March among them, would not forgive him easily the monstrous treatment he had inflicted upon them, upon Chu Teh and Lo Juiching, and Ho Lung.

And there was Chou Enlai; whom Mao now called 'the manager', who had kept China going, and who since 1968, with the condemnation of the 'ultra-left', could no longer be openly attacked. However, Chen Pota and a group of military men in the Central Committee did attack Chou Enlai openly, for not subscribing to the total cult of Mao, at the second session.

The meeting was held at Lushan, the cool mountain resort where, in August 1959, Peng Tehuai, then Defence Minister, had criticized the Leap, and been demoted as a 'right opportunist'. Lin Piao's ascent to Peng's post had taken place there. And now in Lushan, Chen Pota attacked Chou Enlai for questioning the 'genius' thesis. Mao was a genius, and therefore every word of his was infallible.

What they did not realize was that Mao, with the perversity of greatness, was getting tired of his own cult. He had used it,* and would now proceed to undo it. 'Give me back my aeroplanes,' he had shouted, staring at bosoms bedecked with Mao badges made of aluminium and other metals; 'I'm tired of being out in the sun and rain,' he had said of his statues in every public square; and he suggested that visitors in the hotels 'should see more art . . . not only my face'.

Yet for Lin Piao's purposes Mao had to be a god, for how otherwise could Lin Piao be his prophet and sole expounder? Mao's every word must be infallible, even if quoted out of context, even truncated. How else would Lin Piao rule over the minds of China – as Mao did – after Mao's death? And now Chou had contested the 'genius' theory, the infallibility, and Mao actually backed Chou, destroying his own infallibility!

Chen Pota attacked Chou on this theoretical point, affirming that Lenin had recognized the principle of 'genius'.

Besides this abstract polemic there were also very concrete issues. One was the question of the Head of State. Liu Shaochi had become Head of State in 1959, as well as being Vice-Chairman of the Party. Mao had been Chairman of the Party, having relinquished the post of Head of State to Liu Shaochi. Now Lin Piao wanted to be Head of State, for apart from being Mao's heir, Vice-Chairman of the Party, and Minister of Defence, he had no way of controlling the State Council and hence the Establishment – Chou Enlai ranked above him in such matters. Only the National People's Congress and its Head of State could prevail over Chou Enlai. But Lin Piao was not desirous of calling a National People's Congress before being sure that it would ratify him; he was not at all certain of that, and the National People's Congress was the supreme body in China. He had sent 'investigation teams' all over China the previous year, and realized that he did not have total control of the members of the National People's Congress.

*As he told Edgar Snow. See *The Long Revolution* (Hutchinson, 1973).

Lin's scheme could not be voiced directly. Hence he and Chen Pota tabled a request that Mao Tsetung be Head of State as well as Party Chairman, 'for then all words have weight'. Lin Piao, as Mao's heir, would then automatically became Head of State in his turn.

The second major point in dispute was foreign policy. American signalling to China was getting almost frantic ('We still don't get any reply,' a chagrined State Department official would tell me). And Chou Enlai, since the Bandung conference in 1955, had been identified with the policy of opening out to the world, including America.

Lin Piao, and later the Gang of Four, were opposed to any contact with America. The edict of 1969 forbidding all communication with Americans had certainly come from them. Lin Piao was for improving relations with the USSR, despite the attacks on China's borders in 1969.

But in that autumn of 1970, Edgar Snow was in China and on October 1st he and his wife stood by Mao Tsetung on the Tienanmen gate, showing themselves to the Chinese millions.

There could be no more pointed evidence that Mao was for responding to American signals. He had received a letter from Nixon, secretly transmitted through Bhutto of Pakistan; and he would reply, through Edgar Snow, with an invitation to Nixon.

At the session of August–September 1970, Mao Tsetung, after having watched the 'political blitzkrieg' of Chen Pota against Chou Enlai, wrote six hundred searing words, a document circulated 'inside' only after Lin Piao's death in 1971, which I would be given to read in 1972.

'We do not need a Head of State . . . I have said it many times . . . I do not want to be Head of State,' wrote Mao. He refuted the genius theory. He pointed out that Chen Pota 'has never agreed with me in many ways . . . and now acts as if the earth would stop turning, and the mountain of Lushan would be blown flat . . . but this will not happen, the earth will continue to turn, and Lushan will not be blown flat.' He then referred to Lin Piao in veiled terms. 'We both . . . must still study this question (of genius); of whether one stands on the side of idealism or materialism.'

Lin Piao, in his preface to the little red book, had mentioned Mao's genius, and now Mao was refuting the whole concept of himself elaborated by Lin Piao!

The quarrel over 'genius' may appear small, but to Mao, as a theoretician, it was fundamental to a whole philosophy. Hence the many articles which then appeared, refuting that 'history is made by geniuses'.

Mao was now suspicious of Lin Piao; of the whole trend of his thinking. Within weeks he had called upon Chen Pota, and the military members of the Central Committee who had supported his move against Chou Enlai, for their self-criticism.

I think Mao was greatly saddened when he started to move against Lin Piao; saddened because he had truly cared for and trusted the younger man; and they had had many years of friendship together. He now waited for Lin Piao to come to him, to change, to own up . . . but Lin Piao did not do so.

Lin Piao's wife, Yeh Chun, said openly, 'If there is no Head of State, what guarantee of power is there for us?'

As in a tragic play of the Renaissance, Mao and Lin Piao went on appearing together, acclaimed together; Lin Piao went on waving the little red book and shouting 'Long live Chairman Mao'.

And on October 1st Ed Snow, blissfully unconscious of all this, addressed Lin Piao who stood by Mao, and asked him for an interview. Lin Piao turned to Mao for his agreement, and Mao looked straight into the infinite distance, as if he had not heard.

What attitude did the Shanghai Four – Chiang Ching and Wang Hungwen in the Central Committee, and her two helpers in the Politburo – adopt towards the assault upon Chou by Chen Pota? Nowhere has this ever been mentioned. Yet they were still closely identified both with Lin Piao and

Chen Pota. They appeared, in fact, to form a coherent, solid 'Left'.

Perhaps, after Mao's six hundred words, the Shanghai Four hastily dropped Chen Pota and Lin Piao, 'unloading the general's chariot', as they had done with the young Red Guards who had served their purposes. Possibly they also realized that Lin Piao's overvaulting ambition would not hesitate to sacrifice them when the time came.

Towards the end of my stay in Japan, Hatano, one of the able correspondents of *Asahi Shimbun*, who spoke excellent Chinese and whose wife taught Chinese cooking on television, came to tell me that Kung Peng had died. Her death had now been officially confirmed.

I remained impassive, since for me she was already dead, and I had exhausted the externals of sorrow. For me she had died the day I had seen her in the hospital bed, her face so calm and her hair so neat, and all those tubes going in and out of her. Keeping the body alive when the mind is totally gone seems to me the height of superstition, of self-indulgence.

Hatano, being Japanese, understood me. He did not react like a Westerner, concluding only from outside appearance. 'You knew,' he said. 'I knew.' It is something we share, the art of non-exposure; reticence. I had loved Kung Peng too much to exhibit grief outside China.

CHAPTER 6

New Tartary: 1971

In February 1971 I went to Algeria, invited by some Algerian writers I had met in 1962 in Cairo, who had now become officials in Algiers.

There was a cocky headiness, very marked among the young in Algiers. They walked tall, and my remark that everyone had a good straight spine pleased the susceptible Algerians (they are a most susceptible people). 'We have fought, we have stood up to a great war. We had a million dead out of eleven million people.' I roamed as far as I could, delighting in the Kabyle villages perched on the crests of the Djurjura ranges and in the beautiful white cities of the desert, Mzab, where women are all wrapped up, leaving only one eye with which to confront the world outside their bodies.

I gave lectures and met Houari Boumedienne. He had incorruptible gravity, the demeanour which Malaya had taught me to associate with an Islamic upbringing. He spoke intelligently about his country. But he was a military man, and in Algeria, unlike China, the word 'military' was antithetical to 'intellectual', owing to the French influence. The Algerian intelligentsia were very 'French' in habit and attitude and method of reasoning, even when opposing French colonialism. They could enthuse over de Gaulle's superb style, but not Boumedienne's excellent Arabic.

Algeria was well placed for prosperity. It had petrol, a small energetic population; excellent ports. Its valleys were fertile; agriculture would thrive when and if wheat took the place of the French-created vineyards. If only it could harness and utilize the abilities of its intelligentsia. This was the problem everywhere in the Third World, including China. But French colonialism had done little to train a professional élite: doctors, engineers, technicians. Their numbers were appallingly low. Of course, there were writers; but a writer's usefulness is limited in the technology-hungry Third World.

'Our tragedy is that we are much too close to France. For many of our élite, the attraction of Paris remains overwhelming,' said Boumedienne.

How would Algeria (and so many other developing countries) reconcile the need for Western technology in the utilization of its resources, with its own cultural traditions? How would it allow the élite's demand for all Western freedoms which are but a concomitant of Western wealth – when this meant losing its élite, and very fast, to the seductive West?

In April 1971 Vincent and I were married in Madras. 'It will please your father,' I said. Vincent, like all men, had forgotten the legalities. Vincent's father, although President of the Catholic Association of India, was the most tolerant of men; he was beaming with happiness at our civil ceremony, held in his house opposite the Cathedral of St Thomas, where reposed, in the crypt, the bones of my favourite saint, Doubting Thomas the Apostle.

At India's independence in 1947, Vincent's father had fought for tolerance of all religions to be written into the Constitution. A strong clamour for making India a Hindu religious state had started; and Hinduism with its caste system, is one of the most intolerant and repressive of all religious creeds. Nehru was too modern-minded to agree to this, although he was of Brahmin origin; and the Constitution proclaimed that India was a secular state. But today's Indian leaders are more inward-turning. Militant Hinduism is on the march, as militant Islam is from Bangladesh to Algeria. Should the warlike, intolerant Jan Sangh Party of India – a paramilitary arm of the Hindu religion – come to power, India's 9 million Christians and 80-odd million Muslims may be exterminated by 600 million

Hindus, as Buddhism was exterminated by India's great religious wars of the past.

In May 1971, Edgar Snow came to see me in Paris. Ed's interview with Mao of December 1970, during which Mao said that President Nixon would be welcome in Peking, had been published in *Life* magazine. Ed had tried the *New York Times*, but they had dawdled, and *Life* had snapped up the story.

We talked about Chou Enlai. Chou had called for Ed one night, and spoken to him for hours, not complaining, simply thinking aloud. 'He was under great stress,' said Ed, the most discreet and trustworthy of friends.

Now it was certain that America and China would get together. Ed was working hard on his book, *The Long Revolution*. He left me, complaining of backache. A doctor pottered with his kidneys. Only at the year's end would it be discovered that Ed's backache was cancer of the pancreas. I still have Ed's letter about it, received when I returned from China in December. 'I was felled by something,' he wrote. He would be operated on, and would die in February 1972, the very month that President Nixon went to China to see Mao Tsetung.

Ed's death was for me almost like the passing of my days of youth and strength. We had known each other so long, so long; meeting at last in person in London in 1942 – through Dorothy Woodman of the *New Statesman*. Both of us had, behind us, decades of involvement with China; we had shared these extraordinary and inspiring years, through letters, meetings, concern, fascination. Ed's spirit lives on; many Americans will be grateful to him. He had the courage to fight against cowardice, obscurantism; to maintain whole and clear a vision of the future. A vision shared by Mao, when he told Anna-Louise Strong, 'I place my hopes in the American people.'

To Yugoslavia and to Italy, to attend meetings of writers and meet my publishers, and then off to New Delhi, to see Indira

Gandhi. Indira was kind, but evasive. She was, that year, leaning towards the Soviet Union for reasons which would become clear: the revolt of East Pakistan against West Pakistan's rule.

Mujibur Rahman of East Pakistan led the revolt, and was openly supported by India. Bhutto of West Pakistan jailed him; but subsequently released him. Bhutto sent troops to suppress the 'rebellion', and these troops committed atrocities, or so it was profusely reported. This produced immense indignation, not only in India but throughout Europe, and the propaganda was most effective because the Soviet Union helped, through all its 'progressive' sympathizers in West Europe. Refugees from East Pakistan poured into India's Bengal (East Pakistan was actually the other half of Bengal, sundered by the British at Partition in 1947). Ten million refugees were said to be coming out. 'We cannot afford them. Our own people are starving,' clamoured the well-fed ladies and gentlemen of New Delhi to me (I was lecturing at the Press Club).

In Europe the cause of 'Bangladesh',* the new name for East Pakistan, aroused disproportionate emotion (but who remembers it now?). André Malraux announced that he was setting out to fight for Bangladesh. He desisted, however, a week later.

My visit convinced me that East Pakistan was indeed shabbily treated by West Pakistan. But the furore engendered had another motive, as had the exaggerated refugee figures. Mujibur Rahman, India's favourite, would establish the independent state of Bangladesh with the help of the Indian army in November. This action would only be undertaken, however, after a treaty of friendship and alliance between India and the USSR had been signed in August that year; the treaty was meant to 'warn off' China and Pakistan, should either of them intervene.

Mujibar Rahman did not last; he was assassinated within

*Meaning East Bengal.

two years, and relations between India and Bangladesh were strained, since the real issues – as always – were economic: the control by India of the waters of the Main River and the monopoly of Bangladesh jute production by the jute companies established in Calcutta. Exchanging one despot for another was not the object of the people's uprising in Bangladesh. But like all Third World countries, the way to a better future would be long and dolorous.

Meanwhile, the 'treaty' between India and the USSR would have far-reaching consequences: it would help to establish the USSR as a power capable of interfering in the whole of South Asia.

Late June in Peking; the sky heat-pale, and in the parks the strong smell of insecticides sprayed on the trees. I had asked to tour the landmark sites of the Long March for a chapter in my book, *The Morning Deluge*. I had also asked again to visit Tibet. Regretfully, Tibet was 'not available', but the Long March sites were, and would we like to visit Sinkiang later in the summer, instead of Tibet? Vincent and I were elated. Sinkiang had been closed for many years to visitors. We would be the first to go there since 1959.

But we went first to Shanhaikuan, the seaboard town, to see the end of the Great Wall there, a tiered gate which had just been repaired; for Vincent was fascinated by the Great Wall. Then on to Manchuria, where Commander Liu Tetsai once again welcomed us, as did Li Suwen and Wen Chuming, and other members of the provincial revolutionary committee. Somehow, I had favourably impressed Chiang Ching in my 1969 interview, hence the reception. By then Chiang Ching and her group went scouring round for intellectuals to serve them. In the universities, already, they had recruited a few, who would thereby escape 'cattle sheds' and long imprisonment by putting their pens at the disposal of the Four.

We went to Dairen, and sailed with the fishing fleet, and saw the harvest of the largest and best sea-cucumbers, with five rows of knobs on their backs. Commander Liu took us into a mountain's heart, to view the installations against a nuclear attack: schools, a hospital, dormitories and food stores, canteens and water tanks and toilets – everything for the survival of a population of 200,000.

Vincent's advice was eagerly sought in the factories and plants, but not always well received when he gave it with his usual forthrightness. 'In India the factory inspector would not allow such unsafe working conditions,' he would say in Dairen of the glass factory, which produced marvels, but in most primitive surroundings. I reminded him that in India there were appalling sweat shops and factories, and that Untouchable children worked in the most terrible conditions in the leather industry. 'I'm talking of India's public sector,' said Vincent with indisputable logic.

We were back in Peking for Army Day and its banquet. Huang Yungsheng, the acting chief of staff and Lin Piao's right-hand man, made the main speech. Huang had been nicknamed 'the butcher' by the young in Kuangtung province, because of his drastic methods of restoring order there. He was to leave, during his years of tenure in south China, quite a network of his men behind; and even in 1978 a clear-up of 'Lin Piao influence' was still proceeding in Kuangchow.

In that summer of 1971 an unconfirmed rumour went about that Army Day would be changed from August 1st to September 18th. The reason given was that Mao Tsetung, the 'True Creator' of the Red Army, had started the peasant insurrection called 'The Autumn Harvest Uprising' in September 1927. It was the first skirmish utilizing Mao's basic strategy of 'the countryside surrounding the cities'. And Lin Piao, in 1965, had pinned his reputation on a pamphlet entirely backing this strategy, but extending it to proclaim the Third World the 'countryside', which would surround and destroy the affluent world in a maelstrom of revolution.

August 1st, however, commemorated the Communist

Party's first armed resistance and military exploit, the capture of the city of Nanchang under the direction of Chou Enlai, and with professional forces. In this episode, which had been a breakthrough from the policy of supine non-resistance to Chiang Kaishek's onslaught, Chu Teh, Chen Yi, Lo Juiching, and Ho Lung had also distinguished themselves. And Lin Piao was attempting to efface from history all other commanders except himself and his allies. Already Chu Teh had been 'rubbed out' at the first base created by Mao in the mountains of Chingkang in 1927. After many battles against Chiang Kaishek, Chu Teh had led his remaining battalions there, to join with Mao. Now a large oil painting had taken the place of the monument previously set up in memory of this historic event. The painting showed only Mao and Lin Piao meeting there.

Ho Lung had died of 'natural causes' (some people whispered: of diabetes and starvation) in 1969. Chen Yi was dying of cancer. Lo Juiching was denounced as a counter-revolutionary . . .

But apparently Mao had refused to move the date of Army Day. I listened to Huang's speech on August 1st, and was surprised because it made only one reference to Soviet 'social-imperialism' but denounced repeatedly 'American imperialism'. Usually a speech even-handedly denounced both. What did this mean?

In the newspapers an insistent debate castigating idealism, and 'the theory of many centres' continued from the previous winter. Chen Pota had disappeared from view. But praise of Lin Piao continued. And not even the keenest China-watcher in Hong Kong guessed that the articles were slings and arrows directed against Lin Piao.

I received a telephone call: Comrade Chiang Ching would like us to attend a new ballet that evening. We had tea at the British Embassy, and went on to the theatre. We were ushered into a private reception room and found it full of people waiting for Chiang Ching. There was Joris Ivens, and

Marcelline Loridan, and also Yao Wenyuan and Chang Chunchiao, Chiang Ching's two allies, and Wu Teh, to become later acting Mayor of Peking, and a number of other officials, interpreters and translators.

I sat by Chang; Yao was on the opposite side of the room, talking with Marcelline and Joris. Joris had come to make films, and would begin to plan and to prepare his magnificent series of ten films on China.* I thought Yao repulsive to look at; his teeth were jagged, and he had a bad skin. He wore a cap screwed to his head at all times, until suddenly, in 1975, he appeared at a formal banquet with a thick, shining head of hair: wig or graft, for he was, despite his youth (he was forty), extremely bald.

Chang, on the contrary, looked like an intellectual, with a long, intelligent face. He had wavy dark hair. Born in 1916 of a mandarin family, he had started writing in school magazines when he was fifteen; and gravitating to Shanghai had joined the League of Left-wing Writers there in the 1930s. After 1949 he had become the director of the literary department of the Party in Shanghai; and had then recruited Yao Wenyuan, who specialized in politico-literary criticism. Both joined forces in the 1950s to denounce the 'rightists' in the aftermath of the Hundred Flowers; and by exhibiting ruthless revolutionary purity Chang had become the cultural tsar of Shanghai.

In 1963, Chiang Ching, furious at the cold shouldering she received from people like the Vice-Minister Hsia Yen, and Mayor Peng Chen, in Peking, went to Shanghai and there obtained all the support she wanted from Chang and Yao. Thus would start the nucleus of the Gang of Four. Shanghai's cultural and propaganda apparatus was mobilized for theatre reform, but also to serve Chiang Ching.

Chang had ascended the hierarchy of the Party very swiftly since 1966. He was chairman of Shanghai's

How the Foolish Old Man Moved the Mountain.

Revolutionary Committee, member of the Politburo, and he would accumulate other posts. He had now recruited the Seventeenth Textile Mill 'worker', Wang Hungwen, who had led the seizure of Shanghai in January 1967. There is no doubt that he was clever as well as ambitious; in fact, he was the brains behind the organization of the Four.

Chang said to me, 'I've heard of your interest in the model operas. Comrade Chiang Ching has worked very hard. She has many interesting things to teach us. We all learn from her . . . her life has been entirely in the cause of revolution.' I have never had such a direct hint that I should interest myself not only in the operas but in Chiang Ching's life story. And before I had thought what I would say, I replied, 'Unfortunately I am very busy at present . . . I am writing a big book on the Chinese Revolution.' This was the most brutal and, from the point of view of anyone intent on getting into the good graces of the rising constellation, the most stupid thing I could ever have done. Thus did I turn down the second, and the most outspoken hint to write up Madame Mao's life, a hint which had certainly come from her. She had planned to recruit me. I did it not because I had any feelings against her at the time but out of stark candour, stupid ignorance of 'how to get on'.

In came Chiang Ching, like a small whirlwind, buzzing in a suit; her voice loud and imperious. She sat down and stood up, sat down again, wiped her face, wiped her arms to the elbows, wiped her neck to the armpits, with hot towels handed to her; as if she had just come from the fields and a spell of harvesting or threshing. She had, in fact, stepped down from her car. There was a blown-up exaggeration in all this physical activity which compelled one into a feeling grotesque and unreal. But Chiang Ching did have the power to transport her viewers from solid common sense into her own world of make-believe.

Behind Chiang Ching someone carried a pile of new blouses. 'I want to reform clothing . . . our women are too strict in their ideas. They should wear flowery materials.'

This was meant to be, like the model operas, a major innovation. I forbore to say – though I was tempted – that I had seen flowery blouses throughout north China before the Cultural Revolution. Marcelline was handed a blouse, and the other women present too. Came my turn: Chiang Ching hesitated, then went to the toilet, came back with a fresh blouse on and handed me the one she had worn. A most signal honour. 'The very blouse Comrade Chiang Ching wore, on her own body,' whispered Vincent's interpreter to him, in an awed voice. I expressed my thanks. Chiang Ching went on talking, or rather exclaiming about the opera, and actresses, and other topics; disconnected phrases. She put on and took off her glasses. I had with me a small chain to keep one's spectacles round one's neck, and I handed it to her.

'What is this for?'

I explained. But the chain did not please her.

'It's gold,' she said, looking at it suspiciously.

'No, it's gilded.'

'I don't like anything round my neck, like a necklace,' said she.

And this conjured up for me a scene three years old: that of Liu Shoachi's wife, Wang Kuangmei, being humiliated by two thousand Red Guards at Tsinghua University, and forced to wear a necklace of ping-pong balls – because she had worn a necklace on official visits to potentates abroad. Perhaps it was Chiang Ching who had remarked on Wang Kuangmei's necklace when haranguing the young Red Guards, at the time devoted to her. Hence they had singled out this detail against Wang Kuangmei.

Chiang Ching rose, looked round at us, a satisfied circular glance. Now she started comparing our heights. A young actress was there, following her with clasped hands, as in prayer.

'We have a number of tall women here,' said Chiang Ching, and addressing herself to me, 'How tall are you?'

'I don't know,' I replied.

Silence. Thick, no sound. Chiang Ching could no longer

say a word. I think now that her chatter had annoyed me, but neither Vincent nor the Ivens realized what had taken place, and no interpreter translated. Chiang Ching glared, speechless; she could not find her voice. She simply waved her hand to usher us into the auditorium. We followed her. She had put on her jacket again.

The hall was packed with a select audience of actors and actresses and musicians, and soldiers in uniform, all 'cultural workers'. They clapped and clapped. Chiang Ching waved the little red book she had taken out of her pocket, and looked round, with a gleam of triumph on her face. Joris sat on her right and I was at her left. Throughout the next two hours she kept her back firmly turned to me, and addressed herself solely to Joris Ivens, or to the row behind us, where some officials sat.

The ballet started: Chiang Ching talked steadily right through it, and all the time she talked, she wiped herself, going over her neck and face and even under her armpits, as if she sweated abundantly. And she told Joris, at the top of her voice, the story of her life; or rather, those parts of it that she wanted me to hear. For it was quite obvious that she wanted *me* to hear them. She would not otherwise have talked so loudly. Behind Joris an interpreter translated into French. Joris made cooing sounds. He was always amiable, and slightly bored.

She told Joris about her family; its poverty; how people talked 'maliciously' about her, had calumniated her and continued to do so; how she had always fought to produce revolutionary films and plays. Constantly she came back to the theme: 'People lie about me; they tell tales about me . . . they seek to destroy me.'

The ballet proceeded.* It was about a heroic peasant woman who finds a wounded PLA soldier lying in coma and gives him her own breast milk to drink in order to save him. Of course the dancer went off stage, returning with a cup in

*It was *Yi Meng Song*. It was shown several times but never really caught on.

her hands. The soldier quaffed the beverage and from a prone position started to leap about. Suddenly Chiang Ching interrupted herself to shout, 'Red shoes, not green shoes.' (The heroine was wearing green shoes.) 'Red shoes, not green shoes,' said a resigned voice. It was that of an official seated behind her.

At the end, we trooped on stage to applaud and shake hands with the dancers and be photographed with them. Chiang Ching had Joris and Marcelline stand next to her; I found a place a little further from her. Vincent, meanwhile, had tried to speak to Yao Wenyuan, but Yao had turned away and pretended not to hear him. Then it was over. Chiang Ching left, after another circular glance at all of us. Chang and Yao went with her, and did not shake hands with me. We went back to the hotel and to bed, and suddenly we were whispering, as if there were hidden microphones in the room.

'She's odd.'

'Yes.'

'Arrogant.'

'Well . . .'

I lay awake, thinking: what kind of a person had she become, and how could Mao have such a woman to live with, next to him? But these were sacrilegious thoughts which I did not share with Vincent at the time.

I went with Hsing Chiang to Papaoshan, the hill of burial for revolutionaries, to salute the ashes of Kung Peng. Most Party members were cremated; non-Party people, like my father, often chose burial. Right through north China grave mounds still pock-marked the fields; and peasants burned paper money on them at certain times of the year.

Each time I entered the modest-sized hall where, on shelves, the ashes of Party members reposed I felt moved, remembering the past, and their deeds of valour. We found Kung Peng; a photograph adorned her casket, and Hsing

Chiang and I bowed, and sorrowed. Such a small box, to contain what had been so much grace and fortitude.

In 1972 I would again come to salute Kung Peng, and I would see, further along the rows, the casket of Chen Yi, the merry and honest warrior and poet. Chen Yi died in January 1972 of cancer of the caecum. I would never hear his cheerful laughter again. George Wu, the cancer specialist, also missed him greatly. 'He noticed everything. He would say to me, "How do you stick it round here? We push you around, we criticize you – yet you go on. Why?" 'Because, I guess, I love China,' Wu had replied. And Chen Yi had said, 'You overseas Chinese, you have much to teach us.' Chou Enlai had delivered the funeral oration for Chen Yi, and Mao Tsetung himself had attended. A friend of mine told me how Mao had stayed on after the ceremony, staring at the wreaths, just staring, until, gently, Chou Enlai had led him away.

'Every day there are several hundred people, on Sundays a thousand or more, who come here to salute Chen Yi,' said the keeper.

I went to salute Papa's grave, now repaired after the depredations of the Red Guards, and then to see Anna-Louise. She had a magnificent marble tombstone. 'Rest happy, Anna-Louise. What you wanted to bring about has come to pass. China and America will be friends, and already the world is changed.'

Central Asia begins at Sian, the ancient Tang dynasty capital on the elbow of the Wei River. We flew over a million square kilometres of loess, silt brought down by the Yellow River, which has built the north China plains. Deforestation and erosion have made this solid mud a macaroni tangle of knotted cliffs and gullies, harbinger of the desert it would have become within the next century, had not the present government started taming the river, rewooding its upper reaches, building dams, making the desert shrink. It will take a century or two of work, an awesome enterprise. Meanwhile, in the limitless yellow churn, were sudden plateaux bulldozed to evenness, intensely green and fertile; state farms, communes, reclaiming the canyons, terracing the cliffs, and each terrace bearing the seed of forests to come.

I like the Islamic quarter of Sian, where an ambling goat, an occasional two-humped camel, rare as a fabled beast today, could still be accosted in the 1960s. Sian is enchanting, with its willows, the roar of its noon cicadas, its temples and museums and palaces, its delicious local beer and civilized people. From here we set out on our journey to modern Tartary, Sinkiang; we shall follow – by aeroplane – the Silk Road, as did the caravans launching themselves to cross the deserts to India, to Iran, to Tyre and Sidon, to Rome and to Alexandria.

Lanchow, capital of Kansu province, is the first oasis on the desert's edge. It nestles in a coil of the Yellow River, here a monstrous stream of ochre.

Our hotel is full of boisterous Mongols; a football team from Ninghsia has arrived to play a match with the local team. In the streets squads of people shouldering spades and pickaxes march to plant ten thousand new *mus* of land; there is a new canal, its water supply pumped up from the river.

The city is cool (1,400 metres above sea-level) and we are mothered by Madame Li of the revolutionary committee. I shall go back four times to Lanchow; which fascinates me. It is now an industrial city, the centre of China's atomic industry. Kansu was the poorest of all provinces before 1949, ruined by famines and wars since the nineteenth century. Now there are four times as many people in the city as in 1949. The railway only reached Lanchow in 1952, but it has since been built, from oasis to oasis, to reach Hami, and Urumchi, and onwards to Karamai.

In Lanchow the Cultural Revolution has been grim and fearful. 'The workers in the factories shot at each other,' says Madame Li. And this year there is a drought. 'Many trees have died . . . We did wrong to plant on slopes. It is difficult to water them.' Blanket directives to grow cereal anywhere and everywhere have produced friction; for Kansu province contains national minorities: Mongols and Tibetans and Huis, whose grazing land has been reduced, to grow cereal. 'We must not go on doing it,' says Madame Li. Because of the Huis (Muslims), pig breeding is not favoured. 'Sheep and goat meat are still available, but the drought has killed a lot of animals.'

I have never seen such scrawny, dejected horses and mules as in Kansu province: almost as skeletal as in Old China, whereas one of the things I love in New China is the way the peasants' horses and mules are sleek and well-fed.

Next we fly off to Hami, two hundred metres below sea-level, renowned for its delicious melons. Once known as Qomul, on the Silk Road, it was a great trading emporium. Now it is an industrial city, as is Lanchow. At Hami airport I saw a fleet of ships upon a sparkling sea, and palm trees on the horizon. A desert mirage. Vincent, more prosaic, saw fighter planes aligned, and said that Hami must be an air force base.

Hami is the threshold to the majestic Gobi Desert. The aeroplane followed the Heavenly Mountains across the Gobi Desert, dividing Sinkiang into Zungaria in the north and the Tarim basin and the Taklamakan Desert in the south.

We took the northern route, and the oases along the mountain slopes were few; the southern slopes were the true main line of the Silk Road, swinging along the basin of the Tarim, to Turfan and Korla, to Kuche and Aksu and on to Kashgar where began the Pamirs and Afghanistan. We flew over black Gobi, a landscape of the moon, the mountains of the moon, torn by a wind already at noon wild and strong, tossing our aeroplane and rearranging the sand dunes below us into crescents and circles; shifting great tides of gravel which changed colour with the hours. And the mountains sat in vast crinolines, skirts of their own substance which had slid down their slopes and mantled their bases. 'It's the alternate heat and cold . . . sometimes a mountain explodes,' said the pilot. 'The Gobi is a young desert and it is still being sifted and split by wind and sun.'

There had been a plague of donkeys around Hami some years past, said the pilot. 'We don't need them any more. We have jeeps and trucks, so now they run wild.' Once they had been the mainstay of the Shansi carters who plied up and down the Silk Road. Now, below us, a procession of lorries swirled immense dust clouds, climbing the desert dunes. The leaf-vein pattern of desert streams run dry, coming down from the mountains, ended in a pulverized mass of sand.

The Heavenly Mountains rose in height and dignity, and then there was a snow cap and many more patches of emerald green: oases, valleys. Urumchi was twenty minutes away. There towered Bogdan, God's mountain, twin-crested and radiant.

Urumchi seemed in the grip of a local flood, although there had been no rain for six months. 'Underground water.' The inhabitants had been digging air-raid shelters (all China was digging shelters that year), and a spring had been broken into and had flowed into the streets. Ismail Emet, the Uighur representative, a delegate at the Ninth Congress, welcomed us. He was thirty-four years of age, a mild and handsome man with a fair skin and curly dark hair. He wore a thick corduroy jacket and trousers and he did not sweat. Throughout our stay in Sinkiang I would be amazed to find the Uighurs heavily clad, wrapped in clothes and shawls on the hottest day.

'Urumchi is sinister,' Owen Lattimore had written; to him, it was the most thief- and dog-ridden city in China. But of course it was not so when we saw it. Like all cities of China today, it was two cities, the old and the new. And the difference is far more marked in national minority areas, such as Sinkiang, or Tibet, or in Yunnan among the Pais. Both in Urumchi and Kashgar, the old towns with their small desert-style houses, thick walls of mud bricks, shuttered and cool, painted white or ochre, might have been anywhere in Islam's great domain; and narrow lanes through which skirted women hurried were timeless,

Biblical. But there were also modern Urumchi and Kashgar, with drab, functional buildings of grey and red brick, with schools and hospitals and supermarkets and factories. Inelegant, but with running water and electricity.

The Uighurs are of the same origin as the Turks; the word Turk came into being in the fourth century, when their tribes came down from the Altai and into Sinkiang. 'That was six centuries after the Silk Road had been established by the Hans,' Ismail reminded me. For a while, here were great kingdoms and empires; there is no more fascinating, adventurous history than that of Central Asia.

It was not before the eighth or ninth century that the Turks went westward and began to settle in today's Turkey. The Uighur language still bears a very strong resemblance to Turkish.

There are altogether thirteen national minorities in Sinkiang, Uighurs and Tajiks, Uzbeks and Kazakhs, Tartars and others; but the whole area of over $1\frac{1}{2}$ million square kilometres, only contains eight million people: $4\frac{1}{2}$ million Uighurs, half a million other nationalities, and three million Hans. Sinkiang is now known as a Uighur autonomous region.

How beautiful the Uighurs were! Truly one of the most handsome people on earth. And how they loved to dance, to sing, to play music! All their movements were graceful, and the girls with their thick plaits, in their flowered short-sleeved dresses, were enchanting.

This is where frustration came in. We had to battle – politely – with a fairly fat military man, Comrade C., who was a security maniac – and alas not the only one. He was so careful of our safety that we could not move near anyone, and would have spent our days in Sinkiang being briefed in our guest residence, or whirling about at great speed in cars which we were not allowed to leave, had we not rebelled.

I understood the concern of Comrade C. There had been bloody episodes here during the first years of the Cultural Revolution, and he was still jittery. But it was dreary to go to a factory or a supermarket, and find that everyone who was an ordinary person had been shooed away; that we could only be approached by a handful of people duly tutored. Mr Ma, the very able and erudite Foreign Ministry official who accompanied us on this trip, and Madame Yeh also a diplomat, did their best. But the thwarting produced awkward moments.

I remember one 'arranged' occasion in a store for native handicrafts. Not one of the 'buyers' gathered there, waiting for us to arrive in order to pretend to buy, was anything but a cadre in training! They were all young, well-dressed, and they acted their parts very badly.

We stayed outside Urumchi in a beautiful guest house, once a warlord's residence, around it a garden with willows and camphor trees and running water. Beyond it was the main road to Hami, bordered with tamarisk and poplars. And along it were communes, some of mixed Uighur and Han families, some of Uighur only.

One day at the road's edge I saw a marvellous sight. Harvesting. A high-wheeled horse cart, and the Uighur women throwing the sheaves of wheat with lovely gestures on to the cart. 'Stop, stop,' I cried, and got out of the car, and Vincent and I walked into the wheat stubble, and like a great rise of birds all the Uighurs in the field, children and women (the Uighur male seems to leave this work to women and young boys), came running towards us, laughing and cheering. I still have the scene on film.

Many of the women had babies tied to them; they crowded round us. They had none of the Confucian reticence of the Hans; they *wanted* to be filmed, to be photographed! They wanted to touch us and to be near us, and this great hunger for friendliness was something unforgettable. Marco Polo, who had come along the Silk Road in the thirteenth century, had already commented: 'They are the most friendly people.' They had not changed. Gaiety and the body's grace was theirs, always. They burst into song on invisible impulse; I had seen boys dancing in the street with the sheer joy of being alive.

And so the meaning of *oasis* came to us; of life which had dominion over gaunt death, over the dread of the terrible desert. The people were like those springs of water one discovered spurting from arid rock, unquenchable in their passion for joy.

But Military C.'s car caught up with us, and the security men surged out and started shoving the people away. 'Don't push, don't push,' I shouted angrily. It would happen a good many times. I would go back to Peking and complain about this, and say that this was not the way to treat national minorities . . .

I did not know then – but I would find out the next year, when I returned to the oases and the desert – that Sinkiang was indeed an area of 'major security', not only because there was still trouble, purportedly with 'Russian agents', but chiefly because Sinkiang had become the bastion of Lin Piao, one of the regions of China in his power, and no rising of any kind could be allowed.

Vincent, who had not spent a childhood as I had on alert, avoiding warlords, escaping raids and danger; who had never been bombed, nor had had any of the experiences of my exciting life, became angry; he felt it was all childish and ridiculous. But I realized that it was not clever not to see the point of view of Comrade C. There might indeed be a terrorist attempt on us, to discredit the military holding Sinkiang. It was best, therefore, to compromise. I spoke in a conciliatory way to several people, and security slackened considerably.

It was in Kashgar that I had a wonderful experience, when I was allowed to visit, publicly, the great mosque.

The mosque was being regilded. Basil Davidson had noted in the early 1950s that the mosque was in sad disrepair, owing to the ravages before Liberation.* Obviously it had suffered some recent damage, probably from the Red Guards sent out from Peking to 'make revolution' in

*See *Turkestan Alive* (Cape, 1957).

Sinkiang. I saluted the venerable men who came to greet me at the gates of the mosque, and I bowed towards the edifice (of course I did not enter it) with the deference of a woman. And when I walked out there was an immense crowd on the square, cheering, and suddenly I was crying as the crowd broke through a cordon of unarmed Han policemen, and children and women ran towards me. I picked up a toddler and the little boy did not cry. He looked like me. They all looked like me. They were all Eurasians!

Policemen tried to push back the crowd and the crowd went back like docile water, pliant and unbeatable like water. Mr Ma came and said it was time to go, and docile as water I re-entered the car. But Mr Ma was pleased, and so was I. After that Ismail Emet, who had been somewhat silent, somewhat subdued by Military C., blossomed. 'We are a great people, we the Uighurs,' he said.

'Of course you are.' I added, 'And I am a member of China's smallest minority. A Eurasian. There are not more than a few hundred of us about. But I have always been so terribly proud of being Eurasian.'

And so we met through words, in our dream of a world to come. For this is the desert, which lifts the ordinary into the extraordinary; or rather shows how extraordinary everyday life is, and makes words glow as stars in its velvet night sky.

Kashgar is a marvellous place; once a great city, and destined for greatness again as China develops the whole area up to the Pamirs. Here, and all along the oases from it two great cultures, the Chinese and the Greek, met. Not only trade but religion and art; Buddhism from India and the Greco–Buddhist art of Gandhara. And Nestorians, Zoroastrians, so many others. There was glamour just in the names. They rang of splendour and adventure.

I went to see the grave of Hsiang Fei, the Fragrant Concubine. She was a Uighur, her loveliness so great that its fame reached the eighteenth-century Ching Emperor, Chien Lung, who desired her, and she was brought to him. The tradition of having Uighur wives and concubines in the imperial household was an old one; in fact the Tang dynasty was more than a little Uighur.

Fragrant Concubine's voyage across the desert took two years, but the patient Emperor was ravished. So enamoured of her did he become that he built for her a palace, and a swimming pool; and because she was forever sad, thinking of her country, he built mountains and a desert in the palace gardens. Her body gave out perfume; even the waters of her bath carried the scent; whether or not it was attar of roses is not recorded. But she pined for Kashgar, rode on horseback, wore boots and a dagger in her jewelled belt, and was painted in helmet-and-armour by the court painter, Giulio Castiglione, an Italian.

Emperor Chien Lung went on a trip, and his mother had Fragrant Concubine strangled, alleging that she possessed a dagger and planned to kill the Emperor.

Her tomb in Kashgar is an edifice in Arab style, with glowing blue-tiled domes. Inside it she and her parents lie. An annual fair lasting a week is held here. Tents and stalls are erected all round the monument; families come from afar in their big-wheeled carts drawn by donkeys and horses. The men ride on horseback and race; the young girls titter and glance at them; and there is dancing and music and much singing of love.

A hedge of cactuses and desert date trees surrounded the garden. On the flat spiked palettes of the cactuses Red Guards (who had come perhaps to destroy the grave as 'feudal', but they had been stopped) had engraved the words: 'Destroy Wang Enmao', 'Wang Enmao is a counter-revolutionary.' Wang Enmao was the commander in charge in Sinkiang before Lin Piao took over.

Kashgar was no longer the 'sinister city' described by Sir Eric Teichman. But it was still a Central Asian city; along its lanes came women looking like the Virgin Mary, wrapped in great mantles which covered their hair. The houses were pale grey and ochre, of straw and clay bricks, bricks such as had been made by the Jews in Egypt in the Pharaohs' time; the same bricks from which the first battlements of the Great Wall of China had been built.

At one time Kashgar was such a caravanserai that each nationality had its own walled enclave, but now all the walls had been taken down. The new Kashgar had bicycle and tractor and textile and wool and fertilizer and petrochemical and heavy machinery factories. The road to it was busy; it ran from Aksu and Kuche to the north and Yarkand and Khotan south-eastwards. Trucks and lorries passed frequently, with their motors exposed to cool the engines and prevent the sand clogging them. Above the road towered the great ranges of the Karakorum, and from the slopes came many streams, making fertile valleys with grassland for pasture, and fields, right on the edge of the Taklamakan Desert.

The Kashgar middle school had as many girls as boys. Uighur was being romanized, said the headmaster. Previously the Arabic script had been used; then Cyrillic had been introduced, owing to Russian influence, from 1954 to 1956; but in 1958 Premier Chou Enlai had it changed to the roman alphabet. The headmaster told me gravely that 90 per cent of the text-books were now romanized, but he read his own speech from notes in Arabic script, and when I pointed this out he said, 'I am too old to study romanization.' Outside, all posters, banners and painted slogans were in both Han and romanized Uighur. This was the gap between rhetoric and reality, official façade and everyday life. I told the headmaster that the Turkish language had been romanized some decades ago, and he nodded again. 'It is not for an old man like me.' He was forty-two.

We lodged at what had once been the Russian Consulate; a gloomy assembly of enormous rooms separated by thick velvet hangings and draped, so many carpets on the walls and on the floor that all sound was muffled; Vincent and I spent much time seeking each other and shouting, 'Where are you?' without an echo in reply. The toilet and bathroom were furnished with giant porcelain equipment, as in every place where Russians had lodged. Were they truly so large-bodied? Or was it merely the fashion of the times?

I lost my temper at the Kashgar hospital. The army man in charge had forced all the doctors to turn out, to sit and listen while he talked and talked about the hospital and how much it had improved now after ridding itself of 'the capitalist line'. I looked at the impassive faces around me. They were tired and thin. I got down to questions. How many nurses were there? How many beds? How many patients? Then I got angry.

'You can't run a hospital like that. There are not enough nurses for the patients – the doctors' health will break down.'

'With Mao Tsetung Thought we can do *anything*,' replied the army man fatuously.

'You can do a lot but you cannot revive people who are dead . . . Your doctors are overworked.'

I left in fury.

'I'll report to Peking about this. It's sabotage,' I said to Mr Ma.

'Oh, please do,' said Ma happily.

And then I realized that that was the reason I had been sent. Not to approve of everything, but to pick faults. And I remembered that Chou Enlai had often said, 'We are not always well-informed.' I was not here just for a good time; I also had a responsibility. To see clearly, and to report what I had found, but not to collide with local authority. I must keep my temper, if possible.

We went by car to the oases of Kuche and Aksu, and on to Shohotze in the Tarim basin reclamation area. 'The women of Aksu are the most beautiful in the world,' said the very nice military man from Kashgar who came with us. He had become thoroughly Uighurized after six years in the country. 'I don't think I can live anywhere else now. My spirit needs the desert.' His gestures had unstiffened; he would almost burst into song and dance. He probably yearned to marry a Uighur girl from Aksu.

All along the roads of Sinkiang are rock caves with Buddhist and Manichean frescoes; the latter with the double eagle emblem, which was a religious symbol before it became the emblem of Tsarist Russia. But alas, we could not stop to see those priceless relics of the past.

Shohotze was once centre of the reclamation area of the Tarim basin. In summer when the river's many tributaries from the Heavenly Mountains and the Karakorum are in spate, the valley, six hundred kilometres long, is bright green, and there are poplars and groves of tamarisk and scrub and reeds. Since 1950 it had been under development by the army, and it was now an enormous collection of fertile fields with many tree belts, state farms. Three hundred thousand Hans from Szechuan and other provinces, and forty thousand 'educated youths' were settled here in 1964–5. Chou Enlai and Chen Yi had come to visit the youths, many from Peking and Shanghai, and to enquire about their living conditions.

From all I had read of previous travellers, the area was indeed unrecognizable. There had been merely swamps and some skimpy huts. Now there was electric light, telephone, running water; in this depth of Central Asia an expanse of modernism, ball-bearings instead of exotic backwardness. But then all Asia wanted ball-bearings, and the word exotic was a European invention.

Here grew cotton and wheat, and sunflowers for oil, and maize, and rice to improve the alkaline soil; for the soil was laden with salt. Date trees of a tenacious kind were grown, to anchor the sand dunes, and mushrooms. There were straight avenues lined with poplars and young firs and white wax trees; and many irrigation canals. And of course there were factories. The population was organized along military lines, as the commander told us. 'The dependants of our workers', which meant the families, 'produce secondary articles needed for the factories.' He said that the educated youths 'adapt well'; they received 30 *yuan* 30 *fen* a month; a worker received 58 *yuan*.

This was one of the many 'army resettlement camps', designed to implant a population in remote uninhabited areas. From the overcrowded provinces of China, millions would be resettled here. 'Life is better here than in many regions of east China.'

I got up early in the morning. Some women were walking on the road, and they stopped and we began to talk. They came from Szechuan.

'I go back to see my family every New Year,' said one woman. Her children were in Szechuan. 'They are used to the city. My parents look after them.'

A military man came up fast behind me and our talk was over. The woman walked away, grinning cockily.

'Really, there's just too much security,' I said to Mr Ma. 'As if I did not understand that we have to plant new settlements, to shift people. I even talked about it with Chen Yi some years ago. And to pretend that *every one* of these people comes willingly – that's nonsense. There must be both stick and carrot. Incentive and pressure. I understand all this. Why not let me speak to the people?'

After that there was no more interference, and I saw a good many families. The standard of care was very high.

We visited the Karamai oilfields, encompassed by ranges in a vast horseshoe, called the mountains of Genghis Khan; they looked like an advancing horde. The oilfield was an old one, and had pipelines to several cities of Sinkiang. The army of course ran the oilfield. Keiyoumu Maitimiyaze, a Tajik in charge of the Karamai garrison, told me that here the struggle had been 'acute', and 'the ultra-left used knives and guns and mortars . . .' The army had crushed them, in March 1967, and production had been resumed. There were wells some 4,000 metres deep; Soviet experts had said that Karamai was finished, done for, there was no more oil, but Keiyoumu said that was not true. 'We are prospecting and there may be new gushers soon.'

* * *

We went from Urumchi to Turfan by Big Wind Pass, a narrow-throated gorge though which the sinuous road wound by a river. We sweltered, and I could imagine the whinny of horses and the lugubrious scream of camels in the hot wind which sandblasted our faces. From the grey metallic sheen of the Gobi into another desert, where the air quivered like flame and the land was red, and the low-lying horizon was red too: here were the Flame Mountains of legend. Through this furnace the monk Hsuen Tsang had travelled, accompanied by the legendary Monkey,* to seek the Buddhist scriptures in India.

All security had vanished; leaving the gorge, Ismail and I now loitered by the river bank, dipping our hands in the stream as an act of worship to the sparkling water.

Down the road came a horseman, beautiful in his saddle, saluting gravely and behind him also on horseback a woman with a wimple on her head, as in fourteenth-century Europe.

From some ten minutes away, dancing in the heat, Turfan appeared like a green haze on the horizon, a mirage to cool the eye; and first there were its lifelines, the long ridges of *kereze* underground wells like mole burrows, bringing it water in tunnels, an irrigation technique practised in Iran and here for more than five hundred years.

The oasis of Turfan is 160 metres below sea-level; February is the sowing season and the sand wind blows burning air two days out of five. It has been described as hell by so many travellers that perhaps it is hell, but the people of Turfan call it the Vale of Paradise. Or at least so did Joshe Turudi, the head of the revolutionary committee of Turfan, who came to greet us.

Turudi was six foot two, weighed two hundred pounds and had green eyes and curly hair. From Spain to Afghanistan he would have been at home; he even looked like a Roman centurion in search of spoil. He spoke both Chinese and Uighur, and he was exhilarated by water. The

*See *Monkey*, translated by Arthur Waley (Allen & Unwin, 1942).

way he said the word was blessing, wonder of moisture, and the glamour of Turfan in the days of caravans came to us in that single word.

There are no industries in Turfan; it is still the oasis, and the houses are mostly baked clay and reed and straw, which can be sculpted into delicate patterns. Along the ridges of higher ground, are the barns for drying the grapes, a lacework of walls like sieves to let the air through. Turfan produced the wonderful seedless grapes renowned throughout the world, from Peking to Victorian England.* The mosque of Turfan was green-tiled and small; it had been derelict when Basil Davidson came here in 1956. It was now repaired, and on Friday capped men congregated in the narrow lane leading to it, obviously waiting to pray.

How green was Turfan, green and restful to the eye after the grey desert and the red desert! And here were tales of demons and ghosts, goblins of the sands and the scalding winds. We almost forgot (although it was forty-two degrees Centigrade in the shade) our aching skins rubbed raw by sand gusts. The guest house garden was pleasant and shaded, but there was a Shanghai housekeeper in charge of it. She was thin and depressed and she kept saying, without a pause, 'Oh how hot it is how hot it is please do not move too much here is a fan or you will be too hot.' All through the time we spent in Turfan she would cry unweariedly of the unbearable heat, and her voice was an uninterrupted sad scream. The heat terrorized her; she could not forget it for a moment, and she had been in Turfan eighteen years. 'I came here when I was twenty . . . to serve the people of Turfan.' But she could only utter her querulous and maddeningly monotonous cry, like a stranded curlew.

With her, to look after guests, was a most beautiful Uighur girl. She wore a multi-coloured dress and she did not even sweat; her skin was like a golden peach and her hair

---

*In Christina Rossetti's poem, *Goblin Market*, 'pellucid grapes without one seed'.

concealed an auburn glow in the coils of her heavy, sensuous plaits.

Vincent could not stand the heat at night; though he bore it well during the day. He was provided with two fans, both turned on to him as he slept. 'But it gets cool at night,' said Turudi, wondering that an Indian did not find Turfan pleasant.

In Turfan's great trough now flowed a new canal, the Tarlan canal, three hundred kilometres long; it had been dug 'by our Han brothers,' said Turudi, and the oasis had doubled in size. There was electric light and running water now. 'Turfan *is* the Valley of Paradise,' insisted Turudi. But it only rained twelve millimetres in a year, and in winter the temperature went down to minus ten degrees Centigrade. All the houses had *kangs* of clay, and in winter the families huddled together upon them; the *kang* was in use all over north China.

Around us the desert smoked and boiled, and one could cook an egg in the sand of the Flame Mountains (fifty-two degrees Centigrade) when we took the forked road to the ancient city of Karakhoja; which, at one time, some Greeks who had wandered here had called Ephesus, in memory of another Ephesus. The palaces and teraces, buffeted by the terrible wind, showed their dead windows; but it had all become part of the rock and the sand and anyway we were not allowed to tarry. We had come to see the new, not the old, and once more 'security' intervened. The new was exciting; it was greenness eating into the desert; the oases extending; the first line of small young trees, their boles slender and younger than in the middle of Turfan with its old lanes: trees aligned straight as though drawn with a ruler. These were the green shelter belts and the new fields wrested from the desert would now yield cotton and wheat and maize and there would be orchards 'enlarging Paradise'. Rice too was being tried here for the first time in history. Turfan had been a Han garrison in the Tang dynasty, but the north China soldiers ate wheat, not rice.

We went about the oasis through shaded pathways with willows and running water; we met women and girls; none wore the veil; though older women still had their heads covered with a shawl. The girls wore earrings and plaits and the beautiful embroidered Uighur caps on their heads. We ate sitting on carpets spread on the ground under shady trees: mutton and great heaps of melons and peaches and apples and grapes. At night boys and girls with guitars and clarinets and timbrels came to sing and to dance in the gardens. But at the guest house we could not escape the Shanghai woman's gentle moan: 'It is hot, it is hot.' She wore long trousers and a buttoned jacket. She did not turn up the trouser legs to the knee, as did the Han men, who fanned their bare legs and thus cooled themselves. She did not wear the light short-sleeved dresses of the Uighur women. Her face expressed only utter lassitude. Yet she valiantly continued to serve the people in Turfan.

'This was a poor and devastated oasis. Now it is rich,' said Turudi. Former travellers, like Owen Lattimore, and the two dauntless Englishwomen, Mildred Cable and Francesca French, wrote of hopeless misery;* the misery had gone. The average income of an oasis dweller was much higher than in China proper; it averaged 2.50 *yuan* per labour day. There were 230 pumps for new irrigation, 530 *kereze* wells. Turfan now had over 120,000 people, of which the Uighurs made up 95,000, the Huis 10,000 and the Hans 16,000.

Turudi had had a terrible childhood. His mother had been killed by the water lord in front of him. All his life had been controlled by water, or the lack of it; and in the cool night, I sat with him for hours as he told me his story. 'The Revolution has been good for us; it has made us men, it has given us pride.' He also praised the Cultural Revolution. 'Without it we were being forgotten; there was too much bureaucracy.'

One afternoon we went to the Valley of Grapes. It was a

---

*Owen Lattimore, *Nomads and Commissars* (Oxford University Press, 1962); Mildred Cable and Francesca French, *Through the Jade Gate and Central Asia* (Hodder & Stoughton, 1950).

most famous valley; over our head in thick clusters hung the grapes; so many of them, so many, almost theatrically too many, heavy, translucent, nacreous grapes. Below them we sat and ate, and then we danced. On both sides of the narrow valley were the cliffs, deformed, disintegrating, sitting in grey dust. They looked like demons watching us ready to pounce, to bury us in their dust. But the Uighurs made music with tambourines and the beautiful girls of the valley danced, and we had travelled back many centuries. If Paradise is relief from grief and want and care, when the caravans came here and the poets wrote love songs, then indeed Turfan was Paradise.

Up we went to the lake in the Heavenly Mountains, to spend a day with the Kazakhs; to drink mare's milk freshly fermented in large copper pots. A woman, booted and with ample skirts, knelt to turn and stir the milk with a ladle and to spoon it out into drinking bowls. Vincent drank six bowls and earned the admiration and affection of the Kazakhs. I could not manage even one. And then there were games on horseback, races: and we went from tent to tent, talking with the families, admiring the children. The unmarried girls wore a little tuft of owl feathers in their caps. Tzeya the Tartar was the leader of this settlement, now known as the East Wind Pastoral Commune. Tzeya said how much better off they were than in the past. Here the workpoints are high. A commune member earns something like three *yuan* a day; seven to eight times as much as the average peasant in Szechuan. Everywhere in China there are differences in earnings, but among the national minorities it is policy to raise the earnings; they are uniformly higher than in the Han areas, except among the Yis and the Miaos of Kweichow and Yunnan, where they are extremely low.*

*These two provinces are reckoned to be 'cheap' areas, where the cost of living is low. There are fourteen 'grades' of living standard in China, and people are paid accordingly. Peking, for instance, is only Grade Ten, while Shanghai is Grade Fourteen. A Shanghai worker will automatically be paid more than a Peking worker.

East Wind Commune is wealthy; it owns glossy stallions from Illi. All the men are elegant in corduroy; the women and girls wear layers of petticoats, boots and stockings. Abiola is the midwife of the commune, and Tunkien the teacher. Tunkien teaches on horseback, following the herds and their families; she wears brilliant pink stockings, and handles a gun with practised ease.

On the road back, single families of Kazakhs come riding down the Bogdan with their felt tents tied upon the backs of their cattle. The women carry their babies on the high saddle in front of them.

We are honoured on leave-taking. Lung Shuchin, the top military man in Sinkiang, gives us dinner. He is tall, thin and quiet. He commanded the unit which forced the crossing of the bridge over the Tatu River, under terrible fire from the Kuomintang, during the Long March.

We have been to Tartary, we have learnt much; we have met the Uighurs, and we feel as Marco Polo did, who loved them on sight.

On to Chengtu; and here at last is Sixth Brother and his wife; it is five years since I have seen them. They look well. I want to see Third Aunt, but it is hinted that she had better come to see me. We are lodged outside the city in a spacious villa; I take the hint. There is no point in forcing things. But in the end, we do go to her house: I want to make sure that she is well cared for.

Third Uncle died in 1968. Sixth Brother affirms that it was of natural causes. However, Sixth Brother does not tell me much that year. Only the next year, 1972, will he begin to tell me, in morsels, in very small fragments, how he was grilled and grilled for weeks, accused of having 'illicit connections abroad'(which meant being my cousin!), accused of having passed secrets, and of having had other evil intentions. 'But I never gave in, I always repudiated their accusations.' Finally 'they' could not do anything to him, except cut his salary and take away all his clothes and his wife's clothes, so that the two had nothing to wear except what they had on their backs, and winter was coming. And 'they' took away his watch, saying it was foreign. He had bought it in 1962, with money I had brought, in the overseas Chinese shop.

As for Third Aunt, she said nothing to me that year except that she was well. All I could do was give her some money and hope that all was indeed well. But in 1972 I heard in Peking from Jui that Third Aunt was accused of being from a landlord family, and she had been put 'under supervision of the masses'. This meant that an old worker, Comrade Wu, was supposed to watch her every move. I would make great friends with Comrade Wu and his wife, and they looked after Third Aunt with affection and care, so that finally what could have been unendurable turned out for the best. I also protested and I was assured in Szechuan that Third Aunt had never been accused of being 'landlord class'. All this took patience, and forcefulness at the right time, and also weighing judiciously what must be said and what must not, and above all not losing one's temper. And because it was my Family, I kept my temper remarkably well and did what had to be done.

It was obvious that Chengtu had suffered a good deal. There were damaged buildings, and in the factories the machinery was ill-kept. There was an unkempt look; and when I asked Sixth Brother he said, 'Some days we could not go out at all. There was fighting on the streets . . . they killed people.' Who were 'they'? The May 16ers, he said.

The bookshops were almost empty. And there was no Szechuan opera, none at all.

'Why?'

'Because the cultural workers are in the countryside, learning from the workers–peasants–soldiers.'

I think of my dear friend Miss Chen, she of the crystal voice and the beautiful face. There are no plays to see, nothing, whereas in Sinkiang, there was every night some entertainment or another.

* * *

One morning (it was September 11th), Mr Ma said he had to return to Peking immediately, for there was business to attend to.

'Madame Yeh will look after you,' said he. Ma's face was sombre. Something really worried him.

'Mr Ma, are you feeling well?'

'Oh yes, yes of course.'

'Has something serious happened?'

Travelling in inland China, not allowed to read the local newspapers (the *People's Daily* arrives three days late), we are out of touch with what happens anywhere in the world, even with what is happening in Peking.

'Nothing serious,' says Mr Ma, smiling with great effort. Then he adds, 'One can never tell, about anyone . . . A person can always change . . ' He leaves that evening.

Madame Yeh tells me that instead of taking an aeroplane we shall go by train to Chungking and proceed to Kweiyang, and from there we shall go to Tsunyi. Tsunyi is the famous city in Kweichow province where, in January 1935, the Red Army arrived after the staggering losses of the first lap of the Long March (due to bad military tactics). Mao Tsetung became, at Tsunyi, the leader of the Long March and thus it became an epic, a major triumph.*

We were a day in Chungking and in every shop there were slogans posted: 'Destroy the ultra-left!' 'Down with the ultra-left!', 'Catch the ultra-left, do not let them escape!'

It was September 13th when we arrived in Tsunyi. I watched the way the rice was planted; helter-skelter, unevenly as in Malaya, not in the beautiful tight symmetry of Szechuan. This was the way national minorities planted rice. On the roads were Miao women carrying baskets on their backs, supported by a belt on their forehead, as is still done in Nepal by mountain porters.

We went to the house where in January 1935 the Party held its famous meeting, a turning point in the history of the Revolution and in the career of Mao Tsetung.

*See *The Morning Deluge*.

We sat in the room where it had all happened. Above us hung a large oil painting; the triumphant conclusion of the Tsunyi meeting. There was Mao, rosy, impeccable in a well-pressed uniform, and by his side, of course, Lin Piao. Only Lin Piao. I could not make out anyone else in the painting.

The briefing was in keeping with the painting. Lin Piao had stood staunchly by Mao while Mao exposed the errors made. No one else was mentioned. This posed a serious problem: Lin Piao had indeed been in command of the army divisions in the forefront of the March. He had captured Tsunyi, which made the meeting possible. Was this military superiority utilized to force a decision at Tsunyi? I do not think the cadres realized what they were saying; it distorted what Mao had tried to do: which was, in his customary way, to have Party sanction for the condemnation of the 'erroneous military line', and for his own accession to authority. The people who briefed us forgot that Mao had always insisted on Party dominance over the army; even if Party decision was 'helped' by the presence of favourable army commanders.

At the end of the briefing Vincent and I exploded.

'Tell me,' said Vincent, 'were there only Mao and Lin Piao at Tsunyi? Nobody else? What about Chu Teh, and Premier Chou Enlai?'

I said, 'I have read about the Tsunyi meeting; there's been quite a lot about it printed abroad . . . I have consulted historians. Everyone is agreed that other people, such as Premier Chou Enlai, also played a major role at Tsunyi. It is not historically correct to mention only Vice-Chairman Lin . . .'

Silence. Madame Yeh kept an impenetrable expression. The local cadres looked at each other. 'Of course others had a role . . . but Vice-Chairman Lin was the one who made Tsunyi successful.'

That night, the local cadres drank a great deal with Vincent. Everybody became very cheerful.

We left Tsunyi on September 14th. I do not know whether

by then the local cadres had learnt what had happened on the night of September 11th–12th to Lin Piao.

We went by car to Juiching. And thus we saw much more of the hinterland than we would have done otherwise. We discovered mountain roads; hydro-electric power stations; exciting villages where no one had ever been. We did part of the Long March through the Miao regions, and throughout I met many Long Marchers, the rank and file ones; ordinary soldiers of those days, retired. I filled notebooks with their reminiscences: what it was like to slog on foot through passes and the mountains; to fight, to fight, to suffer from dysentery and to fight.

We arrived in Juiching, which had been the great base for the Party and army from 1929 to 1934, and had resisted four major campaigns by Chiang Kaishek. Juiching was a pretty little city; the hills round it were mantled with new trees; they had been seeded by aeroplane but the peasants of the communes, independent and wilful, cut the young trees down for fuel. No visitor had ever come here before. We entered the peasants' homes freely. And the flexible manner in which the directives from Peking were locally interpreted never ceased to amaze me. We shopped in Juiching town; small and delightful shops; and obtained lacquer pillows, which had disappeared everywhere else. I could compare with the past, and things were much better: not only electricity and running water and fields glossy with well-being, but also people. China's elasticity – its inherent suppleness, which makes it independent of the crises of the outside world, and which absorbs its own paroxysms – I rediscovered here. It is not true that the best showpieces are reserved for visits of foreigners: on the contrary, much the best has never been shown to visitors from abroad.

From Juiching we went to Changsa, and there I interviewed Mao Tsetung's old bodyguard, Chen Chang-fong, who for many years, including those of the Long March, had looked after him. He had written a book, *On the*

Long March with Chairman Mao. I asked Chen Changfong only personal questions; about Mao's food and habits, for instance. Mao was a rice eater, and in the north, with millet and sorghum, he developed acute constipation, so that Chen had to give him rectal enemas. He kept a rubber tube with vaseline or oil ready for use. Mao also could never get accustomed to the *kang*. He used a southern type of wooden bed, much colder to sleep on.

My days in Juiching meant not only notebooks to fill, but a whole era to understand: so many deeds of bravery, casual and unrecorded; so much heroism taken for granted. Who shall write the immortal epic of China's Revolution as it ought to be written? The Long March alone is as magnificent as the *Iliad* and I longed, as I talked to the simple soldiers (I interviewed forty of them), who merely slogged and fought without any idea that they were doing something extraordinary, to write it up as it ought to be written, in verse. The number of those who had taken part in this epic was dwindling fast; I had not world enough and time left to do it. But perhaps, if I took many notes, someone would come along, young enough and dedicated enough, to do this work. My notes would be used. The world needs grandeur, honour, a record of man's nobility. A poet – Chinese or American or European or African or Arab or Indian or Japanese – would do it one day.

Suddenly there were aeroplanes; and we flew back to Peking.

It was September 22nd.

Mr Ma was at Peking airport to greet us, and as we drank tea while waiting for our luggage, he told us that unfortunately Vincent's request to go to the Great Wall could not be granted for the time being. 'Anyway, you have seen both ends of the Great Wall,' said he, smiling expansively. He also told us that the government had decided not to hold a parade on October 1st this year, as had been customary, but to let the people enjoy themselves freely, in the parks, and everywhere, for three days.

We went back to the hotel, and immediately were deluged with information. One Japanese friend, and then others came to see me. Something had happened, something very important. Either Mao or Lin Piao had had some accident . . . all aeroplanes in China had been grounded for a week . . .

'So that's why we went everywhere by car,' I said to Vincent.

A very important meeting of the top leaders was being held in the Western Hills, beyond the Great Wall . . . all the heads of Party provincial committees and the Central Committee were assembled there.

'So that's why I couldn't go to see the Great Wall,' said Vincent to me.

Now we began to worry. What had happened? Was Mao dead? Had something happened to him? 'That would be a major catastrophe for your country,' said Vincent, and we both worried so much that it showed in our faces.

In Peking people walked about, outwardly impassive. But there was that solidity of silence which held worry. We all felt the same way, all part of the same body of unease. No one would discuss anything. No one laughed or smiled either. 'Yes,' Hualan said, 'I am as worried as you are, my dear . . . I don't know . . . I only hope that nothing has happened to Chairman Mao.'

Third Brother was back in Peking, but he did not know anything. The French correspondent for Agence France-Presse came to me, and in a voice that could be heard ten metres away, stated, 'Mao is dead. He has been killed.' I met another Frenchman. He had come expressly to write a book on Lin Piao; he was going round asking the Chinese to arrange an interview for him with Lin Piao. The Chinese just smiled and said, 'We shall see.'

I went to see Rewi. He had lost his tail. 'The old cadres of my organization came back and they liberated me . . . I'd got quite used to my tail . . . he was nice.' He walked slowly with me down the street, and at the end, in a small voice said,

'Cheer up, lass, it isn't too bad.' Which meant that Mao had not died.

Chiao Kuanhua had two dinners and a further two meetings with me. He asked about my trip. I told him everything about Sinkiang, about Juiching, and then Chiao asked what had happened at Tsunyi. I told him that it was wrong to distort history. 'Premier Chou is the one who really turned the balance of forces at Tsunyi by throwing his influence on the side of Chairman Mao,' I said.

Dangerous words, dangerous . . . because of what we had said at Tsunyi, it was somehow suspected that I had an inkling of what had happened to Lin Piao. Otherwise, who would be so bold as to question Lin Piao's outstanding role at Tsunyi?

I went back to Peking University to show Vincent my old campus. Professor Chou Peiyuan received us, and spoke of the crushing of the 'ultra-left' at the university. Professor Chou was still carrying on his battle on behalf of fundamental research. 'It will now go on. It will pick up where it left off in 1966.' Backed by Chou Enlai, the professor would produce in 1972 important articles on the need for research; and this would arouse the fury of the Four, when once again they rose in power and influence.

Yang Chengning, the Nobel Prize winner, came to Peking. He was an American citizen and had lived in America since the late 1940s and was apprehensive. 'Please don't publicize my visit,' he said to me. By that time Kissinger had come and gone, and President Nixon was coming; but people like Dr Yang, in America's scientific community, had suffered from the McCarthy pressures in the 1950s, and they were still worried. Dr Yang had shown courage in coming to China so early: for everyone knew that his brain carried a treasure for China.

Dr Yang was duly received by Chairman Mao, and even Chiang Ching and her associates received him. He would begin a trend among scientists of Chinese origin to return to China, with the assent of the United States, in order to speed up China's development.

I thought of the humdrum, anonymous courage of those who had returned much earlier, as had Third and Fourth Brother. Three years of Third Brother's good brain wasted stoking the fires of a cook in a canteen!

I thought of the parable of the labourers in the vineyard; those who come at the eleventh hour are just as useful as those who have toiled all day. But the pioneers, those who did not count the cost, who gave their all when it was dangerous to do so – they should be remembered.

September 30th: usual banquet; and prominently, Premier Chou Enlai was there. With Chiang Ching.

I saw many old friends sitting at tables whom I had not seen for a long time, and I walked about to speak to them. I felt the Premier's eyes on me. Nothing ever escaped Chou Enlai.

I sat at one of the tables in a row near enough to the main table. Chou Enlai and Chiang Ching went from table to table, lifting their glasses and toasting each guest. When they came to me they both glared, and Chou Enlai frowned heavily.

What had I done wrong?

On September 30th the news that a Chinese jet had crashed in Outer Mongolia, and all the nine passengers aboard had been killed, came through. The Outer Mongolian government had reported the matter. It was in all the newspapers abroad.

On October 4th I saw Premier Chou Enlai. He said, 'You must have heard a good deal of gossip about our change of plans for the October 1st festival.'

'I have heard nothing, Prime Minister.'

'That's strange. You've usually got your ear fairly close to the ground in such matters.'

'I've heard nothing, Prime Minister.'

He frowned a little, and then he knew he had made his

point, as I had made mine. Whatever I knew, I knew nothing.

I had submitted a list of questions, and now Chou Enlai answered them most fully. None were about the crash. How could I say, 'Please, Your Excellency, do tell me: Is it Lin Piao who has died, or Chairman Mao?'

'In the last twenty years,' said Chou Enlai, 'we have known that never for a single moment can we relax our vigilance. Always there has been struggle, *inside the Party and outside it*. It will be so again. A revolution can easily be lost, more easily than it is made. Look at what happened in the USSR.' The Vietnam war had shown the two imperialisms, Russian and American, contending and colluding in a desperate race for superiority. 'America is trying to keep what she has: she is on the defensive. Russia is on the offensive everywhere in the world.' Europe, the Middle East, Japan, were bones of contention between the two superpowers; they agreed to transient 'arrangements'. Nevertheless, the rivalry went on.

'We were always prepared for the worst . . . prepared to be attacked by both the superpowers plus India and Japan . . . but this will not come to pass.' Negotiations with the USSR about the border with China were taking place. 'We do not worry if negotiations are protracted . . . ten years, twenty years . . . we have been negotiating with America for sixteen years; and in the end it was President Nixon who suggested that Sino-American talks be held at a higher level . . . in 1970 we received a message from him. Hence he was invited to China.'

At no time did Chou give me the impression that he believed that China would be attacked by the USSR. 'China is tough meat. They prefer soft meat. There is soft meat about.'

As for Taiwan, it was an internal issue for China to solve. No one else. There was a bourgeoisie in Taiwan, as in Hong Kong and Macao, and there must be a 'transitional period' for them to integrate. 'In the early years of China, after 1949, we even supported the national bourgeoisie with subsidies when there were not enough raw materials to keep the factories working.' No cotton had been available for the textile mills of Shanghai in 1950, 'but we paid the workers, and the managers too, even when there was no work to do.'

The total value of the national bourgeoisie assets had been estimated at 2.2 billion *yuan* by 1955; on this, 5 per cent interest had been paid until 1966, not counting salaries, emoluments and compensations. 'We shall certainly proceed in the same manner for Taiwan, Hong Kong and Macao,' said Chou Enlai.

A certain school of Sinologists insists that Chou Enlai had 'engineered' the fall of Lin Piao, and that he was strangled by Chou Enlai at the turn of a dim corridor in a villa in Peitaiho.

High fancy must yield to plausible concreteness. No two witnesses of an event ever tell quite the same story. Hence my personal calendar for the events leading to the death of Lin Piao.

Huang Yungsheng, Lin Piao's right hand man and acting chief of staff, made his last appearance in public on September 10th. On September 11th, Mr Ma returned in haste to Peking. On September 11th, a scheduled meeting between Premier Chou and a Japanese parliamentary delegation was postponed (I met the Japanese delegates at the hotel). On the night of September 11th, rehearsals for the celebration of the National Day parade were stopped. No further rehearsals took place. It was on the night of September 11th–12th that a Chinese Trident crashed in Outer Mongolia with nine people aboard.

The presence in Peking of the American heart specialist Paul Dudley White led to rumours that Mao had had a heart attack. The cancellation of the parade seemed to confirm it. Then came other rumours: there had been an assassination attempt on Mao as he returned by train to Peking . . .

All aeroplanes in China stopped flying from September 11th to September 18th.

On October 4th, Lin Piao's name was dropped from radio broadcasts. On October 8th, Mao appeared in a photograph in the *People's Daily* welcoming the Emperor of Ethiopia, Haile Selassie. Mao looked well.

All China sighed in relief.

I went to Hualan that day, and we hugged each other.

'He is not dead, Hualan.'

She had tears in her eyes. 'All is well, yes, my dear.'

'But then, what has happened, Hualan?'

'Who knows? Maybe someone else has died . . .'

By November, the world outside China conjectured that Lin Piao, his wife and some of his supporters had died in the plane crash. But percolation of information in China from top level to bottom takes time. And the secret was well kept. No one who knew about it said a word.

It was October 18th before the picture of Lin Piao was taken down from above the main Peking bookstore. *China Pictorial* had a special October issue on Mao and Lin Piao, which could not be withdrawn from circulation in Hong Kong. It would be July 1972 before an official pronouncement about Lin Piao and the manner of his death would be issued by China.

In October a small quotation appeared in the *People's Daily*: 'I fear not what my enemies do to me . . . but the sinister arrow fired at my back by my ally, and his smiling face after I was wounded . . .'

All of us understood. Mao was grieving, wounded by Lin Piao's treachery: for Mao had believed in him, and loved and trusted him. From that time on, Mao suddenly began to grow old, and sick, and tired.

Lin Piao had indeed plotted to seize power by a military coup. He committed his plan to paper in March 1971. This document – which I saw – set down the forces at his disposal: nine of China's thirty armies. Because of the other commanders loyal to Mao, he would have to rely on the air force, of which his son was in charge, on parachute drops and raids on major cities, the capture of key points such as air fields and railway stations, radio and television centres. There could be no general military uprising; only regional insurgencies. Lin Piao listed the areas where he held sway: among them Kuangtung and Szechuan provinces, and Sinkiang.

His 'unbounded love' for Mao, the father figure, turned to hatred. He called Mao a feudal tyrant, and 'B-52', a bomber destroying all before him. 'He trusts people of the pen more than people of the sword.'

But Mao had not been inactive or unaware. In December 1970, a major conference in north China reorganized the military garrisons, including that of Peking; this weakened the chances of a military coup in the capital.

In July, forty minutes before he was to receive Kissinger, Mao would see a high official and discuss Lin Piao. 'What shall I do? He is plotting a coup.' After the Kissinger visit, Mao went on tour, to see the regional commanders, as he had done in 1967.

Mao Tsetung's talk with the regional commanders was circulated througout China in 1972, as an internal document. 'We must try to save Lin Piao,' said Mao. 'When I get back to Peking, I shall go to see them [the conspirators], and discuss with them . . . If they don't come to me, I'll go to them. Some can be saved; others it is not possible to save . . .'

Mao told of the care he had taken to pre-empt the coup: 'Throwing stones, mixing sand with mud, and digging the wall's foot'. 'Throwing stones' refers to the numerous articles castigating 'idealism' and 'many centres', which had poured out steadily in the press. Mao had also diluted the Military Commission with new commanders ('mixing sand with mud') and changed the garrisons of major cities ('digging the wall's foot'). Mao then coined a phrase, famous because five years later it would be used against the gang to which his wife belonged: 'Practise Marxism, not revisionism. Unite and do not split. Be open and above board; do not intrigue or conspire.'

Late in October 1971 I went to the French Embassy, and the French Ambasssador, Étienne Manac'h, and I drank champagne.

'To that great man, His Excellency, Prime Minister Chou Enlai,' said Étienne Manac'h. 'The hour of Chou Enlai has come, and it is a good hour for China.'

CHAPTER 7

The Hour of Chou Enlai: 1972–1973

I flew to New York directly after leaving China, on October 25th, 1971. *The Morning Deluge*, my first book of Mao's impact on the Chinese Revolution, would be published in 1972. Harry Sions, the chief editor of Little, Brown had taken a gamble on this book, for anything favourable to Mao Tsetung challenged anchored prejudice. But he was a courageous man and an excellent editor, and he was delighted with the chapter on the Long March, although he thought some others too flattering to Mao. His death three years later much afflicted me.

I gave some lectures in America, in Belgium and France, and in London, but I have totally forgotten what I said. By now I had given so many lectures that I could talk without any preparation; but as soon as a speech was over I had rubbed it out of my mind. Thus I preserved myself from being submerged by my own activity.

On May 4th, 1972 I was back in China. My friends the Yangs were out of jail. Yeh could have me at home for dinner. How wonderful it was, to see some of my old friends again! 'Chou Enlai,' they said. Of course it was Chou Enlai who had opened the jail gates for them. In the next two years many hundreds of thousands would be released . . .

Gladys and Hsienyi did not talk of their jail experience for a long time. Gladys had had the worst of it, for she had been in solitary confinement. And this not through viciousness, but through respect for her higher status as a foreigner! This Englishwoman stood the ordeal nobly and came out luminous, calm, and sane, ready to serve China again (although she could have asked to leave). What strength of character! What fortitude! 'I now understand the quirks of a revolution much better,' said Gladys in her quiet upper-class voice.

But she was worried about her son. It had been a great strain for her children; parents in jail as 'counter-revolutionaries', and the children Eurasians. Her daughters were adapting remarkably well; they would marry excellent Chinese husbands of the new kind, who accept woman's equality. They would pursue university careers, and exhibit no trauma of any kind. But her son, after having been an extremely enthusiastic Red Guard, was now bitter, cynical. He had wanted to be all-Chinese; now he wanted to be all-English. It was quite understandable. Among the Eurasians, the male children often were the more vulnerable.

'Girls do seem more resilient, more able than boys to take catastrophe and tragedy. They live through them and come out enriched, matured . . . perhaps because women have always had to confront so much daily unpleasantness,' said Gladys.

Hsienyi said he had known about Lin Piao's downfall probably before many other people in China. 'Each one of us had a copy of the little red book in jail. One day our jailers asked all of us to give them back. The copies were returned the next day, but the preface page written by Lin Piao had been cut out of each one. That's how we knew. He was erased, effaced. We looked at each other with big smiles. We thought we would be out very soon.'

The Yangs had returned to their flat, redecorated for them at government expense. Nothing was missing. They were paid their back salaries in full. And the next year Gladys would go to England, and her English sister would come to China to see her.

Simon and Irène Hua had also had problems. Their eldest daughter had been jailed in 1967, on her return to China from Paris.

I had seen her in Paris that year. I had made a speech defending the Cultural Revolution (and I was right to defend it; I am more convinced than ever that it had to be). But I dissuaded her from returning to China. 'Although the *principle* of the Cultural Revolution is correct, history in its faltering is never straightforward, and you may be misunderstood.' I added, 'We Eurasians are much too easy targets for anyone's attack, at any time.' But Monique was in love with China, and she was patriotic. She had been sent by the Chinese government to France as a university student; she did not understand all the complexities and contradictions of the land she loved. Not as I understood them now. She was young, as I had been in 1938. She plunged into the tempest as I had done when I was twenty-one, armed with nothing but love and enthusiasm. I had reaped a harvest of pain, she reaped three years of jail, although no ill-treatment.

One of the reasons for jailing her was 'bringing in pornographic books'. It was Sika Meyer, the Chinese wife of Charles, Sihanouk's secretary, who told me. Monique had returned via Phnom Penh; she stayed a few days with the Meyers. Sika took exception to the books Monique read. 'All those sex books ... she should not have taken them with her.' I checked. They were not pornography; merely the ordinary run of French love stories. Monique's judgment about what was acceptable or not in China had become muddled in Paris. 'I tried to warn her,' said Sika.

I could well imagine what happened. Monique, back from France, thought the Cultural Revolution in China was a festival of youth, liberty and loving kindness. Which in some ways it was, so protean a phenomenon, embracing all contradictory statements and proving them all both true and false.

Simon and Irène came to see me about Monique. They too were in trouble, but it was nothing very serious. Irène had lost her temper after many hours of being harassed and criticized by a woman cadre, and had slapped her. They were moved from their Western-type flat to a small, typical Chinese home. But their servant stuck loyally to them and continued to serve them. A privilege they were refused was to spend the summer months at the seaside, but Irène bore it with great fortitude. 'I do not mind being deprived of this privilege. My Chinese comrades never enjoyed it.' But why was their daughter in jail?

I was approached by some of Monique's French friends in Paris. 'If you make a row, she'll be in jail much longer,' I warned them. 'Illicit connections with foreigners' would be confirmed, and she would be in greater trouble. Simon wrote to Premier Chou Enlai, but there was no answer. 'Chou Enlai ignores no request, forgets no one. Perhaps he cannot move at the moment on this matter. Trust him and wait,' I said. And sure enough Monique came out of jail, and was assigned a job, and the Huas were once again given a good flat.

Chou Enlai was pulling China together after the strain, the tosses, the upheavals 'Readjustment, consolidation, elevation' were the key words; also a condemnation of waste and extravagance.

There were visible signs of a return to normality in each factory. The emphasis was on quality; no more shoddy work; there were rules and regulations. Technical and industrial exhibitions were held in the major cities. A swarm of Japanese businessmen hove into Peking.

The painters returned. Huang Chou, condemned to going about with an ass, because he had painted the charming donkeys of Sinkiang, was 'liberated'. I saw his paintings once again, albeit only in the small shops, because it took time to reverse in people's minds the condemnations which had been issued so liberally during the first years of the Cultural Revolution.

Chou Enlai would in 1973 call for a meeting of China's best painters and ask them to create three hundred works to decorate the new hotels and other places of interest, because China was now expecting a major influx of visitors. Mao's face disappeared from the hotel rooms (with Mao's approval). 'We are going to open up many more new sites in China for visitors,' said Chang Ying, of the Foreign Ministry, who accompanied me on my travels that year. She was the wife of the very able Ambassador, Chiang Wenching; I liked them both very much.

There were many more books in the bookstores, among them the major classics, *The Dream of the Red Chamber*, and *The Scholars*. The ravenous Japanese bought up all the old books they could find. There was the return of seal carving; and of seals, and a lot of beautiful handicrafts. Once again there were flower shops, and lovely silk and ivory pieces for sale, and everyone breathed easily. One thing would not return. In Peking, on both sides of the houses' street doors there always had been carved stone lions. Almost all of them had been broken as 'feudal', and now only deformed lumps of stone remained.

The parks were again full of strollers. Suddenly in 1973 my favourite park, the Peihai, was closed to the public. 'Repairs.' 'Why? I've been to it. It is not in bad shape.' 'Repairs,' said someone firmly. Only at the end of 1976 would I know that the whole public park had been taken over by Chiang Ching, to become her private garden. She rode in it, on a white horse, imitating her favourite star, Greta Garbo, in *Queen Christina*, a film of which she was very fond.

Timidly, from the provinces, came certain new operas and plays in 1972 and 1973; some of the local folk art came back in the cities. But Szechuan opera remained firmly banned in Szechuan, and in Peking and Shanghai only the 'model operas' could be seen.

There was talk of the Hundred Flowers being revived. Professor Chou Peiyuan of Peking University wrote boldly in support of fundamental research; artists painted, some writers started to write again.

The Mao badges disappeared from all chests (the little red book had gone by November 1971). Only overseas Chinese, visiting their relatives and not up to the latest fashions in politics, still wore badges or carried the book. But once with their families, they gave up what was now called 'formalism'.

Was this 'demaoization'?

Panting like greyhounds after a race, China-watchers in Hong Kong and elsewhere, some of them possessed by a burning hatred for Mao and of China's socialist system, were already announcing 'demaoization' in 1972. But Mao was not Stalin. This was Mao without the crazy cult of Mao, Mao 'demaoized' by himself, whose visions were implemented by Chou Enlai, as I would write articles for the *New York Times* in those years.

Had Mao not suffered, after Lin Piao's death, a series of small strokes, which cut down his mobility, made him half blind, and increasingly helpless; had Chou Enlai not been struck with cancer at the end of 1972 or in early 1973, the Gang of Four would not have emerged, to destroy so much of what had been accomplished.

In 1972, none of us knew this would happen. All we knew was that universities were starting to function; that by the end of 1971 examinations had been restored in Szechuan middle schools, in Tientsin's Nankai middle school, and in higher institutes, for the next student intake. The Cultural Revolution was being assessed calmly, its losses and gains. It was not a question of returning to the pre-1966 days; it was a problem of how to 'summarize experience', as Chou Enlai said; of finding out what was valid and what did not work, always with the same object in view: to chart China's road to swift development, to speed her progress.

I have travelled a great deal up and down China. I too was 'summarizing experience', trying to reach a comprehensive appraisal of events.

The outburst of intellectual energy, the scientific expansion which I had noted in 1964 and 1965, continued to have effect, despite the turmoil of the years 1966–9. For instance, in July 1966, a type of radioactive isotope gauge, automatically regulating the thickness of steel plates, strips and sheets during processing, had been produced. There had also been advance in the development of nuclear weaponry, and the production of a hydrogen bomb, and in 1970 of an earth satellite.

But these, the results of previous years of effort, having occurred during the Cultural Revolution, were claimed to be due to an outburst of ingenuity on the part of workers–peasants–soldiers inspired by Mao Tsetung Thought. Despite the harassment of many scientists and researchers during the Cultural Revolution, the majority of these dedicated men continued to work, even if less efficiently. Therefore the picture is not clear-cut; even in 1974 economists abroad could justly claim achievements and commendable performance in Chinese industry and agriculture during the Cultural Revolution; which in today's backlash is not recognized. But then the continued forward movement of a country on the march, especially such a huge country as China, seems to swallow up all these contradictions; the residue is what has been achieved.

'The gap between China and the advanced nations was narrowing before 1966,' Teng Hsiaoping said to me when I saw him in September 1977, 'but because of the sabotage of the Four, it is now much wider.'* Already in 1972 I had discussed the 'gap' in the economy, and in industrial development, and with Chiao Kuanhua, the Foreign Minister. 'Yes, there is a big gap,' he had said to me. 'For almost six years there's been very little studying . . . and that means almost a generation of university students has been lost to us. Yet we need so many technicians, so many doctors and scientists . . . all lost. There's a very big youth problem now.'

I found out in 1972 and 1973 that 'ultra-left' ideas, at the time solely ascribed to Lin Piao (since no one accused Chiang Ching), persisted, despite all exhortation. It had become a habit – pleasant, since it was part of their revolt against a millenarian parental authoritarianism – among many young people, to label older ones (forty seemed to be

*See article by Han Suyin in *Der Spiegel*, November 1978.

the watershed age). They shouted 'reactionary' or 'counter-revolutionary' whenever any mention of study, discipline, or abiding by rules (including rules of hygiene) was made. There was such a loosening of discipline that since the young now crowded the organizations, efforts to get proper work done were hindered. There was also the problem of the 'reversal of the correct verdicts of the Cultural Revolution'. What did this mean? It meant that many older cadres had been wantonly accused – without any evidence – of multiple crimes, and that anyone arguing for them was in danger of being looked upon as an 'unrepentant capitalist roader', trying to 'reverse the correct verdicts'. In this context, Chiang Ching was the prime mover: any word from her had the weight of an accusation, and no accusation could be proved or disproved; word became fact. Chou Enlai therefore moved cautiously, yet courageously, rehabilitating competent older officials and reinstating discipline.

In the new Party constitution of 1969, a grievous lacuna had occurred. In it was a clause which did not admit intellectuals to the Party, only 'workers–peasants–soldiers' of approved revolutionary demeanour. There was also a clause that renegades and spies, and power-holders who 'had followed the capitalist road' should be expelled from the Party and not allowed to rejoin. It was based on these two clauses that the return to effective work and to authority of certain high-calibre officials was proving very slow and difficult. Yet so many of them had been accused without evidence, and in these wanton accusations the 'Shanghai troika'* – as they were then known – had played an outstanding role, especially Chiang Ching. She would leave no one alone. Thus the able and devoted Liao Chengchih was called by her a 'playboy' and 'untrustworthy'. As a result he had, for years, not been able to function properly; and this because so much authority in China is also a question of personal influence, of being accepted by one's

---

*Chiang Ching, Chang and Yao. Wang Hungwen was not involved in 'cultural' affairs until 1973.

colleagues, and especially one's subordinates. In the absence of any functioning legal system, wanton denunciation had the effect of a virtual judgment. It plunged the cadres into a catatonic stupor, and it sterilized effectively any attempt to counter baseless accusations.

However, in 1972, the Shanghai group appeared to unite with Chou Enlai, at least in the matter of facing the aftermath of the Lin Piao affair. It was very difficult for Chou at the time to fault them. Had they not been 'recuperated' by him from the 'ultra-left'? How difficult to start immediately criticizing them and perhaps bringing about a crisis in the badly mauled Party, in dire need of stable, constructive leadership.

Chou Enlai had, with supreme ability, succeeded in managing the post-Lin Piao interlude. There had been no uprisings, no armed strife, from the nine armies of Lin Piao; no recrudescence of disorder among the people; no increased tension with Moscow over the Lin Piao affair. The Kremlin showed itself non-provocative and prudent, although it could have claimed that it had adherents, even up to Mao's heir, in the Chinese Party.

'There is no more struggle for power now,' wrote the China expert, Robert Guillain, in France's *Le Monde*. He could not have been more wrong; but at the time it really looked peaceful, and I was much relieved. I wrote a letter to Harrison Salisbury, saying that now I would have no more worries. All was plain sailing, with Chou Enlai back, the great manager of China. 'Now I can go back to writing love stories.' I hoped that the Cultural Revolution would soon be wound up, and of course that rehabilitations, reassessments would take place. The Chinese Party had always made reappraisals of its own performance and policies, which is what I liked about it. Then wrongs would be righted – in fact, Chou had already begun. Rewi, Ma Haiteh and Hans Miller, the German doctor who had worked devotedly for China for fifty years, rejoiced with me. In that year, they would be able to go to the seaside in August, and Rewi would travel up and down China again, and this walking encyclopaedia would delight me with his true and sharp assessment of the accomplishments, and also the deficiencies, of the past seven years.

'There's just been too much empty talk of politics . . . Now there will be efficiency, production, science, technology once again,' said the scientists I met.

The year 1972 was one of triumph for Chou Enlai's foreign policy, not only because of President Nixon's visit in February, and China's entry to the United Nations in the previous October, but also because of the resurrection of Mao's old slogan, 'Let foreign things serve China', presaging a wide opening to the West; and a vast surge of sympathy, enthusiasm and admiration from all the nations of the earth.

Chou Enlai looked well, he moved with lithe elegance, he reminded me of mercury; he was seventy-three, and he bore the weight of twenty-three years of governing China upon his shoulders without, apparently, any strain.

The new Japanese Prime Minister, Kakuei Tanaka, signed an agreement in Peking; this was a breakthrough for the future. Twenty-two American editors visited China. Some of them were fascinated. 'A garden of Eden' one man called it. 'The change is miraculous,' wrote the historian John Fairbank. 'No other group of 750 million people has ever been held together . . .' The Americans, so emotionally involved with China for over a century, understood the miracle accomplished since 1949. They knew, deep in their bones, that it could not have been done without the Communist Party, without Mao and his companions, and they did not lie to themselves. 'The Maoist revolution is on the whole the best thing that has happened to China in centuries,' wrote John Fairbank.

I was no longer being reviled as a 'Red' and a 'Maoist', except by some envious 'Sinologists'. It all seemed worthwhile now: the lectures, the running about, the sacrifices too (although mine were minuscule in the Chinese scale). Chou Enlai had spoken well of the Cultural Revolution to Edgar Snow, emphasizing its gains, not for a moment letting on to the bitterness of the attacks against him. Unlike so many subjective people who think that what happens to them is all that matters in the Universe, Chou Enlai had tremendous self-abnegation; he would have cheerfully agreed to being slow-roasted alive if this was good for China. Chou's immortality began that year, when people began calling him Our Beloved Premier Chou.

I wrote a small Op Ed for the *New York Times*, stating that Chou Enlai had 'saved so many lives' during the Cultural Revolution, and that he was very popular.

In 1973 Mao's popularity went down perceptibly; a decline which was not signalled in words, but in a certain pulse, heartbeat, silence, tone of voice. People still cared for him, revered him, but they also felt strangely sorry for him. And some felt resentful. They referred to him as the Great Chairman Mao. It was respect, but not that total giving of the heart which had been his for so many years, as China's true liberator.

Unworded, as an odour which strikes the nostril, detected under all conversations, mostly by the fact of silence, was the unease and dislike of Chiang Ching. Never did I hear a word against her; and it was precisely because of this wordlessness that the feeling came through, strong and unimpeded. No one wanted to converse about her. Dislike is mute as the grass, or a stone.

And because of his wife, there was in the patient, oh so patient, minds of the Chinese people an unworded question: how can Mao Tsetung have a wife like that?

Nevertheless, having from the start got her hands on the formation of mass public opinion – and there I think the Four showed themselves extremely aware of the enormous power of press, television, all communication media which are mind manipulators, whether in the East or in the West – Chiang Ching had her photographs in the newspapers, her eulogists, her adherents. The campaign for her was superbly orchestrated; it deserves a book on its own. And her particular success was to project an image which attracted to her potentially half of China's population: the women; not all, of course, but a certain kind of woman or young girl. It took me almost two years to recognize the type, not through secondhand reading, but through direct contact.

The women who picked – or were picked by – the Four were all personable; garrulously persuasive; forcibly active; and endowed with great imagination and a transporting element of disregard for fact. I had interviewed Li Suwen in Manchuria, and Wang Hsiuchen in Shanghai; and now I met a great many others, at all levels. Edgar Snow and I exchanged data. He had interviewed the woman worker Wu Kueihsien, in Sian. Wu Kueihsien would later become a Vice-Premier, yet she was barely literate. She was interviewed by Roxane Witke, who wrote an article about her.* Ed huffed: 'Silence is beautiful in a woman.'

Docile crowds (there was a ticket distribution in every factory, school, organization) clapped at the model operas. At first no one minded them; not until 1974, when we realized that nothing else was being produced! Chiang Ching in 1972–3 was a pain in the neck, but we all put up with her because of Mao, because of Chou Enlai. We did not realize the considerable foothold her Shanghai Mafia had gained in the mass media, and also in the organs of power, the revolutionary committees, through the new cadres. Between 1966 and 1976, the Communist Party had doubled in number, from seventeen million to thirty-five million, and many new cadres owed their Party membership to the Four.

But not one of the cadres, the writers, the diplomats like Huang Hua, out from the 'cattle pens' and the May schools, said a word against Chiang Ching in deference to Mao. All the violence, everything that had gone wrong, was ascribed to Lin Piao, and to Liu Shaochi. And in those last years of his grace and strength, Chou Enlai too sought to win Chiang Ching, as he had won so many enemies and turned them into friends – to form a collective leadership, for the sake of unity

*China Quarterly, No. 64, December 1975.

and stability. China badly needed unity and stability.

In Hong Kong there was a rumour, uncorroborated, that Mao was angry with his wife, and that she now had a separate establishment in Peking, as well as houses in Shanghai, Hainan Island, and the hot springs near Kuangchow. But despite this semi-official separation, Chiang Ching continued to preface her speeches and public appearances with the words, 'I bring you greetings from Chairman Mao.' And no one knew of the separation. She was still able to control Mao's environment (more so, as Chou became ill) and the people he saw. By the end of 1974, his nephew, Mao Yuanhsing, and two young nurses chosen by Chiang Ching, became, with her, the only people who had unlimited access to him.

Chang Chunchiao had started a major strategy. He began to recruit, in 1972–3, in all the universities, able 'pens' to write for the Four. By 1974 they had organized, in Peking's two universities, some forty to fifty top intellectuals.* Chang also acquired a collection of writers in Shanghai Futan University (which used to be the famous Jesuit University Aurore). Scholars found themselves serving – sometimes unknown to themselves – the purposes of the Gang of Four. Finally, the Gang began making advances even to older cadres, and to veterans: 'Only serve us, and we'll look after you.'

A Japanese ballet company had come to Peking, and danced *The White-Haired Girl*, and also *The Red Regiment of Women*. Some of the dancers had trained in China during the Cultural Revolution and had learnt the new ballets. They were excellent performers, and would go on to win international prizes. But the Japanese choreographer had made some changes in *The White-Haired Girl*, expanding the love scenes between the heroine and her rescuer, who was also her childhood friend.

*They wrote under pseudonyms, the favourite one being Liang Hsiao, which phonetically meant 'the two universities'.

Chiang Ching had already begun to 'improve' ballets and operas, cutting out anything faintly related to ordinary human emotions. Thus in the opera *Shachiapang*, a scene showed the heroine, captured by the Kuomintang, asking herself, 'What shall I do?' when hard pressed to betray the Communist cause or to see her mother killed in front of her eyes. Chiang Ching cut out the words. 'A communist never doubts,' said she. Never must a 'positive character' falter, or be anything but thoroughly positive. I would see *Shachiapang* at least eight times through the years. I noticed the stultification of the script and mentioned it.

'Why cut this out? It added some humanity to the character.'

'But it was not good politics,' was the reply.

Another opera, *Azalea Mountain*, I first saw in Szechuan in 1972. When I viewed it again in Peking, all the humour had gone. The lines where the peasant guerrillas, discovering that the Party comrade they had come to rescue was a girl and not a man, the byplay when she gives orders and they feel affronted – all this was now erased. It was replaced by much vigorous hand-shaking and fist-waving.

It was the same with *The White-Haired Girl*. I had seen it three times before 1966; and in the years under Chiang Ching I watched the beautiful work, which had contained love and passion, become shorn of all emotion except wrath. The rape scene, which was the point of the whole story, was cut out. All that remained was 'revolutionary fury', and people shaking hands repeatedly with piston-like movements of their arms, and then marching off, up a ramp, to the sounds of the 'International'.

The Japanese choreographer's changes were, artistically, an improvement, but I noticed the stern faces around me. Then Chou Enlai spoke about it to me. He told me that the sentiment of the ballet had been transformed; that the 'greatest emotion' was meant to be that of the old father towards his daughter, and not that of the two young lovers. Chou did not speak for himself; he cared about people, their lives and loves. But he expressed the objection – probably Chiang Ching's – to the changes. I had noticed the absence of Chiang Ching at the première of the ballet, although she had been expected to attend.

Chiang Ching would never authorize any change, even the slightest, in what she had laid down. All over China, no artist was allowed a gesture, a word, a tone, not even a button, or the colour of the shoes, or a patch on a coat, which was different from the 'model' laid down by her. 'Everything had to be exactly the same,' said my friend the Szechuan opera singer, Miss Chen Shoufang in 1977. Because the tones of our monosyllabic words alter the meaning, and each province has its own tones, a great deal of silliness occurred. For instance, the phrase 'I have waited a long time' in Peking tonality would mean 'I've got some good wine' in another province. The misinterpretation was worst in Kuangchow, Cantonese dialect being totally different.

I replied respectfully to Chou Enlai that I felt the Japanese had the right to modify the ballet when they danced it . . . such modifications are constantly made in the West . . . every ballet troupe interprets a piece its own way . . . Chou Enlai, straightening in his chair, looked relieved, and immediately spoke of other matters.

I had been captured, entranced by the desert in 1971. Now I wanted to visit Tunhuang, the famous Buddhist painted caves on the Silk Road,* and in 1972 went with Chang Ying. Hsing Chiang was at the time doing her manual labour in a May 7 school. Sending a senior person like Chang Ying with me was Chou's way of saying, 'Don't believe everything you see; keep your eyes open', just as Mr Ma and Madame Yeh had kept their eyes and ears open in Sinkiang the previous year.

Chang Ying and I talked freely of many things, including

---

*The earliest known painted caves dated from AD 366.

the problems of youth and employment. The State Council was recruiting young people from among the Red Guards who had not committed crimes or brutalities (the majority had been very well-behaved). Some of them had even been to jail, or to 'study and labour' camps, for having resisted the 'ultra-left', protested against the brutality towards old cadres and refused to undertake beatings and destruction.

'But we have some bad young people,' said Chang Ying, 'and we have to ask ourselves: How did it happen? What went wrong with our education? At one time we thought that automatically, any child born "under the red flag" must somehow be better than us, we the old people who come from the old society . . . but then we discovered that it was not so.'

'Too much pampering.'

The most worrying thing was 'the gap'. Successors in the fields of science and technology were not there. 'How to train them well, yet not create an élite and lose the revolution? That has been the problem all along.'

The deep stir and turmoil of the Cultural Revolution had spread, however, and enlarged the hunger for many things which China was still too poor to afford. There were rising expectations – but a diminished sense of the necessity of study and knowledge among the young. The 'ultra-left' ideas, that to study was 'revisionist' and landed one in trouble, were strong among them, and there was also discontent, because so many felt cheated by all that had happened.

My way to Tunhuang was circuitous. I meandered, visiting communes; seeing everywhere the 'five small' of alternative technology: small fertilizer plants, small iron and steel making plants, small electric plants, methane gas installations, processing factories. In that year, each production team was confirmed in its private plots, in its storage bins, in its manpower. There were fairs and free markets, but the harvests would not be excellent. Drought.

We went by car from Lanchow, following the Silk Road's string of oases, Tienchu and Wu Wei, and Shandan, where Rewi Alley had laboured so many years founding the Gung Ho co-operatives.* Shandan – in the eighth century AD – had been famous for its city walls, its trees and palaces and running fountains, described by Arab travellers. A great commercial centre, it produced cinnabar, and it had a big Nestorian church.

On to Changye and to Chiu Chuan, the Fountain of Wine, which had been a Han garrison outpost in 115 BC. I would meet on the way Oriats (or Buriats), Tibetans and Mongols, and in the Muslim quarter of the Fountain of Wine we ate delicious dates. They had been the staple food of the oases in the Chou dynasty.† Here also was the jade called Light in Darkness, worked for many centuries; cups of it had been given to barbaric chieftains, and the jade was said to 'show', to change colour, if poison was used. Poems had been written in Persia about its glow. Now a co-operative with seventy-five workers turned out, by hand, 4,500 cups a year; for each there were twenty-two separate grindings.

In the morning I rose to look at the snow-capped Tsilien Mountains which gave birth to the jade, green and black and white. 'This is the false Gobi Desert, layers of black gravel but with good earth under it,' said the head of the revolutionary committee of the district, a Mongol with a face like burnished copper. We were 1,500 metres above sea-level, and the Yumen oilfields were quite near, and there was a pipeline from them; the new city of the Fountain of Wine had a petrol refinery. There were only 70,000 people in the whole district, but 900 million trees had been planted in the last twenty years. 'We could open more fields if we had more people.' There was no family planning here at all.

From the old town stemmed the worn battlements of

---

*See *Yo Banfa*, by Rewi Alley (New Zealand–China Association, Auckland, 1976).
†770–221 BC.

former Great Walls, almost melted into the sand. I went to see the western end of the Great Wall, the Gate of Prosperity, repainted and restored, terminus of the Wall's 5,000-kilometre journey from the sea. On the road were some carts pulled by camels, but they had rubber tyres.

On to Tunhuang, 400 kilometres away. The wind scorched our faces, the scalding sand blistered the skin. To Kara, where there was a spring which had allowed the Han garrison to survive in 300 BC. And then we crossed the Pass of Jade. 'The breath of spring does not reach beyond the Pass of Jade' was a line in an ancient poem. The famed General Tso Tsungtang had consolidated Sinkiang against the encroaching Russians* and then had rebuilt the Silk Road, making it five metres wide and planting trees along both its sides, on his march. He had written his reply to this poem, many centuries later:

I have planted three thousand *lis*† of willows
And brought the breath of spring beyond the Pass of Jade.

On the hills were the sites of ancient beacons, for warning of invasion by barbarians from the West. Each site had been guarded by a village oasis. At Ansi there were communes, producing wheat and linseed oil, and here too a great number of children. A doctor in Peking had told me, 'When we went into that region to introduce family planning the inhabitants threw us out. "Don't come back or we'll kill you," they shouted.' The doctors had withdrawn. Here, as in Szechuan, every child born received a full ration of grain and oil. 'All our families have more than four children,' said Ma, the Muslim head of Ansi, with great pride. 'In the past, all our children died. Now they live.'

We reached Tunhuang one late afternoon, in a desert splendidly pink with sunset. I turned to watch the desert

*The campaign of 1873–9.
† 1 *lis* is 0.5 of a kilometre.

road marked by its interminable march of disfigured stupas,
as if along the wind-blown track would come a slow-paced
caravan of camels and donkeys and mules; and the voices
singing their gladness as they approached the Buddhist caves
and their spring of live water, their promises of the spirit's
and the body's ease.

My host was the incomparable professor Tsang Shuhung,
who was also a painter, Paris-educated, as was his wife. Both
had been in Tunhuang for thirty years. Professor Tsang's
whole life was caring for the cave paintings, deciphering the
writings in the caves and restoring and preventing the
ravages of time. He spoke agreeably of history; he was most
learned. The great tidal waves of peoples in this land ocean
of Central Asia fascinated me. He told marvellous tales: of
the kings of the Huns, who were red-haired and blue-eyed
warriors and who used human skulls as drinking cups.

For the next week we went from cave to cave, visiting over
a hundred of them. And in the dimness we shone our
flashlights, to gaze upon the incandescent swirl and whorl
and cascade of ecstatic elongated bodies; rapt faces, a
firmament of longing, outburst of man's desire for the
sublimity of God. Dug in the friable cliffs, which crumbled
even as I looked at them, they were splendour and passion
and a total absence of stiffness; and although from
Tunhuang I went on to other Buddhist caves, to Yunkang,
and then to Lungmen, there was something incomparable in
Tunhuang, the great shock of universality.

Every night we sat and talked in the charming guest house
with its lovely roofs. By day we went from cave to cave, or
strolled by the brook which flowed near by, under sycamore
and camphor trees. Professor Tsang would point out the
herbs along the pathways, among them liquorice, or
suddenly pounce upon a mushroom, for they grew wild, and
we often had fresh mushrooms for dinner.

Enchanted hours: the name of Alexander, the tale of the
Roman garrison that lost its way and obtained asylum from
the Chinese emperor somewhere near Tunhuang . . . I went

to see the village called Five Beacons, where the last Romans had quartered; but the inhabitants looked Chinese, except that some heads were curly (and that might be Tibetan blood). Five Beacons fed me with wonderful dates and grapes. There were sand grouse and small eagles in the desert and the oases. 'The desert is not dead. It lives a most intense life,' said Tsang.

Only in 1977 would I know that my coming had been Professor Tsang's deliverance. He was still being criticized and made to 'stand aside' because the local authorities dragged their feet over his case for fear of being accused of 'reversing verdicts'. Then they heard I was coming, and Tsang was hastily rehabilitated. A good dentist came to fix his teeth, which ached. And after my visit he could not be criticized again. In 1978, aged seventy-six, Tsang painted a picture of Mount Everest, which is now being exhibited in the national gallery in Peking.

Tsang was worried about the decrepit state of some of the cave paintings not because of destruction by the 'ultra-left', but because of the poor quality of the rock in which the caves had been dug. Much work propping up the cliffs had been done since 1949, but there had been many decades of neglect before that, and also of theft, both by visiting Europeans and by local warlords. The sand wind chipped away at the rock, and some caves had fallen. 'But we shall save Tunhuang, for it is one of the great miracles of art,' said stubborn Professor Tsang.

To him China was a universality; it had been a welcoming land for many centuries, asylum for the persecuted from the West. Heretics of the Christian religion, such as the Nestorians and the Manicheans, had found refuge here. The Tang emperors sent their travellers abroad to discover and to describe for them the customs of other nations, and their resources, and to make maps. They had built roads for commerce, and there were people from Honan province in Arabia, and a Jewish community in Kaifeng city. Paper was sent from China through Samarkand to Alexandria. 'In the

Sui dynasty, the Emperor Yang Ti came here to see twenty ambassadors of as many nations. He gave them silk and gold, and a banquet lasting fifteen days, with eighteen thousand musicians,' said Tsang. But the Ming dynasty in the fifteenth century had been inward looking and Tunhuang had started to decay, and gradually with the rise of the West no more silk went by the Silk Road. The Manchu Ch'ing dynasty had tried to revive Tunhuang. But then had come wars and the colonial powers in China.

Skirting oases with tamarisks, we visited the pleasant town of Tunhuang. The calligraphic curves of the jujubes with their delightful fragrances and small, close flowers were about us. And three kilometres by jeep across the sand from Five Beacons village was the Crescent Moon Lake which Ian Morrison, my dead love, had spoken to me about. Tsang and I sat by the azure lake's dwindling curve – for it was getting smaller, it was shrinking – and we walked on the dunes to hear the song of the sand. Alas, the lovely Ming temple which had been erected on a small island in the middle of the lake was no more. Ian had shown me a photograph of it. It had been destroyed during the Cultural Revolution. Nothing was left of it but a few hacked balustrade pillars. The island was planted with rye and buckwheat, and a donkey went round and round the well, which had once been the temple well, turning a winch in endless pacing.

In all this area no rice was eaten, only bread made from flour. People resented maize, saying it gave them a bitter stomach. Because no snow fell, the winter wheat was covered with sand and mule and donkey and horse manure.

Everywhere the walls of the small towns had been destroyed, which was a great pity, for the sand now swept in unhindered, and wolves had roamed around the streets, until killed off.

Yumen town was well laid out; with water and electric light; tarred roads and a population of 50,000 . . . But it was 2,400 metres above sea-level and Chang Ying, who had mitral stenosis, became blue in the face. I enquired about babies; and was proudly told that last year 835 babies had been born among the 4,000 families 'with breeding possibilities'. This was a record low!

We left Yumen, and in the faultless blue sky was a dark blot of hawks; and suddenly a bar of white wing as an eagle circled above us. We caught stupid, pretty sand grouse. Their little heads shook and their golden eyes trembled, and I was sorry for them, but the drivers were happy, thinking how tasty they would be.

Back in Lanchow, I met another Long Marcher, Comrade Chang. He described the battle he had fought at a pass so narrow that the sky was but a thread of white above, and the Long Marchers were attacked by Tibetan cavalrymen. Comrade Chang was doing a survey of the Yellow River's upper reaches. 'We must tame it,' he said. 'All this area will be electrified one day.'

Kansu province had been unpeopled by war and plague in the past. The present birth rate was 42.2 per thousand among national minorities, and 29 per thousand among the Han; obviously Kansu was not doing much family planning.

We went to bow to the Yellow River – or rather to look at its new pumps. 'Look how much clearer the water is now,' said Madame Li, pointing to the thick ochre slush delightedly.

I returned from the desert rejuvenated, my vitality increased. This would also happen to me when I went to Tibet in 1975.

Vincent arrived, and at Peking airport we met Chou Enlai who had come to greet Prince Sihanouk, back from a trip to North Korea.

Chou stepped down from a small black car, a fairly decrepit one, not a Zis, but one of those Shanghai-made models. He carried his own briefcase, and almost ran, followed by one bodyguard. He crossed the tarmac and then he saw us. He grinned and shook hands. And he asked Vincent, 'How was Singapore?' Then he was in the waiting room, as we were, ignoring the 'top sofa' and the protocol and sitting with us.

Vincent had taken an aeroplane which stopped in Singapore; he thought of looking up my adopted daughter, Huei Ying and my old friends the Lokes. But the unwritten ban still held: he was surrounded by police with machine guns at the ready, and hustled back into the next aeroplane after a few hours' detention.

Chou had heard of it. Vincent said, 'Singapore is just the same as ever.' Chou laughed. He looked radiant.

I watched him striding up to the aeroplane, his right arm a little crooked from that old accident in Yenan. It was an Indian doctor* who had set his elbow, but it remained flexed. I thought, 'He is getting thinner.' That night, at dinner, Rewi also said, 'Chou is getting almost transparent. He works too hard. How can we stop him from working?' But he was as zestful as a young man of twenty. And all of us loved him and felt safe with him; and untiringly told stories about him, as people do about someone they love. And perhaps Chou knew it, and was buoyed up with the love and trust not only of the old, the middle-aged, but also of the young. Those who had now seen through the 'ultra-left' and its cruelties, millions of young people, now turned to Chou Enlai because he had never betrayed them. Neither did he come down hard on them, nor seek revenge. In the end, he would be the only one to help them.

Yungmei and Karen, her daughter, arrived. I had said to Yungmei, 'Why don't you come to China this year?' Now it was safe, and so they came. I took them to Szechuan, and I asked Yungmei whether she wanted to see her own mother. The government of China was ready to trace her mother for her. But Yungmei said no; which is something I do not quite understand. For in her place I could not have resisted, just through sheer curiosity, even if it had hurt me greatly. But my family, for my sake, now adopted her as my true daughter. And they have been good to her ever since.

*Five Indian doctors went to Yenan in 1937, to participate in the Chinese Revolution.

The trip to China did Yungmei immense good. She immediately integrated, because she knew Chinese; and now she understood why I had forced the language into her. Third Aunt, seeing Karen, was delighted and would not let go of her hand – for her it was like having a great-grand-daughter. For Karen too it would be achieving a wholeness, coming to terms with the wealth of her double heritage.

On my return to that other world outside China in which I also lived, I lectured in Paris at the Military Academy (Cours Supérieur Inter-allié). I would lecture there once a year for four years. I made another lecture tour, in early 1973, in the United States. It was successful and happy. By then the greatness of Mao and his enterprises, the boldness and vision of the Revolution, including the Cultural Revolution, had gripped me. My faith in the ultimate result remained unshaken; Chou Enlai had infused me with hope and courage. I wished now for a swift normalization of relations with America; because there were still in China people hostile to Mao's and Chou Enlai's foreign policy. If America delayed, dawdled, this would be used by Chou's opponents against him.

I tried to explain this to some State Department people I met in Washington. A liaison office with David Bruce as its head, was set up in Peking, and there could not have been a better choice. But then Watergate began, and this would delay some major decisions. Another cause of hesitancy – on the part of America – would certainly be the rise of the Four, and the confusion it introduced both in domestic and foreign affairs in China.

In New York in April 1973, I went to see Huang Hua, now Ambassador to the United Nations. And we had lunch with Shirley MacLaine, who wanted to go to China, and did so shortly afterwards.

Huang Hua had been a very famous student leader at Yenching University,* and at times still made pointed hints

*See *A Mortal Flower.*

at my 'waywardness' when we were there as students together in the 1930s. He had been devoted to Edgar Snow, whose interpreter he had been in Yenan, and had stayed by his side through Ed's agony after his operation in Switzerland. He was a seasoned, careful, hardworking diplomat, and his wife Lilian was gifted with intelligence and charm.

One afternoon, a telephone call came from Huang Hua's secretary: had I time to see a Miss Roxane Witke?

'Who is she?'

'She has just come back from China.'

I thought Huang Hua must want me to see her and so I said, 'Ask her to come to dinner with me.'

Into the flat came a tall, auburn-haired, good-looking woman. Conversation was easy. Roxane Witke was an historian; she told me that in August 1972 she had gone to China, and had seen Chiang Ching, and had had long interviews with her; almost sixty hours on tape. She had obtained a visa to China when she had told Huang Hua that as an historian she wanted to gather information on the women's liberation movement in China, a most worthy task.

In Peking, she had met many women leaders including Teng Yingchao, Chou Enlai's wife; she had also briefly seen Premier Chou Enlai. She said that it was Chou who had agreed, or suggested, that she see Chiang Ching. (It is not clear to me whether she had asked, or whether Chou had suggested it to her.)

The rest is related by Roxane Witke herself in her book, *Comrade Chiang Ching*. She met Chiang Ching, and instead of writing about women in China she became Chiang Ching's biographer. 'You will be my Edgar Snow,' Chiang Ching exclaimed, or so I was told.* Apparently Roxane Witke and Chiang Ching also discussed me.† I prefer to

---

*By witness, present at the interviews between Roxane Witke and Chiang Ching.
†Ibid.

ignore what they said; however, this had probably prompted Miss Witke to come to see me.

Roxane Witke thought that Chiang Ching was 'somewhat imperious'. The court around her reminded her of the Empress Tzuhsi. 'Yao Wenyuan looks just like a eunuch,' she said. We both laughed. But she was carried away by the feeling that Chiang Ching would be a most important person. She told me so. I demurred. 'No, Chiang Ching is not going to be a very important person.' 'I disagree . . . I think she will be a very important and influential woman in China's history,' said Miss Witke.

We were walking back along First Avenue, and it was time to say goodbye. I had something to tell her and I said it. 'May I give you some advice? The Chinese people do not like the lady very much, so do be careful.'

Instantly I regretted warning her. Supposing she repeated to Huang Hua what I had said . . . and supposing Huang Hua repeated it . . . already, I shared that all-pervasive feeling of being scared of Chiang Ching.

I saw Huang Hua the next day. He was worried, he said, about Miss Witke's work. After all, she had gone to China to write on women's liberation. She should stick to the subject for which she went. 'How can she?' I said. 'She's been given all this material. Of course she'll use it. It'll be a sensation, and all America loves a sensation.'

'Regular as the swallow,' said Chang Ying, hugging me, as in May 1973 I was back in Peking. I mentioned Roxane Witke to her, because Chang Ying had been present at the interviews given to Miss Witke. Chang Ying said, 'What top leaders do is beyond our control.' She was not going to comment upon the intensely personal character Chiang Ching had given to her outpourings. But it was very clear that she disapproved. There was a precedent. Had not Mao himself spoken to Edgar Snow in Yenan, telling him all of his life? In both of us the thought that Mao's wife was trying to

emulate her husband was present. This could only have one
meaning: she wanted to succeed him.

My son-in-law Sidney now came to China and every day
recorded, on a tape, his impressions for his daughter Karen;
being one of the most devoted fathers one could wish for. He
had brought some of his films with him, just as Vincent had
brought some records of Indian music. We duly offered the
lot to the respective authorities, to transmit to Madame
Mao. But we were met by stony silence; not even an
acknowledgment.

Somehow the matter of a book on Chiang Ching became
known among the Chinese public; but the story was
distorted. Not Witke, but I, said the 'small lane news', had
written a book entitled *Empress of the Red Fortress*,
criticizing Chiang Ching. By 1975 this 'news' would be all
over China, all the universities; passed from mouth to mouth
among the young. 'Of course it is Han Suyin who has written
a book . . . a friend of mine has seen it in Hong Kong . . .'
The number of copies sold was even mentioned: thirty-five
thousand at the first printing. It had now been translated
into several languages and was a best-seller. As usual, the
last person to hear the 'news' was me. It would be September
1975 before a very bold friend would inform me. My
relatives, Hualan, everyone had heard it, and for a while had
been uneasy. Yeh and his wife, Yen Wenching, and Heart of
Ice and her husband; all the writers had heard it. But all of
them said, 'Han Suyin would not do such a thing.' They
knew I could not, and would not put them all in great danger
through such utter foolishness. And so they did not avoid
me, which was very courageous of them.

Fourth Sister, back from two and a half years in a May 7
school and with a sick husband, was a trifle worried at first,
but she checked up, and was assured I had not perpetrated
such a book. She did not, however, tell me of the rumour, so
great was her fear of the Dragon Lady, or 'Three Drops of
Water' – Chiang Ching's current nicknames in 1973–4, and
until she was called China's calamity, in 1976.

The rumour was based on wishful thinking. Many young people, frustrated and resentful, let down by Chiang Ching, were hoping for such a denunciation. Only in December 1976 was it possible for me to deny the rumour, and through the same 'small lane news' the denial went right through China within a week.

Other 'rumours' at the end of 1973 were that Mao was furious with his wife because she had not had the approval of the Politburo before she had launched her biography upon the world, and that Chiang Ching lived at Tiaoyutai, a residence for official guests, and not with Mao.

In 1975, other items about Chiang Ching, began to circulate; ugly stories, about her treatment of Mao's son, Anching, who went mad, and the persecution of Li Ming, his daughter by his former wife.* So widespread were the rumours that the monthly magazine *Red Flag*, came out with a warning against 'small lane news' and in 1974 and 1975 the public security bureau received orders from the Politburo to investigate rumours and pursue 'fabricators' with the utmost severity. Anyone 'betraying state secrets' or 'concocting rumours' was counter-revolutionary. This would clamp most effectively what is now known as 'the Terror of the Gang of Four' upon China.

I had the surprise of seeing Teng Hsiaoping in late 1972. I forget which occasion it was; and my notes do not give the exact date. There was a party; Party officials were there, and among them the recognizable short, squat figure topped by the big head of Teng. And he had a tail. The security man with him was young and tall (they all seemed young and tall). At the end of the party, Teng and his tail walked out, not through the door used by other officials, but through the

---

*Ho Tzechen, who has now reappeared (1980) and become a member of the National People's Congress. Chiang Ching's own daughter, her only child, Li Na, is a schizophrenic.

equivalent of a back door. But there he was. And then the news became semi-official. Teng Hsiaoping was back. Mao wanted him back. 'Talent is hard to find,' Mao said. By April 1973 Teng was able to move about. And he no longer had a tail.

I did not see Chou Enlai in 1973. But his wife, Teng Yingchao, honoured me by receiving me, surrounded by about twenty people from the Foreign Ministry and the Friendship Association, and talking to me for two hours about women's liberation, family planning and many other topics.

She was called Big Sister Teng. Everyone loved her. There was a warmth in the voice and a smile when people talked of her, and in China, where silence is eloquent, the overt fondness for Teng Yingchao was meant to show up the way no one ever pronounced the name of Chiang Ching.

On March 8th, Women's Day, a reception took place for the Western experts living in Peking and in other Chinese cities. Chou Enlai was host; he gave a talk none of them would ever forget. As so often happens in China with a 'breakthrough' speech, there was no official report of it. But the people present would write to their friends abroad, would speak about it.

Chou Enlai said that 'bad elements', such as Lin Piao and others, had taken advantage of the dislocation in the first years of the Cultural Revolution, and done many evil things; one of these was the jailing of Westerners on false charges, or even no charges at all. On behalf of the government, he apologized to the Westerners who had thus suffered, and promised them redress. Chou then walked to several tables, shaking hands and hugging people, among them an American woman who had indeed suffered a great deal, yet who continued to work in China, of her own free will. 'What happens to me is quite secondary . . . it is what happens to China which matters,' she said. 'If Chou had asked me to go to jail I would have done it, so long as it advanced the Revolution,' said Simon Hua. 'Then I understood much better how complicated the Revolution was, and we wanted to stay in China more than ever,' said David Crooke, an Englishman who had been jailed on spurious charges for almost four years.

Thus Chou Enlai suddenly transformed their doubts and questionings and their torments into something quite different. Just as the Long March, with its losses and sufferings and agony had been metamorphosed into an epic of human endurance and a triumph, so the wretchedness, the puzzling punishments, acquired meaning and nobility. They were not senseless ordeals, time wasted, never to return; they became part of this creation, the creation of a new and better world. And this was fulfilment.

Chou Enlai went further. He said there was chauvinism and racialism in the treatment of foreigners in China. 'What is wrong with a Chinese and a foreigner getting married?' said he. Mao Tsetung had castigated his own people for their tenacious conservatism and cliquism. 'This attitude won't enable China to make her proper contribution to mankind,' said Chou Enlai.

Throughout 1973 there were echoes of Chou's speech. Elation, enthusiasm, optimism. But so far the speech has not yet been published. The forces of conservatism are indeed strong in China. In 1977 it would take a great deal of pushing to get permission for a Chinese and a foreigner to marry; finally it would be Teng Hsiaoping, following Chou Enlai, who would declare marriages between foreigners and Chinese perfectly acceptable.

'Young girls still seek a matchmaker to introduce a young man to them,' said Gladys Yang.

Gladys knew a girl who had been 'noticed' by a young man, but he could not approach her until properly introduced; a matchmaker was found, who arranged a meeting place at the Summer Palace park. The girl with her brother, would be in a queue for a boat, to glide among the lake's lotuses and the boy and matchmaker would meet her there. But already a queue a mile long of young people, probably quite a few in the throes of introduction was waiting, and it would take three and a half hours to get a boat; the venue was then changed to another park. However, an untoward hailstorm drove them home. The Great Wall was finally selected, with milling crowds, all going there to relax in the beautiful May weather. But by the time this third rendezvous had been arranged, the young man's leave in Peking was up, and it was his last day in the city. He had to get on his bicycle, after scarcely time to say a few words, and leave in order to catch a train. The girl, however, followed him on her bicycle, and it was at the station, saying goodbye, that they fell in love.

We talked about courtship among the young. 'They make their own rules,' said Gladys. A girl had refused to go on after one meeting with a personable boy. 'He did not talk to me of his ideas and ideals, only of love. How do I know what he is, when he only talks to please me?' 'A lot of young people are very serious-minded. A girl feels humiliated if she thinks she's talked down to.'

There were vague reports of cases of rape of little girls; of the acquisition of young mistresses by old cadres. One of the high cadres who thus took a girl of sixteen as his mistress was Mao's nephew in Manchuria. Educated young girls in the rural areas had been raped by peasants in the communes. Hundreds of letters from parents began to pour in to the State Council, asking for their sons' and daughters' return. All the children of higher cadres had been sent to the rural areas, so that none were at university. Chou Enlai's own nephew had been sent down and had now been away five years. He wrote to his uncle asking to return, but Chou said no, he could not favour his own family. Mao received in May a letter from a distraught mother, whose son had been away; now her daughter had married and gone away, and she was alone. The law said one child must remain to look after the old parents. But the mother had to send money to her son, as he was unable to live on peasant workpoints. Orders to re-examine each case were given; but it would take a long time. There would have been millions of cases to re-examine.

The revolutionary committees were also being re-appraised. Stuffed with youths scarcely out of middle school, inexperienced and at times unscrupulous, corruption had set in in some of them. Nieh Yuantzu and other revolutionaries of 1966, now dubbed 'ultra-left', had committed serious crimes, including beating people to death. 'From time to time we hold meetings and have some of them out of jail to criticize them,' said Hualan. Hualan did not tell me until 1976 that during the Cultural Revolution two of her relatives had committed suicide, accused of 'illicit connection with foreigners'. They had been beaten in front of her, and Hualan had cried, 'Stop please stop,' but the squad of beaters were May 16ers, and particularly vicious. Hualan's elation in seeing justice done to the criminals was understandable.

Hualan's painter sister was again teaching students, but it was difficult 'because the ideas of the ultra-left are still rampant among them'. The students brawled among themselves a great deal; they argued as to the propriety or not of drawing the human body. China's traditional painters had not used human models; and since the Cultural Revolution drawing the naked human body was condemned as 'revisionist' and 'yellow', (pornographic), although it had been done before 1966 in art academies teaching Western oil painting. One of the students, in mockery of the prudery exhibited, had drawn a pair of trousers hanging on a washing line and entitled the picture 'Genuinely Human Legs'.

'There's something wrong with our brains, something wrong with our thinking,' said Hualan, smoking furiously. I said wearily, 'Hualan, you haven't married a feudal Chinese, as I have. It's just feudalism. All the time I am reminded of Pao and the way he thought.'

Yeh only had half of his house. In the other half lived a worker's family. His books were sealed off, and he could not touch them. This had also been done to Pa Chin, and to some other writers. But the books had not been removed. It was, however, frustrating to look at one's books, unable to lay a finger upon them or open a page . . . merely stare through the glass pane. But Yeh was unruffled and calm, and laughed in such a jolly fashion that no one thought him distressed. By the end of 1973, the books were released.

Yen Wenching came back from his May 7 school; he wore shorts, spoke of the problems of pig breeding. Three and a half years of labour had followed two years of detention. He had resumed his position as editor, and his house had been restored to him.

I was asked to give talks to several magazines regarding the way to present facts about China to the West. I did have a few things to say – had I not been infuriated by the inanity of some Chinese publications ever since 1956? But nothing came of it; although it was said that Premier Chou had suggested my talking to the people working on the magazines. 'They listen, but hear not, and nothing will change,' said Hualan. The deadly style of writing, the bombast, continued, but in 1978, after much prodding, and because newspapers and publications in Chinese took the lead in telling the truth at last, the magazines for circulation abroad followed suit and are now better.

As for family planning, the educated youth settled in the countryside were producing babies out of wedlock; the babies were taken back to parents in the cities to be reared. It was particularly so in Manchuria, perhaps because the winter nights are long there. In Peking and other cities, from 1973 onwards, doctors were busy performing abortions on demand; a good many of them were on young unmarried girls. Going through the lanes, on dark nights, one came upon couples in dark corners. Curiously enough, it was precisely when, during 1974–6, the ostensible ban on any expression of love reached its peak, and love became almost counter-revolutionary, with foreigners living in China expressing their horror at the sexless lives of the Chinese, that a 'boom' came in the production of babies, and that in the 'small lane news' everyone knew that prostitution was returning, though not extensively.

Stupidly, or artlessly, or both, I said this to friends in Hong Kong; they did not betray me but begged me to consider that 'small lane' rumours were dangerous. I would, however, inconsiderately repeat some of this talk to European Marxist–Leninists. I encountered immediately their indignation and hostility. Of course I was bourgeois, I could not understand theory . . . any innuendo against the so-called 'radicals', at the time, put them on the defensive.

By 1973, the Shanghai Four had got themselves into all the liaison organizations with Marxist–Leninist parties abroad; Yao Wenyuan being in charge of this department. The net result was that Westerners, especially the more idealistic ones, firmly believed that the Four were thorough revolutionaries. This was reinforced by the appearance of the magazine *Study and Criticism*. Originally published in September 1973 as a magazine for internal consumption by Futan University in Shanghai (which had been Université Aurore, run by French Jesuits), it spread abroad, where it was translated into several languages, in Paris, London, Rome and America. It was, so I have been told, extremely well done, and was regarded for three years as the most revolutionary, must truly Marxist theoretical work extant.

I was earnestly advised to read it by two fairly eminent Marxist thinkers in the West, when I ventured to express to them my puzzlement and confusion. This cowed me. I know that I am not a 'thinker', nor do I pretend to be one. I never did get to read *Study and Criticism*, and now it has been utterly condemned. But through this magazine the Four did manage a most effective brainwashing of some of the intellectuals in France, Italy and other places.

In trips to Yunnan province that year I had visited Kunming's major hospital. The doctors there were recently back; they told me that several diseases, practically nonexistent for the last two years, had returned. One hundred and fifty thousand people in the province had died of malignant malaria in the last three years; resistance to the disease, which had been high before 1949, had disappeared because of the long twenty-year period without any cases.

'We have been unable to investigate tuberculosis in our industrial areas for some years now . . . but with BCG being given to all the young people, we hope it is less prevalent than before,' said the forthright doctors. The figures for tuberculosis, however, which had come down drastically since 1954, were now again climbing; and the doctors knew it.

In Kunming University the professors were just back; and the first intake of students – after examinations – was due. But would they now be admitted? 'The standards are low . . . we run preparatory courses.'

Yunnan was obviously a 'calamity' area, which means it had suffered badly from the Cultural Revolution; as had Szechuan province.* Re-adjustment had not yet reached these far-flung regions. It is false to think that directives in the Party were obeyed everywhere automatically, especially at that time, when the Party contained so many new recruits whose only claim to Party memberships was their obedience to Lin Piao, and later to Chiang Ching and her allies.

The return of feudal practices, eschewing all 'legality', the reign of arbitrary personal whim, had now become very apparent. When would constitutionalism, true respect for the law, guaranteeing personal rights, come to China?

'Only when the Chinese people, who are not legality-minded, realize how necessary it is,' said Hualan. And she was right.

'Water too pure breeds no fish, too harsh a master has no pupils.' Mr Pei wrote this sentence down on a piece of paper and gave it to me. I still have the slip of paper and the date: May 24th, 1973. 'From Chairman Mao,' said he. Mao had

*See *Wind in the Tower*. Casualties in both these provinces were high.

lately scolded the 'radicals' with this quotation from a Sung poet. 'You find fault too much . . . with everything . . . every minor defect becomes for you a political crime.'

A famous painter, a poet, a scientist from the Peking planetarium sat with the Peis and me, and our euphoria was that of people who have surmounted some malady and find themselves well again. Mr Pei mimicked with the poet, one of the 'trials' which the May 16ers used to inflict.

'Now confess your crimes,' he said sternly.

The poet pretended to tremble. 'I have not committed crimes.'

'Ha, ah, you are an obdurate, unrepentant counter-revolutionary! Beat him until he confesses his crimes!'

The poet said, 'I used to suffer from constipation, but not once did it bother me during my three years of labour in the countryside.' He told the amusing story of the day when, lined up with other 'criminals', a man next to him suddenly emitted a tremendous snore. 'It was Old Wang; he had actually fallen asleep standing up during his trial.' 'You are not allowed to snore,' barked one of the 'judges'. But already the audience had broken into laughter, and no one could go on with the meeting. 'The people would certainly not condemn anyone that day, and so they let us all go.'

Thus what had been pain and anguish became buffoonery.

A Chinese proverb says, 'One leaf can conceal Mount Taishan.' The reassurance of Chou Enlai's presence, of the measures he took, the return of Teng Hsiaoping, and of other old cadres, disguised the thrust for power of the Shanghai Four, and lulled us into thinking that all would be well again.

The Tenth Congress of the Party took place in August 1973. It was to wind up the Lin Piao episode. Would another successor be named by Mao? Apparently not. However, the rapid ascent of the young worker, Wang Hungwen of Shanghai, was noted; he became Vice-Chairman (one of five) of the Party. Was Mao thus once again asserting the leadership role of the working class, as well as the necessity of having 'young blood' in the Party?

All the year through, people I trusted reassured me that there was now 'unity'. Nothing could have been less true. But it was certain that Teng's return augured a 'collective leadership', for this is what Tang had advocated as Party Secretary-General, since 1956. He had also supported all moves for creating codes of law, a workable legal system. Perhaps now this would come to pass.

Looking at the Politburo composition, there seemed to be a balance between the 'centre' and 'left', just as Mao had envisaged. The Shanghai Four were in the Politburo, and in its Standing Committee were Wang Hungwen and Chang Chunchiao. This would be the chief snag some two years later, for it is the Standing Committee which handles executive affairs; and it is its Secretary – in this case Chang – who gets all the mail addressed to Politburo members. In 1977 letters addressed to other members of the Politburo, confiscated by Chang, would be found in files he had kept in his home.

The only unknown quantity in the Politburo was a man named Hua Kuofeng. Hua had been a provincial cadre from Hunan; both a soldier and an administrator, rising steadily through sheer merit and hard work from the lower ranks; and although criticized during the Cultural Revolution, he had not then been important enough to be jailed. In September 1971 he had been co-opted to Peking by Mao Tsetung and Chou Enlai because he had done much excellent work in Hunan, especially in preventing a seizure of the province by Lin Piao. He worked with Chou in the State Council; and he was so quiet that no one really bothered about him at the time.

'The tree would like to be still, but the wind does not stop blowing.' In 1973, the Shanghai Mafia began its strategy for seizing power. The first move was to get Wang Hungwen to Peking that year – or rather to commute between Peking and Shanghai – and then to be elected Vice-Chairman of the

Party. Another move, in February 1973, was to have the Communist Youth League Congress held in Shanghai first; the second congress was held in Lianoning province, where Mao's nephew, Chiang Ching's aficionado, ruled. This indicated clearly the target of the Four: once again it was the young.

In July 1973, the battle in the sensitive sector of education began. The case of an 'educated', that is, middle school man of twenty-five, Chang Tiesheng, was splashed on the radio in Liaoning province. He had been so devoted to his work in a commune that, faced with studying for an examination or helping with the harvest, he chose the harvest – and turned in a blank sheet.* He wrote to the newspapers explaining that he felt examinations were a way of corrupting youth, turning away the thoughts of the young from caring for the workers–peasant–soldiers. *Red Flag* and the *People's Daily* took up the battle, criticizing the reintroduction of academic criteria for entrance to educational institutions.

This 'blank sheet' case became part of a nationwide debate on how to run universities, middle schools and primary schools; it would play havoc with education until the fall of the Four. With millions of youngsters hungering to get back to the cities and return to study, yet aware that they could never pass the examinations required, the Tiesheng affair was a godsend. 'Why admission to university on questions framed by bourgeois authorities? Why not be admitted on our proletarian revolutionary spirit alone?' Counter articles produced Mao's dictum that there must also be 'knowledge', but this was drowned in the wrath of the millions of youngsters with little schooling but vast ambitions; they would never have more schooling (and were incapable of it) but they felt, each one of them, capable of 'proletarian leadership'. 'We must not cultivate bookworms . . . we

*This was later proved a fabrication. He did sit for the examination, answered the questions, but obtained too low a mark to pass. The author saw the photocopy of his examination paper in 1977.

evaluate the quality of teaching first of all by the political orientation,' the editorials stormed.

In December 1973 another 'incident': a twelve-year-old girl, Huang Shuai, wrote a letter criticizing her school teacher's behaviour, the way she taught, and the content of the curriculum. The press took the case up and published her letter; millions of youngsters of twelve and thirteen started attacking their teachers. So successful was the shambles thus created that by mid-1974 many schools could not function; and this is when, in Peking, in Chungking, in Wuhan and even in Lhasa, the windows of all middle schools began to be systematically broken by 'rebel' students.

Now newspaper articles appeared, praising the 'militia' of Shanghai. The formation of militia corps in every factory was advocated; it did not at first appear abnormal, since militia training had been called for since 1958. But its sinister significance as the power struggle intensified would become obvious in 1976.

Thus every active sector in China was being sucked into the struggle. There is no doubt that the Four did deploy fantastic energy and a very extraordinary knowledge of psychological warfare. And owing to the obstacles placed in the way of the return of the cadres to the cultural, journalistic and propaganda sectors, they now controlled the mass media: the press, films, radio and television, and publishing houses.

The main attack, directed against Chou Enlai, began in September 1973. It started as a campaign, or movement, against Confucius, and it was led by two old and revered scholars: Professor Yang Jungkuo, an expert on Confucius, and Professor Feng Yulan, who had studied in America and had long been known for his reverence for Old Master Kung.

CHAPTER 8

The Rise of the Four and the Death of Chou Enlai: 1974–1976

1974 to 1976 was a time of perplexity and anguish for the Chinese, both in China and abroad. A malaise which remained largely unvoiced. My relatives and friends went on hoping that there would not be another political paroxysm. I continued my efforts to widen the opening between China and the rest of the world. Chou Enlai had said to me, 'There is no conflict of interest between the people of China and the peoples of the world.' I believed him. But if China was to progress, she must admit the contrary winds of other nations. If her system were good, it must be tested in practice, and not shielded from alien encounter.

I now belittled the viciousness and the danger of the Four because I was convinced that Chou Enlai would be able to maintain stability, unity and progress. The shocking exposure of Lin Piao seemed to me sobering enough. It should make all of us more careful. And surely Chiang Ching, as Mao's wife, *must* understand that 'ultra-leftism' was harmful. Had Mao not repeated in 1973 that there must be stability and progress, and that 'the cultural policy of the Hundred Flowers . . . must be applied'?

I sought to bring to China members of the American Cancer Society. Cancer, with heart disease, was now the major killer in China. George Wu and his colleague, Dr Li Ping, and I spent many hours talking of cancer research, and the detection of early cases. Millions of women coming as routine cases to the hospitals were examined for uterine and cervical cancer. Cancer of the oesophagus was prevalent in the Taihang mountain area; of the liver in east China; of the naso-pharynx in the south. Chou Enlai had approved plans for a major hospital and research centre in Peking, endowed with the latest equipment. Fourteen other cancer hospitals were to be built in the provinces.

But for three years I got nowhere with my efforts on behalf of the American Cancer Society. The reason – unknown to me then – was the attitude of the Health Minister, Madame Liu Hsiangping. She was tall and so fat that we called her 'the Hippo'. Her husband was the head of the Peking Revolutionary Committee and also head of Peking's security police. Her daughter was the personable Hsieh Chingyi, in charge of Tsinghua University, whom I interviewed in 1969. The family was devoted to the Four.

I also tried to get Dr Isaac Berliner and his wife Martha into China. Berliner was doing pioneering work in contraceptives. They received a visa, but Liu Hsiangping refused to meet them. And although Berliner lectured in China to medical staff, nothing came of his efforts. 'Some people want a withdrawal . . . to close us in again,' Ma Haiteh would tell me. That year he could not obtain leave to go to America to see his brother.

I went to Mexico and gave the first public lecture on family planning which Mexico City had ever heard. President Echeverria was worried about Mexico's population increase, but the Catholic Church remained adamantly against contraception.

The tragedy of the Third World countries is that revolutions in health and in education have been made before an industrial revolution. Europe's nineteenth-century industrialization, present affluence and technological advances occurred through the exploitation not only of her own people but of other nations, and included black slavery. And this exploitation went on unhindered for many decades. But the Third World, in its emergence from colonialism, devised modern health and education programmes while its industrial development remained centuries behind. It thus brought upon itself demographic problems on an unprecedented scale.

I attended a United Nations meeting on family planning in

Bucharest, and found myself pitted against Dr Mario Peccei of the Club of Rome. His idea of a 'supreme council' of the 'eminent' (Western experts from the affluent countries) to 'organize all the world's resources' evoked anger from Third World delegates present. How could the Third World further entrust its resources to the ruling of the affluent, I said, when their waste, extravagance and spoliation of the world's resources remains the outstanding crime of our era? And while they continue to perpetuate among us poverty and political instability by denying us an equal share of the world's resources?*

Back to China. And to the roller-coaster feeling. A miasma of disquiet in the air. It is due to the Dragon Lady, Chiang Ching. Her nickname this year is Three Drops of Water. My insistence that she is irresponsible, mentally deranged, is unacceptable to my friends. They see in her a wilful demoniac, and the muttering dislike of 1972 is changing into an almost pathological hatred. Everything that went wrong, every cruelty, every death is now her fault. 'There isn't a family in China which has not suffered because of her,' says Hualan. I disagree, of course. She cannot be held fully guilty for everything, I say.

The anti-Confucius campaign was in full swing; it was now called 'anti-Confucius, anti-Lin Piao', *Pilin Pikung*. Mao was said to have launched it. It had become, however, an ambiguous drive.

With a spate of academic and historical articles to give it respectability, the movement had at first been turned against Chou Enlai and his policies. It attacked the return of the old cadres, 'restoration of the past', 'conservatism', and 'the greatest Confucianist mandarin of them all, who is negating the Cultural Revolution'.† The return of Teng Hsiaoping provoked inspired wall posters on the 'return of capitalist

*The Manila conference of 1979 has proved this true once again.
†Premier Chou Enlai.

roaders . . . who interfere in the factories and seek to negate the Cultural Revolution.'

But in March 1974 Chou Enlai foiled the onslaught. The occasion was the visit of Kenneth Kaunda, President of Zambia. In June 1967, worried about China, Kaunda had gone to Peking; Chou had extolled the Cultural Revolution to him precisely when he was subject to its most vicious attacks. Now Chou Enlai extolled the anti-Confucius movement; said it was an 'anti-Confucius, anti-Lin Piao' campaign, necessary to clear people's minds of the feudal ideas instilled by Lin Piao. The implication that it was an attack against him thus became untenable.

Political conflicts in China have always been fought with the weapons of historical analogy and historical allusion; figures of the past are surrogates, to attack present-day persons. This is as true today as ten centuries ago. Round after round of articles appeared in 1974, tracing the history of China as a 'two-line struggle' between the progressive 'legalists' and the reactionary 'Confucianists'. But the qualities attributed to legalists and Confucianists varied according to who wrote the articles. Lin Piao became a typical Confucian, and having been condemned as ultra-left, became suddenly ultra-right. Chou Enlai's weighty words at the Tenth Congress of 1973 were quoted: 'Very often one tendency covers another.' What appears radical and revolutionary might be serving the most reactionary forces.

With consummate skill Chou Enlai and the returned officials seized upon the campaign to push the rebuilding of Party institutions, to promote legality, unity and economic production, since all three had been 'legalist' theses in Chinese history. At the same time, Chou insisted that the campaign was against élitism, bureaucratism and the inferior condition of women.

'When will the National People's Congress be held?' I asked Wu Chienta and Hsing Chiang. Chienta had had an awful time for almost four years. It would take another two years before he stopped looking dazed.

'We shall hold it when more unity is achieved,' replied Hsing Chiang sagely.

'That was giving you a scoop,' remarked Ma Haiteh later. For it implied that a major battle was proceeding in the highest echelon.

'That's the Cultural Revolution's contribution to our people's brains,' said Hualan. 'We, the people, would not have dreamt of questioning unity among the leaders before. Now every child in China knows that they are constantly bickering and battling among themselves; and so no one is a god anymore.'

'But cannot a paroxysm, a climax, be avoided?' I asked her.

'Perhaps . . . but so far we've had a crisis every five or six years. Maybe another one will come . . .'

'Your temper, your temper – it's a flame nine metres high', said Hsing Chiang, sighing. My temper was getting very dangerous. I was on edge. 'It's because the anti-Confucius movement is carried out in a very Confucian manner,' I retorted.

There were troubles in China that year, ignored by the press but whispered about in the 'small lane news'. The situation in Sinkiang was 'ugly'. Lung Shuching, Lin Piao's man there, had been removed, but it was difficult to take in hand every place in Sinkiang, and there were stoppages in the factories, and even some fighting.

Trouble in the factories had actually erupted in several provinces. In Wuhan, the steel workers were on strike. The strike extended to other steel plants by 1975; then it was stopped by Teng Hsiaoping's energetic measures, only to surge again in 1976. In 1977 Teng Hsiaoping would tell me that due to the 'sabotage' of the Gang of Four a shortage of 27 million tonnes of steel between 1974 and 1976 had occurred.*

*Interview published by *Der Spiegel*. I was at the time asked by Vice-Premier Teng not to give the exact figure; it was mentioned officially four months later.

There was trouble in the silk factories of Hangchow. Wang Hungwen was there, and appointed one of his 'Mafia brothers'. Wen Senho, to supervise the factories. But high officials issued statements that the strikes were 'of no importance', which fooled people like myself.

In 1975, shortages of food and consumer goods would occur in certain cities. Taiyuan, Chengtu, Wuhan. No meat was to be had in Taiyuan for a year. In Chengtu, by 1974, there were already eighty different ration tickets for as many goods, and the goods were hard to find. Szechuan had suffered greatly from the Cultural Revolution, and continued to suffer.

I went to see my second-degree cousins, the sons of my Uncle Liu; who had died at the age of ninety-four. My cousins were all workers in factories. They were voluntarily cleaning the sewers in their district, on the Sunday I went to see them. When I left they insisted on accompanying me through the meander of *hutungs* to the main avenue. 'There are bad people around . . . they may try to rob you,' whispered Liu's second wife to me. Liu's second wife was very active in her street committee, spreading family planning knowledge, perhaps because Uncle Liu had bred altogether sixteen children, twelve by his first and four by his second wife.

People that year were inclined to whisper, as if there were microphones about. Everything was 'secret'; I must not repeat a word.

Adolescent gangs: 'They start at twelve or thirteen. Everything now happens at a younger age. Instead of copying the positive characters in the new model operas, they copy the villains . . . Some of the youngsters are even cultivating moustaches, like the bandits in *Taking Tiger Mountain by Strategy*.' The gangs had 'chieftains' of fifteen. They vandalized, they broke windows . . . 'A lost generation,' said Mr Pei.

Yeh's wife, Yuan Yin, was very much in demand by her street committee to solve delinquency problems. In their neighbourhood two 'armies' of adolescents were acting out old tales of chivalry, battling with each other once a week, at night. The prize was the 'princess', a pretty girl who used to watch these tournaments, wearing a white veil on her head. 'She becomes the mascot of the winning side; the boys bring her presents, even steal money from their parents for her.

'The youngsters have no schools to go to; and if they go to school they are told to bully the teachers. To study is to show bourgeois tendencies.' The examples of Chang Tiesheng, and Huang Shuai, promoted by the Four, had been only too effective. But parents came secretly to teachers, imploring them to give private tuition at night to their children.

Chang Tiesheng (Blank-Sheet Chang) was in 1974 promoted to regional representative at the National People's Congress to be held in January 1975. He was sent to Japan as youth representative, and in 1976 would become Vice-Minister of Culture under the Four. Huang Shuai, the thirteen-year-old, was in the same school as one of my nieces. My niece said very little about her except that she 'is often travelling'. Huang Shuai went from school to school to lecture the students; she had a car to convey her from home to school and back.

'The young are told to grow spikes all over their body and horny antlers all over their heads,' said Jui, my sister-in-law. 'Fortunately our children do not listen to this nonsense.' But many youngsters became insolent, rude and lazy, since these attitudes were now virtues. The sales-girls and boys in the shops would not serve clients, and tales of their hostility to potential buyers became common talk. But so many of these youths had jobs in the cities because they must look after their parents; they could not be moved, or fired. So they did as they pleased.

I went to see the painter Wu Tsojen and his wife. Wu Tsojen was a cheerful and talkative man. He had been criticized during the Cultural Revolution, but now he was in deep trouble because he had wanted the works of that other great painter renowned all over the world, Tsi Paishih, to be adequately preserved. Chiang Ching had railed against Tsi Paishih as a 'miser' who could not paint, as she had abused other famous painters such as Li Kejan and Pan Tienshou.

Wu Tsojen was glum. 'I am not well.' A visit to the art shops revealed that neither his paintings nor those of Li Kejan, nor anyone else of renown, were to be seen. Reproductions of their work were no longer on sale, and the salesgirls frowned heavily when I mentioned them.

Only in 1975 did I hear about the 'black' exhibition of paintings held in spring 1974 in Shanghai. Since then rumour has proved true, confirmed event.

In 1973 Chiang Ching, and the other members of the Politburo had approved a selection of the works of famous painters commissioned by Chou Enlai to decorate public buildings and hotels. Mao had expressed the wish that 'a hundred flowers blossom' and that 'my face should not be in every room'.

But in the spring of 1974, the very works which had been approved by the Four were condemned by them as 'black' and 'attempts to restore capitalism'. For instance, a painting of fish in water: if the water were not 'realistic' enough, it meant 'fish out of water', and it was an insult to the working class attaining administrative posts. If a mountain had many rocks, it was a way of wishing they would fall on the fields and ruin the harvest. And so on. Yao Wenyuan surpassed himself by calling one painting 'a revelation of the spy and enemy agent nature of the painter'. The whole episode sounds so paranoiac that it is scarcely credible. Yet dozens of painters, who suffered at the 'black' exhibition told me similar stories, in Szechuan, in Shanghai, and Peking. This raises once again the problem of the mental balance of Chiang Ching; and of the men around her.

Art academies, which had been closed in 1967, and reopened in 1971 were once more closed while the teachers and their students trudged down to 'integrate' in the villages. In the end this descent of eminent artists among the peasantry – which had first occurred in 1958 – did give rise to some excellent peasant paintings, and promoted among thousands of peasants the need and the urge to paint.*

Millie Pei, now a university student, but working in a factory for six months, to compose, with the workers, a new dictionary of Chinese scientific terms, gave me the flavour of the current disquiet. 'The people feel that they are pawns. They are tired of political movements. They say: Today we are told to run in direction A, and anything else is counter-revolutionary. Tomorrow we are told that A is counter-revolutionary and we must run in direction B. We are not punished; we are simply called "the deluded masses". But who has deluded us? Why is it that yesterday's wrong is today's right?' The young were becoming cynical, and the middle-aged were playing safe. 'They don't want to suffer again for criticizing X or Y today and seeing them return to power tomorrow . . . They say: Let's wait and see.'

As for studying, or becoming an expert at anything – it now took courage to do so. 'Have you heard the doggerel: "Expert, expert, that's the way to eat dirt. See not, hear not, speak not, you wear a clean shirt"' Millie told me of the waste and extravagance in the factory she worked in. 'I go around turning off taps, turning off lights, and I'm accused of being bourgeois and "material production minded" instead of "revolution minded". But what is socialism, if not an end to waste, and increased production? That's what Marx, Lenin and Chairman Mao said, but the young workers say, "Better no production than capitalism". Then how shall we live?' asked Millie.

By 1975 there were once again 'study sessions' in all Party units. They centred on a major article by Chang Chunchiao, which became required study for all Party members. The women cadres brought their knitting with them to the

*The Huhsien peasant paintings, exhibited in London, Paris and the United States, are examples of this collaboration between peasant and professional artist.

meetings. 'We have time to catch up with our winter woollies.' This was passive resistance of a kind no one could take exception to; since knitting was a kind of manual labour. In Chengtu and Chungking, girls would walk on the streets, knitting away, their long hair spread on their shoulders in a way thought 'indecent' by the prim northern Chinese. They would explain that they had just washed their hair, and were walking about to dry it.

'Knit, talk food, talk sickness, and you are safe.'

Food was a good topic, unlikely to be suspect, provided shortages were not mentioned. There was the ritual phrase, 'The general situation is excellent', which meant: but the particular situation is quite awful. Everyone understood the sarcastic implication.

Sickness was the other safe topic of conversation. Comparing symptoms could lead a whole group of women, en masse, to leave the office and seek a doctor urgently. Mild epidemics of headache with blurred vision even required a small autocar, to take a group, as to a picnic, to the hospital.

The doctors were almost all back by 1974; even though there were young heads of departments, who knew very little, and older consultants in subordinate positions. But the conscience of the doctors never faltered. The admirable way in which they accepted working in an inferior position, and continued to do their best, makes them true heroes. The endless queues of waiting patients were not surprising. Older cadres, fearing renewed abuse, humiliation and disgrace, simply became ill. The doctors understood that they must remain under hospital care for 'weak heart', neurasthenia or gastric ulcers. They could not be sent to labour or be bullied, for deaths during bullying, and suicides, in the early years of the Cultural Revolution, had been very much resented.

There were professional betrayers, among them a poet; he participated in writers' meetings, then went off on his bicycle to report to 'them'. 'But why on a bicycle?' 'Because if he went in a car it would be noticed.'

My friend, Yen Wenching, back from May 7 school, had

six hundred manuscripts on his editorial desk awaiting publication. He could not send one to the printers.

'Why?'

'Because publication depends on Yao Wenyuan's approval.'

'Why no literary magazines? It was announced they would reappear . . .'

But Yao Wenyuan, now editor of *Red Flag*, would not allow any magazine which might print articles disagreeing with the Four.

'Are there such articles?'

'Hundreds,' replied Yen Wenching, crinkling his eyes at me.

The core of the unease was Chou Enlai's illness. Chou Enlai had been in hospital since April 1974. Some people said that already in 1973 he had been unwell. What was he suffering from? Diplomats said it was cardiac disease. George Wu, who should have known, said that he had no idea, but his face was sombre.

I gathered from George the erroneous impression that Chou would soon get better. This was, of course, not true. But George could not betray what was both a professional and a state secret. And Chou continued to work; daily, high officials came to see him at the hospital.

'Suppose something goes wrong with Chou . . . what will happen to China?'

Rewi was vague. 'The Young Turks are pushing the Dragon Lady on top.'

'Maybe Teng Hsiaoping can manage them now.' Teng was in charge of the daily work Chou could no longer do.

'We all hope so,' said Rewi, looking grim.

Articles on class origin and class struggle, and talk about 'class origin goes back three generations', abounded. If acted upon it meant that my nephews and nieces would have mighty little chance of getting into a university, ever. Now there were nine instead of five 'bad categories', and the intelligentsia was 'the stinking ninth', according to the Dragon Lady.* Articles about 'new Liu Shaochis', warnings of 'erroneous tendencies in the Party', exhortations to 'go against the tide', a phrase used by Wang Hungwen at the Tenth Congress – all this showed a new outburst of ultra-leftism. Going against the tide was a favourite cliché among the young. It meant going against all educationalists. A film, *Counterattack*, would be made, based on the 'blank-sheet' episode of Chang Tiesheng. Another film, *Spring Seedlets*, showed all the old cadres, older doctors (above forty) as rotten, incompetent and heartless. The only heroic, devoted and successful figures were young boys and girls, young barefoot doctors of seventeen, eighteen.

Many absurd slogans were current that year. 'Better a socialist train running late than a capitalist train on time.' This was licence for everything not to run on schedule. City transport became badly disorganized (except in Shanghai) because bus drivers made it a revolutionary attitude to run buses not on time – or even not at all. But in Shanghai the workers were paid 20 per cent more than anywhere else and production was encouraged by the Four, because it was their main bastion, and no strikes or dissent were allowed. Everywhere else they instigated conflict, breakage of machinery, stoppages, to prove that Teng Hsiaoping could not run things and that people opposed him.

Already in summer 1974 the overseas Chinese were leaving in droves. Eighty thousand of them applied to leave China, and 45,000 were given permission. 'They're afraid that violence is beginning all over again. They don't want to put up with it any longer.' A friend of mine from Yenching, a doctor, could not stay. He had been, in 1956, so full of enthusiasm. In 1974 he left China. 'I can no longer bear it . . . I gave up a big job in 1950 to return to serve China . . .'

I went to Tientsin, and down the railway to Chengchow

*Landlords, rich peasants, reactionaries, hooligans, capitalist roaders, the old national bourgeoisie, the bourgeoisie within the Party, spies and people in collusion with abroad, and the 'unreformed' intelligentsia.

and to Loyang. The railway line's terminus was Shanghai. Now I understand that I was, that year, the subject of an operation designed to win me over to Chiang Ching. Almost all the places I visited were under her influence, particularly the railway stations of Tientsin, Chengchow and Paoting. The Four had a long-term plan to capture the railway, in order to move the armed militia they nurtured in Shanghai up north, if necessary, joining with forces from Manchuria under Mao's nephew, Mao Yuanhsing, and capturing Peking.

Tientsin was depressing; the railway station was surrounded by silent, sinister youths. Some wore small moustaches; others were obviously vagrants. I had another shock the next morning. Almost every shop window showed at least one dress, in a pastel colour, with ample skirt and a V neck. It was *the* Chiang Ching dress, designed by her. I knew about *the* dress because Shuan came to tell me of it. Shuan was to create new patterns for the material used in the dress. All the tailors were told they must make only this model and no other. Every woman in China was to wear *the* dress. But Shuan said it took almost five metres of material and cost at least thirty *yuan*, the monthly salary of a young worker, and more than a month's wage for a street factory worker. And breast-feeding women could not wear it, for it did not unbutton, and how and where could they take it off when they wanted to feed their babies? 'Three Drops of Water' had also decided that there would be five basic colours, according to rank: peasant, worker, cadre, woman soldier, higher leading cadre. Ambassadors' wives would wear *the* dress abroad. However, counter-revolutionaries and people of bad origin would not be allowed to wear it. They would have to stick to trousers.

Tientsin was now the Dragon Lady's city. A meeting of national women representatives had been held here. All those who attended wore *the* dress while Chiang Ching spoke to them. 'She said, "Why should not a woman have male concubines? The Empress Wu Tzetien had male concubines . . ." Because of her a woman cadre now openly entertains her boyfriends at home and the husband dare not protest. And a woman and her daughter have started a prostitution ring . . .' Thus my informant, a woman cadre.

I meet in Tientsin Pa Mulan. She is a typical Chiang Ching recruit; good-looking, energetic, and above all prolix. 'Listening to you, I wish I had a tape recorder,' I say. She explains to me women's liberation and its astounding progress, owing to the *Pilin Pikung* movement. All revolutionary committees in Tientsin have 30 per cent women members.

We go to Takang, the offshore oilfield near Tientsin. Young girls are 'in charge' of routine work at many posts in the oilfield. They are between eighteen and twenty-nine years old. The visit ends disastrously. I am shown a very modern machine, obviously either Swedish or Japanese, which just stands next to an older machine. I am told that it was made by the workers 'out of bits and pieces of discarded material'. I explode. 'It just is not true.' Great awkwardness. 'You're pouring cold water on the workers' enthusiasm,' says Hsing Chiang. 'Enthusiasm does not mean telling lies,' I reply, and Hsing Chiang utters a deep sigh, for I make life very difficult for her. She is torn in two, and Party discipline does not allow her to say anything.

The Nankai middle school was established in 1904. Chou Enlai studied there. The Assistant Dean, Chu Ta, is affable. No classes are held because the students are 'going down to help the peasants . . .' Twice Mr Chu refers to 'our beloved Premier Chou', and we look at each other in great sadness. 'His recovery is the fervent wish of all the Chinese people,' says he pointedly. Next to him sits the school heroine, the seventeen-year-old Wei, a disciple of the 'model', Huang Shuai. She wrote a wall poster against her teachers and against the Dean of Nankai. 'We went against the tide, as Vice-Chairman Wang Hungwen enjoined us to do,' says she. Students and teachers apparently spend two evenings a week criticizing Confucius.

The Tientsin railway station workers are writing the history of their railway station and its vicissitudes. An admirable project. 'Are the trains running well?' 'Better than before.' They say it was Liu Shaochi and Lin Piao who stopped the trains. And yet, in 1975, all along that railway line and others, young workers will 'go against the tide' and the trains will be hours late, and accidents will occur on several railroads.

Must I or must I not believe the stories I am told by these railway workers: how they serve the people by selling tickets at the schools and factories, how they strive to make things easier at holiday time for those who go home to see their families? Eighty per cent of the train attendants are girls. Part of women's liberation is giving jobs to girls. I think of the hostile young men outside the railway station.

Siaodjing village near Tientsin is Chiang Ching's model brigade. All the women here have learnt to read and write, and the village practises total equality in workpoints, which is still quite rare in rural China. Poems against Confucius are written on the walls by the villagers, and poetry competitions are held.

A young girl, a 'model' in the fight against Confucius, tells me of the way she 'uprooted Confucian ideas' in her production team. She is twenty-six. 'Do you intend to get married?' 'I have not yet found a master,' she replies. 'What did you say?' I ask innocently, and she blushes scarlet. She has used the old, Confucian term, a slip of the tongue . . .

Evident progress has taken place in women's liberation everywhere in China, but it is simply not true that everything started at the Cultural Revolution of 1966, and that all of it is due to Chiang Ching launching the slogan: Every revolutionary committee must have 30 per cent of women.

In Loyang the tractor factory is a mess. Screws and bolts and spare parts of every description litter the floor in untidy heaps; the engineer who takes me around does not attempt to explain. He shows me one workshop and then says, 'Our production is not too good. We have had ultra-left sabotage.

But it will pick up now.' He hopes, of course, that Teng Hsiaoping will intervene and make things work.

Of all the disciplines, only archaeology has never been obstructed during the Cultural Revolution. Most important archaeological finds have taken place during those years of turmoil. I have been to Tatung, following the tracks of Buddhism, to see the Wei dynasty Yungkang caves. I now see the Lungmen caves in Loyang, and their thousands of carved Buddhas, from the gigantic to the tiny. I am told of 'the great contribution' of Empress Wu Tzetien to the sculptures and treasures of the Lungmen caves. I shall hear a great deal about Empress Wu of the Tang dynasty, and also about Empress Lu of the Han dynasty, in the next two years. Both these women apparently were progressive, legalists, anti-Confucian. Both added great lustre and prosperity to the Empire. So write the 'new historians' collected in the universities by the Four. Does this mean that we shall have a new empress in China?

In Chengchow, in Loyang, everywhere there are wall posters, writings on walls and bridges and atop telegraph poles; in black paint which cannot be rubbed off. Some welcome the army; some call for the start of a workers' militia to patrol the streets; some demand that there be street protection units; some accuse capitalist roaders, 'people like Liu Shaochi', in authority; some say, 'We are not going back to the cattle pens . . .' 'There must be better arrangements for education . . .' 'There are false revolutionaries; all they want is power . . .' 'Down with the ultra-left who wave the red flag to knock down the red flag'. There are also many torn posters. My driver goes very fast through the streets.

The fields around Chengchow are almost eighteen metres below the Yellow River level, and the dykes are constantly added to. The roads are used as threshing floors, and there is a jam of peasant carts. My driver says, 'What is life like in the West? Here we have security, but it is so terribly monotonous . . .' Monotonous! When so much is happening! In Loyang the army called to quell riots and round up hooligans and stop the armed attacks on banks . . .

On family planning, the statistics I am given in 1974 and 1975 are more than suspect, because of 'Hippo', the Health Minister. I cannot use them, except one or two specific examples. The son of a friend, who is now a factory worker, tells me that in his plant the leading cadres all have six to ten children. The workers, urged to have no more than three, have put up a poster: 'In family planning, modestly follow the example of our factory leadership.'

In another city I feel around me a tightening surveillance, as in 1969. Someone thinks there are things I must not know. My friends are more than usually reticent. One person will tell me how he has been warned only to talk to me of 'positive aspects'.

In Peking, Hualan is not reticent. 'People who have beaten and tortured others are now being admitted to the Party . . . the Party's filling up with them. With membership of the Party they can do anything . . . so who dares to complain?' Especially not to someone who might say something outside, and be quoted in the newspapers. Every person I have met will be questioned if I am quoted repeating, for instance, Hualan's phrase.

I can well conceive the following scenario: I am fêted, shown around, and given interviews; although I am somewhat disappointing because I publish so little of what I am told, unlike a good many authoritative visitors who have managed entire books based solely on interviews, interpreters and three solid weeks of conducted tours.

Meanwhile, my friends and Family members are being told what to say to me, and perhaps someone will be incarcerated because I have been indiscreet. I feel my skin crawl with apprehension at the thought. And this could happen now, because Chou Enlai is ill, and Kung Peng is no longer there, and I have no protection . . . I don't know Teng Hsiaoping; as for Chiao Kuanhua, he is always very busy.

Now I am seriously perturbed. Does Three Drops really mean to become Party Chairman, or Empress? Perhaps Roxane Witke was right and I was wrong. I am convinced in my bone marrow that Chiang Ching's access to supreme power will be very bad for China. I think: 'She's like Caligula, the crazy Roman Emperor. Let her mess with culture or whatever for a while, and sooner or later the people will get rid of her. But not, oh not Party Chairman.'

I go to see Claire Hollingsworth, correspondent for the *Daily Telegraph*, whom I met at the Hsinchiao Hotel. I tried to help her with her very unsatisfactory interpreter. 'He's totally inert,' she said. 'He's always tired and going off to sleep.' This inertia was a defensive reaction, perhaps also one of hostility. So many youths are now hostile. I spoke to Chiao Kuanhua about it but Chiao was unhelpful. 'She is a difficult woman,' said he.

Now I plan to ask Claire to write about *the* dress. The best way to attack Chiang Ching is by ridicule; showing her up as a foolish bizarre woman. Anything else, especially as so much is gossip and conjecture,* will only enhance that dread of her which unhinges us all.

Besides the dress, I tell Claire how much people are frightened; how the formerly renowned film star, Pei Yang, has been declared 'an American spy'. I do not tell her of the accusation suspended above my head – or rather, above my Family's head. I know that it can be used at any time against me, but Claire, being English, will think me melodramatic and disbelieve me if I tell her. Claire says that she cannot write the story because she cannot quote me. But she will try to pass it 'through a French newspaper'.

The French newspaper apparently refused the story, deeming it of little value. Claire, as correspondent in Peking, could not be identified with an article against Madame Mao without being thrown out. 'You must understand my

---

*Until 1977, when I made sure of facts, through witnesses and documents in the handwriting of the Four.

position . . . .I have family and friends here; it's a sword over my head,' I said. 'Are you quite serious?' asked Claire. Perhaps I sounded histrionic to her. So I said, 'Never mind.' And we talked of Chou Enlai.

But already our two meetings were suspect. As we walked back to the hotel (for I never talked in Claire's room, of course, only outside), a young girl passed us and said to me, 'Talking to a foreigner – what are you talking about?' and walked on. And Chiao let me know that the less I had to do with Claire the better.

The waitresses of the Peking Hotel blossomed into pleated skirts.

I asked Little Chou, my favourite waitress, 'How much did it cost?'

'A lot. And I've four children.'

Rewi said, 'The Dragon Lady makes life difficult for everybody.'

The latest rumour was about the jailing of a geography lecturer who had a photograph of Armstrong walking on the moon. A friend had sent it to him from America. Someone had reported the fact to Chiang Ching, and she had said 'Investigate'. And so he had been jailed.

I lost my temper. 'Everything is always her fault . . . why pick on her every time? Surely bad things have been done by other people . . .' I could not believe all the rumours; there were simply too many, too many. It was indeed pathological. All the hatred, all the resentment, were directed at her. 'She's not normal, she's mentally disturbed,' I said. But Hualan would not listen. 'She's the most wicked woman in the world . . .we hate her, hate her . . . we wish we could boil her alive . . .'

In September Mrs Imelda Marcos came to China for eight days, and suddenly a lot of women were having their hair done to look like Imelda.

Chiang Ching took Mrs Marcos to the model Siaodjing brigade. 'You had the same trip as Imelda Marcos,' said

Hsing Chiang to me. A great compliment. It is now claimed that Chiang Ching inspired Chairman Mao to instigate the rectification in art and literature in Yenan in 1942 (she married him in 1938).* 'Whoever is against the revolution in art and literature is against the Party' is the theme of an article. Criticism of Chiang Ching is tantamount to criticism of the revolution in art and literature, and that means being anti-Party, therefore counter-revolutionary. It's very neat.

On television I see Chairman Mao receiving Mrs Marcos, who looks exquisite. I am shattered because Mao is old, so old. His lower jaw hangs and his hands shake. I write to Chiao Kuanhua, whom I continue to trust, telling him that Mao appears very ill. I do not get a reply.

Chiao Kuanhua has married again. We, his friends, are happy for him. Chang Handje is very beautiful. She has divorced her husband to marry Chiao. Some people have to wait years for a divorce, but for Chiao it has gone very quickly. For the first time there is criticism of Chiao (who until now has been something of a hero among the people). The son of Chang Handje goes abroad to study, but Chiao's own son and daughter by Kung Peng do not get any privileges. They have done labour in the communes.

I have seen Chang Handje at a sports meeting; she sat behind Wang Hungwen, whose English interpreter she appears to have been.

Chang Handje does not receive me. No more dinners with Chiao, only formal cups of tea and a talk in the official residence.

Prince Sihanouk and Princess Monique give me a wonderful lunch for my birthday, September 12th. The Prince has cooked it himself. In 1973, at great risk, the Prince and his wife went back to Cambodia through the Ho Chih Minh Trail, and spent some weeks with the Khmer Rouge guerrillas

*See *The Morning Deluge*.

in the jungle. Sinhanouk even reached Angkor, and was photographed among its monuments. In 1974 it is obvious that the Vietnam war – and its corollary, the Cambodian war – will be wound up. 'My position is now very strong,' said Sihanouk. 'The Americans are defeated. Victory is ours.'

Kissinger, in Peking to see Mao and Chou Enlai, has asked them, so says rumour, to intercede with Sihanouk. The latter should be 'reasonable', and parley with Lon Nol, rather than let the Khmer Rouge take over in a final and decisive military victory. But Sihanouk tells me now that the Americans are 'duping' the Chinese. '*Vous avez été dupés*,' he says. He refuses to talk with Lon Nol. Boumedienne of Algeria has also written, asking him to be 'flexible'. But Sihanouk will only talk with Washington 'if they get rid of Lon Nol'.

Kissinger's attitude to Sihanouk is abusive and irrational. The two men simply detest each other. But Sihanouk was willing that I should talk to the head of the American Liaison Office, David Bruce, in Peking; which I now proceeded to do.

Meeting David Bruce and his wife was a joyful experience, illuminating that gloomy year when I felt crushed by the emergence of Chiang Ching as political superstar. We talked at the house of a friendly ambassador. Bruce was very shrewd. He spoke about 'woman power . . . something not to be neglected'. He shared the general view that Chiang Ching might come to reign, and the less said about her the better. He had just read an article on Empress Wu Tzetien and another one on women leaders in revolutionary struggles.

Bruce told some funny stories to put me at ease, then said seriously, 'Don't let anyone get their hands on your oil.' About Chou's ill health he said, 'A great impediment at the moment . . . it makes steady negotiations difficult. Neither is Chairman Mao capable of sustained effort.' 'But American hesitation will weaken Chou further,' I said. Bruce's handsome face showed he understood what I meant.

On Cambodia Bruce was emphatic. The coup against

Sihanouk had not been instigated by the Americans. 'We only came afterwards, to prevent a takeover by some of Sihanouk's friends . . . he should know that.' Sihanouk's attitude made it impossible for America to get rid of Lon Nol. 'We can't be seen grovelling too much . . .'

I went to see Étienne Manac'h, the French Ambassador, a friend of great wisdom and vision. De Gaulle had started Nixon thinking of relations with China, and Manac'h had greatly helped. 'Kissinger at one point suggested getting the Russians to approach the Chinese. He had his priorities wrong,' said Manac'h, who thought Kissinger 'slightly hyperactive'. 'As for détente, there is less and less of it, but the Western world is not yet ready to face the fact.' He could not help at all with the Lon Nol problem. 'Both sides are rigid . . . a dénouement must come, which may not be the best solution.'

September 30th, and the usual evening banquet for the celebration of October 1st, National Day.

I was seated next to the famous pianist, Yin Shentsung, one of the two best in China. The other is Liu Shekun, but Liu was then in jail because he was the son-in-law of Marshal Yeh Chienying. It was a way of pressuring the old Marshal.

Yin was trained by Russian masters, and used to play Chopin and Liszt. He is now a devotee of Chiang Ching, and has lavished praise on her in many articles. 'You will enjoy sitting with Comrade Yin,' says the head of protocol, seating me. Yin was an intellectual who had 'reformed' and gone over to the Four.

I congratulate Yin on his playing of *Symphony of the Yellow River*. It was composed in Yenan in 1944, but now is claimed as a 'fruit' of the Cultural Revolution, and of Chiang Ching's influence. At every one of the first two rows of tables I can see two or three actors, film stars or musicians; all Chiang Ching's people.

Suddenly the national anthem sounds and hands are clapping. We rise, the leaders file in, and at their head is

Chou Enlai. He has come. He is there, he is back. He is very thin, but he is there.

Chiang Ching comes in. Dramatic, in *the* dress, black, a big black skirt. Yin Shentsung turns to me amiably. 'Comrade Chiang Ching is *very* healthy now.' He is full of goodwill. 'Pay attention. She is the rising power', is what he means to convey to me.

Only the night before, I have had a conversation with an overseas Chinese who appears to have gone over to Chiang Ching. 'Who do you think will be Party Chairman after Mao?' 'Of course, Comrade Chiang Ching,' she said. And I said, 'Oh heavens!' and left her.

So I reply to Yin Shentsung, 'Yes, she *is* fatter.'

After that, we know where we stand.

Now two young girls, opera stars, both dressed in *the* dress, go from table to table toasting the guests. This has never been done before. And I think of the bitter doggerel I heard in Szechuan:

> It is better to dance a model ballet
> Than to have fought the Long March.
> It is better to sing a model opera
> Than to have a body full of bullet holes.

The resentment against these young upstarts, basking in the sunshine effulgence of 'the Empress' . . . I share it.

Chou Enlai stands up to speak. And we all stand and clap, clap, clap. We cannot stop applauding him and there is love and sorrow and rejoicing in our clapping. We go on and on until our hands are sore. At some tables, the artists of Chiang Ching do not clap. But Yin does. And I am crying, the tears running down my cheeks. When we stop, Chou speaks. His voice is still strong. It is not what he says, but the feeling in it which is utterly poignant. 'Unity,' he cries, 'unity. We *must* unite.' He repeats it again and again. He is making a last appeal, so that another crisis may be averted. I turn to Yin when he has finished. 'Premier Chou is one of the greatest men in the world.' Yin nods but does not say yes or no.

In Hong Kong I ring up Leo Goodstadt, editor of the *Far Eastern Economic Review*, and tell him that my hopes are with Teng Hsiaoping. I see Lee Tsungying and tell him that I feel dubious about Chiang Ching. I repeat some of the things I have heard. He says, 'Wait and see. Wait and see.' He is a little frightened. So is Percy Chen, to whom I talk. 'Mum's the word,' he says. But they do not betray me.

'We could not say anything, even to each other,' says Tsungying, years later. And it is true. Already friends do not trust each other, and parents cannot trust their children. Children are urged to report on their parents; a nightmare feeling of fear and suspicion is being created.

I am asked by Mr Fei of the *Takungpao* newspaper to make a speech on women's liberation in China. I make the speech, but I do it without once mentioning Chiang Ching or her 'standard bearer' role in women's liberation. Not once does her name pass my lips.

In January 1975, the Third National People's Congress is held, and it is a triumph for Chou Enlai, for stability and unity and progress.

Of the Shanghai Group, only one, Chang Chunchiao, obtains a post, as head of the general political department in the army. Chiang Ching is nowhere. In the allotment of vice-premierships, too, the 'Young Turks' are in a minority. Teng Hsiaoping comes top of the list of Vice-Premiers. He is also Chief of Staff of the Army.

Since November 1974 there have been rumours that Chang Chunchiao is becoming more pragmatic, that he is joining the older cadres. After all, he is sixty in 1975.

Chou announces the programme for the modernization of China. It is not a new departure. Ever since 1956, this has been the goal. To announce it now means that the situation is stabilized. 'Everything will be all right,' says Tsungying. And Mr Fei, who is a delegate for the Hong Kong Chinese at the Congress, tells me that unity is restored; that Wang Hungwen behaved with the utmost courtesy to 'old and venerated Long Marchers' such as Chu Teh.

The new man, Hua Kuofeng, also becomes a Vice-Premier. He is known as a very hardworking, very thorough man, and he has no clique, is not identified with anyone. He has no backing but his own merit. He is entrusted with public security, and no one objects.

Why were the Four, so fierce and so assured in October 1974, flaunting their power, defeated at the Congress of January 1975?

There are, of course, two versions. The one favoured by certain Sinologists and Western newsmen lumps Mao with the Four, and explains that he was put in a minority when he tried to give them power at the Congress.

This version – like the one about Chou strangling Lin Piao – is not only fanciful, it is laughable. But it will become part of the sedulous myth that Mao and the Four had one identity until the end. Anyone who studies Mao's personality and vision would not hold this view for a moment. All I have seen, heard, checked and double checked convinces me that it was not so. On the contrary, since 1973, Mao Tsetung had decided that although it was necessary to have an equilibrium in order not to fall back into a mandarin bureaucracy, at the same time, he would not give power to any junta which utilized his wife.

I saw in 1977 and 1978 documents which, because they are in the handwriting of the Four, I cannot doubt. Wang Hungwen went several times to Mao with reports against Chou Enlai in the autumn of 1974, accusing Chou of 'plotting and conspiring'. 'He is not sick at all, he is merely conspiring,' said Chiang Ching to her husband. Mao would not listen to Wang Hungwen. Chiang Ching then sent a personal messenger (who happened to be Mao's own niece, a young woman, Wang Haijung) to her husband. The reason for a messenger was that, since 1974, Mao had refused to see her. She asked her husband, through Haijung, to give her 'responsible work', to promote Chang Chunchiao to the position of Premier and allow him to form a new cabinet; to nominate Wang Hungwen as Chairman of the Standing Committee to the National People's Congress.

Mao refused all of these requests. 'You are far too ambitious', he told his wife. He would repeat an injunction which already in 1974 he had made publicly: 'You four . . . you stick together, forming a gang, like in the bad old days of the Mafia in Shanghai. Do not form a gang of four . . . no good will come of it.'

There are other instances of Mao objecting to his wife's actions. 'She does not represent me . . .' he would say. But how could he stop her from beginning her public speeches with the phrase, 'I bring you greetings from Chairman Mao', which of course meant every word was Mao's own word?

Mao's power had never been supreme; as what I have written so far amply proves. And now he was increasingly limited by his deteriorating physical and mental condition; by his nephew; by his entourage – two young nurses devoted to his wife, who would whip a document from his hands, saying, 'You mustn't read!' After all, the nurses had been picked as 'reliable' by the Minister of Health, Liu Hsiangping.

The Four played a subdued role for a while, before the convening of the Congress. Chang wrote a penitent letter to Mao: 'Henceforth we shall certainly stop making a gang of four.'

This letter was at the origin of the rumours that there was a change in Chang, the wily, ruthless and supremely clever 'brain' of the Four; that he was becoming 'moderate'.

I was back in China in September 1975, and everyone seemed much happier. 'Teng really gets things going,' said Rewi, smiling broadly. Teng was becoming very popular because food was more plentiful, factories were working, and Teng had drawn up plans for industrialization; three documents, on science, technology and economics. More competent cadres were coming back, and working. And old

Marshal Yeh Chienying, whom everyone liked so much, was now Defence Minister. Teng's clashes with the Four in the Politburo meetings, his Szechuan wit and virulence, were endlessly relayed on the people's grapevine. Everyone chuckled when he said of Chiang Ching's cultural attempts, 'A single flower blooms'. And he would say, 'Certain of our comrades slap their cheek until it swells and say: See how fat and healthy I am.' Little Bottle* was becoming a popular hero.

Yet there were ominous signs. Orders for machinery from Western countries had gone down badly in late 1974; production too had lagged, owing to the strikes. I had seen the strikes in textile factories in October 1974. Long rows of peasant horse carts, filled to the brim with raw cotton, standing outside the factories waiting. Hundreds of them outside the gates, and the factories were closed. No one took the cotton in. What would the peasants do if no one was there to pay them for the cotton they had grown?

But by the summer of 1975 the Hangchow silk factories, which had been under a 'small brother' of Wang Hungwen, were working again. Teng had used the army to restore order, and this, although perhaps not quite the way he should have done it, was effective. Abroad the overseas Chinese said that the living standard had been going down and that Teng was trying to bring it up again.

The Party had been studying a new article by Chang Chunchiao, which had Mao's backing – or so it was said – on the 'bourgeoisie in the Party'. It was persuasive, and appeared to me to be a salutary reminder that the danger of a new class, a new mandarinate, was always present. But this danger did not come from the old cadres; it was, rather, the new cadres, the young, promoted by the Four, who exhibited an amazingly swift tendency to become corrupt.

Again a September 30th banquet. I am in the front row of

*A nickname for Teng Hsiaoping.

tables. But now I know (I have been told) what is the matter with Chou Enlai, and that he will not recover.

A man in a wheelchair is pushed in, and some people rise to clap, to crowd around him and shake his hand. It is Lo Juiching, so badly treated in 1966–7. I see Teng Yingchao sitting at a table; she goes up to Lo and shakes both his hands. So I go up to salute her, and to ask her to give Premier Chou my wishes for his health.

The leaders come in, Teng Hsiaoping at their head. There are none of the actors and actresses of Chiang Ching at the tables, as in the previous year. At my table a Western woman leans towards the host, an eminent member of the Friendship Association, and says that she wants to write a biography of that remarkable woman, Madame Mao. She does not know that the wife of the official she is addressing committed suicide and that rumour holds Madame Mao responsible for this death. The official simply nods, and changes the conversation.

Teng's speech was pithy and direct. Unity and stability. And hard work to reach the goal. A speech remarkably free of slogans. But that was Teng all over. He was so forthright that he laid himself open to attack . . .

Wang Hungwen was not there. Teng had just stripped the Hangchow factories of his Mafia friends.

The next evening Madame Soong Chingling invited me to dinner with Rewi Alley and Ma Haiteh. She said, 'Did you see the two sides glare at each other like porcelain dogs?'

When a high member of the Party is ill, to see that all is well done, to procure for him the best of care, a special committee is appointed to supervise the medical staff treating the case.

Why was it that in Chou Enlai's case, the man who headed the committee of supervision was Wang Hungwen?

I went to see George Wu. We both wept bitterly in that October of 1975, thinking of Chou Enlai dying in hospital. His agony would be long and painful.

'Have you seen him, George?'

'Yes, but,' his face screwed up with pain, 'I have been declared untrustworthy by the Minister of Health . . . and that bloody woman is in charge.'

All Chou's enemies were in charge of the case . . . And why was it that the treatment recommended by the best cancer specialist in China was not followed?

'Premier Chou was hounded to the day of his death . . . they would allow him no rest . . . even while we were giving him a blood transfusion, Chiang Ching would ring up and *order* that the transfusion be stopped while she talked nonsense to him, calling it "matters of state".' And George Wu weeps uncontrollably as he tells me this in 1977.

Heart of Ice and her husband, Wu Wentsao, came to see me, and I went to see them. Both of them suffered a great deal, but Heart of Ice never complained. We talked of writing, and of love, of friendship, and of betrayal. Heart of Ice said Chou Yang was now freed, though not yet employed. I told her how much Lu Hsun's widow, Hsu Kuangping, seemed to detest him.

'But she was wrong,' said Heart of Ice. Hsu Kuangping was turned against Chou Yang. Actually he was always good to her. But so many people got turned against each other then.

We talked of writing love stories (she used to write such wonderful ones). 'It's now taboo,' she said, smiling a little. I remembered Hsu Kuangping telling me how, opening a book long after Lu Hsun had died, she had found in it a love poem, dedicated to her.

'Perhaps we must now do this, leave love poems in books to be found by our loved ones,' said Heart of Ice, looking at Wu Wentsao and both smiled, a little shy, startled to find their love so fresh. When they left they walked hand in hand down the hotel corridor.

They are only in their late seventies, and therefore very young.

*   *   *

Norodom Sihanouk was preparing to return to Phnom Penh. I lunched with him and Princess Monique, and with Phoumi Vong Vichit, the Premier of Laos and his wife, on October 1st. Sihanouk looked forward to having a role to play in his country, even if 'the Khmer Rouge are pitiless . . .'

Half the population of Cambodia, three million people, had become refugees in the city of Phnom Penh, which originally held less than 40,000 people. Their evacuation was now taking place. 'It is quite impossible to feed all these people in the city,' said Sihanouk. Some members of his own family had been given spades and told to dig. 'There will be a drastic clean-up. It's not going to be pretty.' In Laos, said Phoumi Vong Vichit, six traitors had been sent out of the country. 'The people were angry. They wanted to execute them.' Sihanouk talked of executions in his country. 'They're drastic,' he repeated, laughing a little nervously. He gave me a tree leaf from the Ho Chih Minh Trail, which I keep preciously.

Before leaving Peking, Sihanouk together with the Khmer Rouge Minister, Khiu Samphan, would see Mao.

'What do you plan to do?' Mao asked.

'We plan to work together,' replied Khiu.

'Good,' Mao said, 'you must be united.'

But instead of using Sihanouk, the Khmer Rouge would hold him and Princess Monique virtual prisoners for three long years. The Chinese were not at all happy about this. 'They're "ultra-left",' they would mutter. The Khmer Rouge was one of the few governments to send congratulations to Peking on the fall of Teng Hsiaoping in April 1976.

In September 1978, I would try to see Sihanouk in Phnom Penh. I wrote to Ieng Sary, the Foreign Minister. Ieng Sary wrote back that I would be welcome in Cambodia, but I could not see Sihanouk. 'In that case I shall not go,' I said to the Ambassador, and wrote back, refusing.

Three months later, in December, the Vietnamese invasion of Cambodia took place. Sihanouk, his wife and their two sons were evacuated, on the very last day before

Phnom Penh was occupied by the Vietnamese, by a special aeroplane from China.

I went to Tibet that year, passing through Szechuan, since the aeroplane for Tibet started at Chengtu.*

Szechua was not doing well. Many thousands of people were going down the river, leaving for other places. There were plays and articles against 'spontaneous capitalism in the countryside'. But Sixth Brother said it was not so much capitalism as ultra-leftism which plagued Szechuan. The private plots had been abolished and the peasants did not like it. He and his wife were once more involved in 'study sessions', and likely to be investigated again.

Third Aunt had everything she needed, and with money one could go into the countryside and buy eggs and meat, both rare in Chengtu. Sixth Brother got on his bicycle at weekends, and searched for food for his mother.

I would tell Chiao Kuanhua of this and other things I had noticed. 'Production seems to be falling.' But he assured me that it had never been better.

I ended my second book on Mao and the Chinese Revolution, *Wind in the Tower*, in the spring of 1975, and on a hopeful note. My euphoria was due to the holding of the Third National People's Congress. Perhaps I should have waited, since there was to be so much change immediately, and all conjectures and conclusions were proved invalid.

My Chinese friends do not blame me for being over-sanguine. They too were caught in the dramatic, the unexpected, the unforeseen. 'In a revolution, people's characters change most swiftly,' they say. 'We learn the heights and depths of human behaviour; and the meaning of loyalty and treachery, in our own hearts.'

On January 8th, 1976, Chou Enlai passed away.

*See *Lhasa, the Open City*.

I was asked on European television and radio networks about Chou; and who I thought would succeed him. 'Teng Hsiaoping,' I replied. 'Everyone in China hopes it will be Teng Hsiaoping. He's hot-tempered and blunt but he's popular . . .'

I would have forgotten my own answer but that my television appearance was reported to China; and that Chang Ying would remind me of it a year later. 'That is what you said . . .' She smiled. 'It was quite right.' It was not courage, but only the fact that suddenly I was on the point of exploding, of exploding as were the people of China, against the Four, and particularly against Chiang Ching. Again I have no explanation; for until then I had tried, despite my dislike, to be fair to her; bending over backwards to defend her . . . But now Chou Enlai was dead. And somehow this released in me what turned to hatred of his enemies.

Even today I weep for him. For no one else, not even Ian Morrison, nor even my father, have I mourned so long.

CHAPTER 9

The Fall of the Four

When Chou Enlai died, I received telephone calls from overseas Chinese in America and in Canada. 'What is going to happen now? We are afraid.' Millions of Chinese were worried. And some even entertained the sacrilegious thought: '*Perhaps* Chairman Mao should have passed away before Premier Chou Enlai . . . then we could have dealt with the White-Boned Devil before she ruined China.' Chiang Ching was now called the Devil, the Plague, the Witch. We all knew the Mao was too old, too feeble, to deal with her; and anyway the bond between man and wife yields not to logic and reason. 'Why does he not get rid of her?' overseas Chinese asked.

We all cared for Mao deeply; and so we kept silent about his wife, although his name and our love for him were besmirched, tainted by her and her companions. And now the hatred proliferated. It extended even into the villages; where in 1974, and again in 1976, private plots were seized, seasoned cadres persecuted, and the production teams were not paid for their sales to the state.

Overseas Chinese abroad kept stoically silent, refused to talk to foreigners, poured out to me their bitterness about the renewed ill-treatment of their relatives . . . one of them condemned to fifteen years of labour for owning records of Western music . . .

And yet, in those years since 1973, Chiang Ching had bought films in America, for her private viewing. My son-in-law, Sidney, had helped some Chinese diplomats to purchase these films, happy in the thought that they would encourage 'cultural exchanges'. But the films were for Chiang Ching's own delectation. I had protested to the Foreign Minister, Chiao Kuanhua, about these purchases in 1974. 'If films are bought the public should see them.' 'Of course, of course,' Chiao had soothed me. But 'of course' nothing was done.

Chou was dead. There was only Teng Hsiaoping to withstand the Four. He quarrelled violently with them at Politburo meetings; he settled strikes with a firm hand – sometimes too firm. 'He shoots all his arrows in one skirmish,' said my friends. 'That's because he is from Szechuan, full of red pepper.' The Four sneered at him: 'How can you trust a man who has to hitch up his trousers under his shoulder blades?' referring thus to his small size. But the people liked him all the better; he had put up major programmes for industry and technology, which the Four condemned as 'poisonous weeds', 'a return of the productive forces revisionist theory', 'the stinking capitalist wind'.

Chou's death elated Yao Wenyuan, who gave a banquet the day after (within a week, I had had the news through the overseas network). But the people mourned greatly. A deep and true sorrow.

Only in autumn 1977 would a film made of Chou's last drive, to his incinerator, be shown in Peking. The Four had tried to confiscate every copy, but courageous newsmen hid parts of the film in their own houses.

A small white ambulance was waiting at the hospital gate. Chou's coffin was taken out; a small simple black coffin, so small. It was placed in the vehicle, which drove off. And suddenly the doctors and nurses who stood there began to wail, and one nurse even sobbed and jumped up and down like a child bereft. It was not faked. And there was no ceremony of any kind.

The little ambulance went on through the wide avenues of Peking, followed by a few cars: Chou's wife, the ministers he worked with, old comrades. No guard of honour. No music. Nothing. It was dusk and all along the avenue, mile upon mile, stood the people. Silent people. The whole city seemed to have turned out to see Chou pass. And in that enormous silence, only the small roar of the ambulance motor was heard.

The million and a half who lined the way had waited many hours for this last glimpse of their beloved Premier. Some had waited since the morning and others had come from work. No outer sign, no lament. Just this terrible silence. And as the ambulance went by, the men took off their caps; the women simply stood. There were no close-ups of faces, the film was too dark. But the immobility was heavy with meaning as was that immense silence in the cold air. It was twelve degrees below zero that evening.

How is it that the Four missed the warning of these unmoving faces?

Chou's body was reduced to ashes, and after the memorial ceremony they were strewn over the rivers and the mountains of China.

Because Chou thus became non-substance, refusing a tangible grave, a monument, embalming, he would remain with us always. From this dust scattered in the air all of us caught spirit and defiance.

The people went home, and in silence grew their anger. Chou became part of themselves, of their ancestors, their family. He who had never had a child was most blessed now; for he became everyone's father, uncle, grandfather. Most blessed in his posterity, all China's children now adopted him. And so the Four lost the people, all of them, even the young and the very young.

In the press – controlled by Yao Wenyuan – within forty-eight hours of Chou's death appeared an article, 'The revolution of education in Tsinghua University occupies all our thoughts.'

Thousands of angry letters were sent to the *People's Daily*. 'We are plunged in sorrow because of the death of our beloved Premier . . . and you dare to put an article on education in Tsinghua . . . what kind of people are you?' Many cancelled the subscription.

The attacks against Teng, 'the unrepentant capitalist roader', and the 'right deviationist wind' he blew, assumed a new intensity.

From January 15th to February 3rd, 1976, meetings of the Central Committee and the Politburo were held to debate the appointment of Chou's successor. It should have been Teng. But such was the opposition of the Four – even Mao Yuanhsin came down from Manchuria to see his uncle and talk ill of Teng – that the end was inconclusive. Mao refused to nominate Chang Chunchiao as Premier, and this is not conjecture, but fact. On February 7th, Hua Kuofeng became acting Premier. Thus the Four, and Teng, were bypassed. A compromise solution.

Hua Kuofeng, the new man from the provinces, had no clique and no powerful patron. But Mao had called him in 1970 from Hunan, to deal with Lin Piao; and he had worked with Chou Enlai since 1971. He had a reputation for hard work and probity. Mao said, 'Hua is noble-minded, not pompous, and good-mannered.' A man who kept his temper, his head, his tongue. He had befriended old Marshal Yeh Chienying, Minister of Defence, when the latter was virtually under house arrest; supplied him with coal and daily necessities.*

'It's us or them . . . heads will have to roll . . . we haven't killed enough,' said Chang Chunchiao meaning: killed enough of the old cadres. 'First bring Teng down, then deal with Hua.'

In April was the Feast of the Dead, *Tsingming*, meaning clear and light. On that day we sweep our ancestors' graves and commune with them; renewing our spirit and strengthening our lives with their memory; for the dead are companionable, benign and powerful if we honour them. And man lives not alone; he blossoms within the fulfilled past and the engendering of posterity.

Already by mid-March, in every factory, school, organization, preparations to mourn Chou Enlai had begun.

*This is celebrated in a painting exhibited in Shanghai in 1978, and seen by the author.

Women came to work with white flowers in their hair. They were asked, 'Why do you mourn?'

'For a relative.'

One cannot arrest two million mourners.

The Four were uneasy. Everywhere incidents: in Kuangchow a young girl suddenly shouting, 'Down with Chiang Ching!' In the night, posters against them: 'Down with the Shanghai gang!'*

The spark came when in the newspapers in Shanghai, Nanking and Wuhan, Yao Wenyuan foolishly caused slanderous articles to be printed against Chou Enlai. Although not naming Chou, they were clearly enough against him; even taking up alleged 'events' in his private life.

The result was immense indignation. In Nanking, in Wuhan, even in Shanghai, bastion of the Four, thousands of letters of protest came to the newspapers. 'Why do you print such filth? We do not believe a word of it.'

Far more was to happen. Nanking city started it. Around thirty thousand people, among them students and young workers, marched upon the newspaper offices in Nanking, shouting and waving banners for Chou Enlai. This also happened in some other cities, although the demonstrations were quickly squashed.

The Nanking garrison was supposed to be under the command of Chang Chunchiao. It is perhaps one of the more feudal features of the Chinese administration – inherited from the past, for the Kuomintang also practised it – that one man should accumulate many diverse functions, which gave him leverage and influence in many quarters. Chang was not only political commissar of the army, he was also the overall head of the Nanking army group.

The military forces in Nanking were ordered to crush the 'counter-revolutionaries'. There were thousands of arrests. But no news of this event filtered into the newspapers,

*They were called the Shanghai Gang or Mafia by the people until it was known, through the circulation of the letters of Chang himself, that Mao had called them the Gang of Four.

although even the train carriages were covered with posters against the Four. By word of mouth, by telephone, or simply by that extraordinary almost biological osmosis which happens in all popular uprisings, people in Chengtu, in Kuangchow, in Kunming, in Peking, knew of the Nanking demonstration almost immediately.

'I heard the news the day after. I went to my room and I was so excited and so enraged with the Four that I started tearing up newspapers and muttering, 'Let them die let them die' . . . I wanted to run on to the streets and shout it to everybody,' said a young girl, an interpreter I met in Szechuan. She had been criticized for trying to keep up her English.

'How did you learn of what happened?'

'A friend of a person I know was on the train from Nanking to Wuhan . . . a friend of mine in Wuhan heard it. She told my aunt, who told me . . .'

The great anger of the people rose, irresistible as lava from a volcano in eruption. In Peking, on April 1st, the children and the adolescents had begun to make white paper flowers, cutting out the petals with scissors, minutely and with love, twisting them skilfully with thin thread or wire. Boys worked on wreaths, with green paper for leaves, and silver foil. All the shops had under the counter supplies of paper, sold by the single sheet. In the textile mill and the post offices and the banks, groups huddled, making wreaths. At night, youths and workers would sit together, composing wall posters; others sat alone, writing poems. There would be thousands of poems, thousands of posters.

My nephews and nieces, and Hualan's nephews, and the children of my friends, and Millie Pei – all the young I know were in this immense people's conspiracy. 'Of course no one organized us. We organized ourselves. All of us wanted to do it. We would have choked with anger if we had not done it.' My niece said, 'In school, we made paper flowers during recreation time. The teachers also made them; and when we had made them, we wrote: To Grandpa Chou, your grandchild who loves you. And then we went to Tienanmen Square, each class walking in orderly manner. We stuck our small flowers on the twigs of the trees.'

When four hundred thousand children between seven and fourteen make four hundred thousand white flowers, pretty soon the trees look as if a snowfall has settled on them. The primary school children now came, school by school marching solemnly up to the square, and no one could stop them. They put their wreaths at the foot of the Monument to the Revolutionary Heroes. They stuck their white flowers on the trees.

Millie said, 'In our university, we were told that we must not leave the campus. The gates were locked. But at four in the morning we went over the wall, hoisting ourselves up on each other's shoulders. Those who had to stay behind handed us their poems. We did this on the nights of April 3rd and 4th.'

By April 2nd, the crowds walking about Tienanmen Square were unusually large. By the 3rd the wreaths were beginning to pile up; and now processions of workers marched into the square, to bring more. On the 4th, the wreaths on the Monument to the Revolutionary Heroes in the centre of Tienanmen Square were piled so high that there was no place left for more. The inscription on the monument was in Chou Enlai's calligraphy.

When the workers saw that no more wreaths could be placed on the monument, they brought their tools and erected scaffoldings; they nailed their wreaths to them. They brought ladders, and hung the wreaths on the lamp-posts round the square. When these were covered, they went further up the avenue; attaching their offerings with stout wire, so that they could not be easily taken away.

The security police came into action. They removed the wreaths. But this also became impossible, especially in the daytime, when hundreds of thousands milled in the square, copying the poems and the posters or reading them aloud for others to write down. People began to sing. 'We went,' say my cousins, 'but we wore mufflers. We knew that the Four had their militia in the square.' The militia now came in lorries to remove the wreaths, the poems and the posters.

On the morning of the 5th, young men and young women stood on platforms and spoke to the crowd, haranguing them with loudspeakers. Groups went about shouting, 'Long live Chou Enlai', 'Down with the pseudo-Marxists'.

It had all been very orderly up to the 5th. But now incidents began. The militia and security police scuffled with and arrested demonstrators; agents of the Four insulted Chou, and were beaten up by the crowd. Later it was alleged that 'counter-revolutionaries' had burnt cars and a jeep, and also a building (a wooden telephone booth). Little damage was done, but many hundreds were arrested on the 5th, and as night came the square was cleared.

The whole incident was written up in great detail by the Hsinhua news agency. And what is quite extraordinary about the write-up is that despite the 'indignation' expressed by the reporters in their article, the delight they felt came through; they even quoted almost in full a poem against the Four:

When I weep, the wolves howl with joy.
I shall shed my blood on the altar of dead heroes.
Lift my head; and my sword shall leap from its scabbard . . .
The Chinese people are no longer ignorant!
Down with false Marxist-Leninists!

Yao Wenyuan was not fooled by the 'indignation'. 'Why did you have to write up this counter-revolutionary incident in such detail?' he raged at the newsmen. He could no longer cover up, minimize, the Tienanmen demonstration after this report.

Thousands of poems – now assembled in two volumes* –

*These two volumes are only a beginning. Every city in China is collecting its poems written for Chou Enlai.

were very clearly against the Four. Posters read: 'We don't want an empress!', 'No Indira Gandhi in China'.

During the next three months the hunt for 'counter-revolutionaries' went on. 'They came to our dormitories, asking each one what we had done on those nights . . . they offered rewards to those who would speak up,' said Millie. In the schools, the children were interrogated about their parents. 'It is revolutionary to unmask the bourgeoisie . . . even if it is your father . . .'

But this 'incident', which was an enormous people's manifestation against the Four, initiated their downfall. Their bluff had been called, and they could only exercise repression. Forty-two youths, it is said, were executed out of hand on the night of the 5th for 'counter-revolutionary activity'. Several hundred were incarcerated. Five thousand were still being investigated when, in October 1976, the Four were arrested.

On Wednesday April 7th, two resolutions in the Central Committee were published. One cited Mao's 'proposal' to strip Teng Hsiaoping of all his posts, but to allow him to keep his Party membership, 'to see how he will behave in the future'. The Tienanmen incident was declared 'counter-revolutionary'. The other resolution was to nominate Hua Kuofeng to be First Vice-Chairman of the Party and appoint him Premier of the State Council.

This was a cruel defeat for the Four, the third in two years. They had shouldered Teng out of the way temporarily, but they had not succeeded in getting 'the seals of power' from Mao; Mao might be misinformed; he was almost isolated by his nephew and his two nurses; Hua Kuofeng and Teng Hsiaoping were denied access to him 'by order of the doctors'; Mao was becoming blind, and unable to walk – but even in his deteriorating state, he would not give power to his wife. It is clear to me that the old man fought, to the last, to keep her from succeeding him.

On April 8th, the Four arranged a counter-demonstration, both in Peking and in Shanghai. Two hundred thousand people were mustered in Peking to celebrate the victory against the 'unrepentant capitalist roader', Teng Hsiaoping. Among those who marched, was my old friend, the Foreign Minister, Chiao Kuanhua.

'Once again they have had their way . . . but in the end, every old door charm shall be replaced by new peachwood,' wrote Chang, quoting an old poem. He had fully expected to become Premier, but he had again been bypassed.

A kind of hysteria now seized the Four. 'All the old cadres naturally become bourgeois,' they declared, as a 'Marxist' truth. This warned of a widespread witch-hunt designed to topple, at all levels, the old and middle-aged cadres, replacing them with youths who swore loyalty to the Four. After all, demography was on their side.

Young gangsters called 'revolutionary rebels' assaulted cadres, stopped workers in almost every plant in China from working, becoming 'slaves of the capitalist road'. In Chengtu, 1,800 youths 'with horns and spikes', specially trained in Shanghai, seized the public security bureaux. They distributed Party cards to anyone who swore fealty to the Four. Out of the thousands of idle youths wandering in the streets (the schools had stopped in summer 1976), they recruited some twelve thousand new Party members in the city. These proceeded to wreck every organization. The structure of the Establishment again broke down.

Yet the people had now realized that the 'wind of capitalism', blowing since 1974, was not due to Teng Hsiaoping, but to the disorder created by the Four, because the only way to survive was by black marketeering, hoarding and bribing; and even printing false money; and Secret Societies, prostitution, everything came back . . .

'It takes ten years to build something, and ten days to destroy it,' the Szechuan cadres would say to me. Beggars and vagrants reappeared; and even opium addicts and drug users among the young, Sixth Brother would tell me in 1977.

Writers and opera stars of Szechuan disguised themselves,

and fled the cities; they went down the great River, as did many thousands of ordinary people, running away from Szechuan. And thus followed a pattern centuries old.

In a hospital in Chungking, a surgeon was called out in the middle of an operation, to be criticized. 'But I cannot leave the patient,' he protested. Nevertheless, he was dragged out to be shouted at. Another surgeon took his place.

A scientist was also attacked. 'When the earth satellite went up in the sky, the reg flag came down to earth . . . down with science, which destroys revolution!' shouted the young who assaulted him. His laboratory instruments were smashed.

The earthquake which started on July 28th in Tangshan had bred waves of counter-shock in Szechuan. The technician in charge of the seismic instruments was told to 'make revolution' and to leave his post. He refused, and was beaten.

In Shanghai a group of 'historians' under Chang Chunchiao rewrote history. Renowned Long Marchers were effaced; or existed only as saboteurs and deviationists, striving against Mao's line. The Revolution had been made by Mao under the inspiration of Chiang Ching.

In Hangchow, again a total stoppage in the factories. Worse, pillage began. The hotels were ransacked. In one factory where the older workers insisted on continuing to work, a woman worker had her hand smashed with a hammer.*

A musician who refused to kneel to the 'Minister of Culture' appointed by the Four, Yu Hueiyung, to beg forgiveness for his crimes was shut in a small room without light for nine months. He came out in October 1976; I would see him in Shanghai. His eyes were still affected.

Some of the young workers jailed after the Tienanmen incident were obliged to feed themselves by kneeling on the floor and lapping the food from bowls, with their hands tied

*Interviewed by the author, January 1977.

behind their backs. 'Never was there such barbarism . . . it was pure fascism,' said many of those who suffered under the Four. 'It was worse than the Kuomintang.'

Breakdown, sabotage, chaos, disorder . . . yet some places were preserved, such as Shanghai; Shanghai had to be shown as *the* model. The factories flourished there, whereas destruction blossomed elsewhere. And this was done to prove that Teng Hsiaoping, and now Hua Kuofeng, could not manage things at all.

I was supposed to return to China in May 1976. But now, with Teng demoted – and it was he who had signed the permission for me to go to Tibet in 1975 – and the Four ostensibly triumphant, I realized that I could not do so without exposing myself to being pressured, or coerced, into serving Chiang Ching.

Because Chiang Ching was a woman, Mao's wife, and because as a doctor, she was for me a medical case, a warped being, I had taken a long time to hate her. I had not understood how dangerous a mean, mediocre mind can be when power is available to it. I said to Vincent and to Cécile Verdurand, and I wrote to a couple of overseas Chinese I could trust, 'If that woman comes to power, I may have to fight against China.'

But this would put my Family in terrible danger. Could I bring disaster upon them and their children, my nephews and nieces?

I went to the Chinese Embassy. The diplomats had their misgivings, but I could not expect them to share their worries with me. I said that, being extremely busy, I would not be able to go to China that year, possibly not before the end of the year, instead of returning, as usual, in May or June.

And that is why, in 1976, I did not go to China until December. I waited. 'There'll be something . . . I can't believe we'll let the Plague run China,' I said to Vincent.

Wind in the Tower was published; I was to be attacked by critics (among them some prestigious Sinologists) for not denouncing Teng Hsiaoping. The next year I would be attacked by other critics for having written some favourable comments on Chiang Ching.

In July and August the frightful earthquake occurred which devastated Tangshan, and caused seven hundred thousand deaths. My niece, daughter of Fourth Sister, went with her nursing team to dig people out, and she stayed awake fifty-three hours on end. 'The earth was all changed. It was as if mud had boiled up in waves,' she said. Hua Kuofeng gathered cadres, sent medical rescue teams, and went personally to tour the earthquake area. The wounded were evacuated to many cities; twelve thousand were taken to Wuhan. Kaimei, a Malayan Chinese doctor in the Wuhan Children's Hospital, worked round the clock for three days, caring for the wounded children.

The Four did not go to the earthquake area. Chiang Ching did not even inquire about it. She was 'resting' at the seaside. Evidence that madness becomes a collective phenomenon, Yao Wenyuan wrote an exultant poem about the earthquake: 'Such natural spasms portend new and wondrous change.' Not a word for the immense desolation, the dead and the wounded, the losses.

The press controlled by him went further. 'Earthquake relief work must not be used as an excuse to stop the criticism of Teng Hsiaoping. Some people want to use relief work to brush aside the mighty surge of revolution . . .' That was actually an attack on Hua Kuofeng.

On September 9th, at ten minutes past midnight, Mao Tsetung died.

The sorrow, the grief at Mao's passing were genuine, deepened by apprehension that China was falling to pieces, that a new era of warlords would come, and civil war. The earthquake and the Yellow River floods – the latter went unreported – were, millions believed, portents of the disasters to come.

* * *

Hua Kuofeng is a quiet man with a mild, deliberate manner.
He had not been inactive, although never involved – as Teng
was – in head-on conflict with the Four.

Since April, as Premier, he accompanied foreign heads of
state to see Mao. He thus managed to meet Mao, and to talk
to him alone. Wang Hungwen, who had been present on
such occasions several times before, was fortunately absent.

Hua Kuofeng obtained from Mao on April 30th a written
and dated message: 'With you in charge, I am at ease.' And a
directive in Mao's hand: 'Act according to past precedent.'

In June, Hua took another step. Mao would no longer be
receiving heads of state; the last occasion would be a meeting
in May with Lee Kuanyew of Singapore. Mao was by then
unable to hold his head straight. It was cruel to keep on
exhibiting him in his condition. Immediately, the Four
attacked Hua in a 'historical' article, comparing him to a
plotting prime minister who had conspired to isolate the
emperor.

In the month from September 9th to October 6th which
followed Mao's death, the fever for the final power contest
was at its height. The Four were now preparing for a 'show
of force'. The workers' militia, which Wang Hungwen had
controlled for some years, would be used; as it had been used
at Tienanmen in April to arrest the demonstrators. There
were three million militiamen available in Shanghai. Each
factory had its militia. The issue of modern weaponry to the
militia began on September 20th. The Four ordered that all
documents sent to the Politburo must come to them. Since
Chang was Secretary of its Standing Committee, this went
unchallenged.

In Paoting, an army corps was told to hold itself ready (the
commander was reckoned a sympathizer of the Four). Mao
Yuanhsin, by then, Deputy Commissar of the 8341 Division
which guarded the leaders in Peking, mustered troops in
Manchuria. Back and forth, between Shenyang, Shanghai
and Peking, went the Four and their allies, preparing a
military seizure of power.

An intensive propaganda drive started, centring on what Mao was alleged to have said to Chiang Ching before expiring: ACT ACCORDING TO THE PRINCIPLES LAID DOWN. Which principles? The principles of the continuing revolution, which they personified. The Four thus claimed to be the heirs of Mao's Thought. Two days before the memorial service to Mao Tsetung on September 18th, this phrase was launched in editorials. At the same time, Yao 'stimulated' letters from all over China demanding that Chiang Ching become Party Chairman. Several hundred such letters were collected . . . pitifully few, by Chinese standards.

But the Four were already outplayed. Hua could show Mao's April 30th handwritten directive: ACT ACCORDING TO PAST PRECEDENT. Also the fact that Hua was nominated First Vice-Chairman meant that he would automatically become acting Chairman of the Party until a new Chairman could be elected by the Central Committee. And as for the distinction between, 'Act according to past precedent' and 'Act according to principles laid down', 'three words in the last formula are incorrect,' wrote Hua. Thus the claim of the Four to be Mao's heirs was denied.

The Four prepared: the coup was to take place on October 13th or 14th.

On October 11th, Monday morning, about 8 o'clock, I was rung up from London by the BBC. Did I know, asked the BBC that Chiang Ching had been arrested over the weekend?

'Is it official?'

'No, just a rumour.'

'Then no comment.'

I could not believe it. It seemed too good to be true.

All my friends in China had the same reaction. 'We could not believe it. Then we went into the streets, walked about, watching to see if other people knew . . .' In front of the wine and liquor shops they saw queues; queues which grew by the minute. 'Then we knew it was true.'

'I went out, and there were people buying wine, so I too bought wine . . . On the street there were people selling autumn crabs: "Three male and a female crab, to go with your wine," they sang. Then I knew that the Four had been arrested. We all bought crabs, and boiled them. We felt that the Four should be boiled alive.' This from my good friend, the eminent painter Huang Yungyu.

And Sixth Brother in Chengtu said, 'I could not believe it . . . but then a friend came and whispered in my ear, and we went into the streets and people were so happy . . . everyone was shaking hands and laughing.'

'Within two days the hospitals were emptying . . . ambulant patients wanted to return to their families, to celebrate . . .' From one of my doctor friends.

China was exuberant. There were monster parades, millions pouring into the streets to celebrate, to beat drums and to dance. 'In Wuhan the steel workers spontaneously went back to work within twenty-four hours. The buses began to run again,' wrote Gladys Yang to me.

'You do realize that this was prepared a year, eighteen months ago? Since April 1975, when Mao said quietly one day to some old veterans in the Politburo, "This problem must be settled . . . if not this year, next year,"' said Ma Haiteh, when I saw him that winter. 'It was Chairman Hua's decision and old Marshal Yeh Chienying. They saved China from disaster by arresting the Four.'

Yeh Chienying, Minister of Defence, was a man of such integrity and discipline that he would not even intervene to save his own daughter or son from jail. For years he had kept quiet, enduring injustice. He saw no one in private. Often he went fishing, all alone.

How the arrests were arranged will probably be revealed one day. But if Hua Kuofeng had not given the order, they could not have been made. And therefore, in my mind, Hua and Yeh cannot be separated in this affair.

In early October, the commander of troops in Paoting –

reckoned a sympathizer of the Four – was told by Wang
Hungwen to march on to Peking. The commander
telephoned the Ministry of Defence in Peking. Then he
countermanded the march. The Manchurian forces were
told by Mao Yuanhsin to march to Peking 'for a change of
garrison'. At a certain point, the commander sat down and
telephoned. Then he marched back to Manchuria.

'It is time.' Yeh Chienying made the gesture of opening his
hand and closing it, as one gathers a handful of grass. Hua
Kuofeng issued the order. The 8341 Division now moved.
They arrested the three men, Chang, Wang and Yao, while
they were preparing to go to a Politburo meeting on the night
of October 6th. They arrested Chiang Ching in her house.

'But I am Chairman Mao's widow, you don't dare to
arrest me,' she screamed.

'You must still come with us,' said the officer in charge.

Hualan told me later, when I was in Peking, that Chiang
Ching's last words before going into captivity were: 'Well,
I've had my revenge on my enemies . . .'

'She gets one *yuan* fifty a day for food, twice as much as I
get,' said Hualan, who loathes Chiang Ching, and holds her
responsible for the deaths in her family. 'I think it's too
much. We should let her starve on three cents a day, as she
did Ho Lung.'

'The Four were duly warned,' said my old friend Yeh. A
week after Mao died, the newspapers began printing mild-
toned articles, quoting Mao's phrase, used in 1971, when he
told the regional commanders of Lin Piao's treachery, 'Unite
and don't split, be open and above board, do not intrigue or
conspire'. This due 'warning' was not heeded by the Four.
But the Chinese people felt satisfied. The Plague had been
handled in a masterly way, 'nobly and with good manners'.
A decent month of mourning was allowed the widow; there
were repeated injunctions not to 'intrigue'; and the arrests
had been swift and clean. No messy conflict. The allies of the
Four were also warned: Give yourselves up, or . . . The
militia, duly informed, turned in their weapons and started

rejoicing with the rest of the population. The art of war is a minimum, not a maximum of bloodshed.

'Never has a new reign begun without some conflict, but this time it has been managed, and this is the most happy augury,' said Lin Lin, my friend. He had suffered enormously for years. He quoted at length from Chinese history, 'Now we are in for a great period, a period of order and harmony, of reconciliation and stability . . . we must not have another Gang of Four. Never again.'

On October 20th I applied to go to China. At the Embassy everyone was smiling; all gloom dispelled.

But I had a nagging, remaining worry. Chiao Kuanhua. What had possessed him to demonstrate against Teng in April? Perhaps he was forced to, and this temporary lapse would certainly be forgiven. Every new reign begins with amnesties, 'great forgiveness'.

I arrived in China and discovered things were not well with Chiao Kuanhua. 'He became a Gang of Four man. But it was the fault of his wife, Chang Handje.' In the midst of the bliss of seeing all my old friends, of listening to their stories, rejoicing with them, sorrowing over the dead, was this ugliness: Chiao's betrayal of Chou Enlai. 'If Kung Peng had been alive this would not have happened,' said Hsing Chiang. And we both were very sad, for now, when we went to Papaoshan to bow to Kung Peng, we would know that perhaps her husband would not be by her side.

Chiao's many friends were grieved. 'How could he do this?' Chou Enlai had been Chiao's protector, mentor, teacher; had elevated him from being a journalist to become Foreign Minister. How could he join Chou's enemies?

'Chang Handje.' She was beautiful. Beauty's snare, weakening a man's resolve. She was ambitious. Some averred that the marriage had been arranged by Chiang Ching.

On April 7th, 1976, the day before the great demonstration against Teng, Chiang Ching had made a threatening speech to all the heads of the ministries and departments of the State Council. 'Some of you have not yet made clear your attitude,' she said. 'We must know where you stand.' And Chiao 'came clear' the next day, shouting 'Down with Teng' and marching, while many other ministers went sick or simply stayed at home.

Chiao would have been forgiven this, I think; so many, so many cadres, had had to outwardly acquiesce, to shout obediently, to wave banners. But he did more. In October, at the United Nations, Chiao made a speech. In his original draft he had used the Gang of Four sentence: ACT ACCORDING TO PRINCIPLES LAID DOWN. And Hua Kuofeng, reading the draft before Chiao's departure for New York, picked out the sentence. 'This is erroneous . . . three words in it are incorrect,' wrote Hua in the margin of the draft.

Since summer's dreadful earthquake, people in China had been cursing 'the Three Witches': Big Witch, Chiang Ching; Middle Witch, the Health Minister Liu Hsiangping (Hippo); and Small Witch, Chang Handje, the Foreign Minister's wife . . .

Perhaps it was fear of suffering all over again, as he had suffered in 1966–7. He was on the lists found in the houses of the Four, marked to become Vice-Premier when Chang Chunchiao became Premier. The Four had lists of those who had to be killed, and those to be promoted. And, in the great renewal of China, I hope he will be forgiven, and will have a place where his talents can be used.

Chiao is not under arrest, merely retired at home.

December in Peking was all talk, talk of Chiang Ching. A wild relief, catharsis, hundreds of stories, some of them exceedingly filthy, about her. 'A prostitute . . . a dirty woman . . . a worn slipper . . .' Even my sisters-in-law Jui and Shuan, so proper, giggle a little at the semi-dirty stories which they hear. Everyone is letting off steam, exhaling jubilant hatred. Third Brother attends the criticism meetings against Peking University tyrants; George Wu attends the meetings against 'the Hippo', ex-minister of Health. They are getting their own back, after years of torment.   In the newspapers, too, there are emotional, sometimes childish tales of the crimes of the Gang of Four. 'They should be tried publicly,' says a Western woman, appalled at the Chinese outburst. These verbal explosions greatly shock Westerners, who think in legal terms. They do not realize that in China 'legality' has never existed. Not in the Western sense.

I do not share in this shattering hatred. I tell Hsing Chiang, 'I know it's relief, and so many have horribly suffered and *must* now talk. But it is not good to do this. Not for Chairman Mao. After all, she was his wife.' But I understand and condone the need for feudal incantation, for exorcism through words of 'the Plague Demons', and especially 'the Woman Plague'. Chiang Ching is the epitome of all evil in China now. But she was also the product of China's evil; of its male oppression, of the thwarted and distorted attitudes to sex and to love in Old China; and she herself, being feudal, acted in turn like a tyrant and an oppressor. I still see her as such: her malady became monstrous evil because of her power. I no longer hate her now, but I hope that she has not hurt too much the cause of women's liberation in China. For now, how easy to fall back into the old pattern: 'See what dreadful things happen when a woman is entrusted with power: In Chinese history always women rulers have been a disaster!' This could have been the reaction of public opinion, leading to a strong backlash against the so painfully acquired new status of women in China.

Fortunately this has not happened. The past cannot return entirely, although there has been regression in the last decade, such as renewed arranged marriages, bartering of brides, dowries, families ruining themselves to acquire an enviable daughter-in-law ... Today the average man in China must give his intended a watch, a sewing machine and a bicycle before she will look at him.

The National Federation of Women has started again to

work. 'The main problems are the alleviation of housework, and family planning,' their leaders say. The women survivors of the Long March, Teng Yingchao, Kang Keching, have picked up where, ten years ago, everything stopped.

Nevertheless, there is bound to be a certain reaction against women, due to the excesses of Chiang Ching. Wife beating, which had been almost abolished, has resurfaced, and was discussed at the National People's Congress meetings in 1979; of course, with the emphasis on the protection of women as equal citizens.

CHAPTER 10

Phoenix China: 1976–1979

Since that freezing December of 1976 after the toppling of the Four when I returned to friends and relatives eager and willing to tell me all that had happened to them, I have not ceased going up and down the land. I have ridden on the new inland railways, visiting out of the way places. I have tape-recorded and interviewed four score of writers, painters, opera stars, musicians, both in provincial towns and in major cities. I have captured their words and their emotions before second thought, prudence, or politics, streamlined them into something more coherent, less revealing. Thus I made mine the happiness and the relief, to which the arrest of the Four gave rise.

For China will never be the same. Everything in its past, recent and ancient, has been exploded and laid bare. In this volcanic eruption, the people have found their own power. They have flexed their muscles and their minds in an exhibition of massive effervescence, and even if there still are persistent attempts to make everything 'as it was before', the present awareness of the millions makes it impossible to return entirely to despotic obscurantism.

The millions of China no longer believe in words, slogans. Words have proved empty, myths have collapsed. 'No more lies.' Everything that is said has to be proved, in action. 'We shall have to rethink and to reword every issue and every problem . . . the language itself must totally change,' I say to my friends. All the questions the people ask must be answered, sooner or later. There must be no more evasion, shirking under pretence of 'state secrecy'. 'The people are no longer ignorant' is the cry of China's workers and peasants, of the young and the old. For the greatest achievement of the thirty years has been literacy at village level; bringing the ability to communicate and to *think*. And the paradox of the Cultural Revolution is that it has destroyed submission, docility, the cowed muteness which accepted that 'leaders' are perforce wiser than ordinary men. So many leaders have proved unworthy: so many acclaimed figures have ended in ignominy. As a result, every child in China knows and feels that he has as much right to his own view as the topmost man in the government . . . for independence of mind, like liberty, must be an experience before it becomes a principle and a habit.

The Cultural Revolution, and the tyranny to which it gave birth, have revealed the Chinese people to themselves. We examine our own twisted feudalist minds and realize that the Four, under cover of revolutionary phrases, were the concentrated essence of what inhibits each one of us still. Everyone says it now.

'We can no longer blame colonialism, the outside world, imperialism, the Kuomintang for what has happened,' say Party members to me. 'We must interrogate our own souls. The fault is there, in ourselves.'

And this clarity of self-knowledge, this widespread self-awareness, means a great deal to China's future. 'Our revolution begins now,' I say to the Yangs. 'Self-knowledge is the threshold we have crossed into the future; now we shall have to think and act in a modern way.'

The feeling that everything must be overhauled – the Party itself, by the Party, interrogating itself on *everything* – is all-pervasive. It gives to the air around us a headiness, and lifts all talk out of conventional courtesy. I am happy and hopeful. If there is one thing that the Chinese Communist Party has shown, through its almost sixty years of life, it is an ability to reappraise, to overhaul itself, its policies and methods. This will now be carried even further. Within the highest councils of Marxist-Leninist philosophers, the topmost cadre schools, a thorough study of the total theory, of all the works from Marx and Mao, will probably have to be undertaken. Already Marxist scholars have begun. After all, the very essence of Mao's innovative talent was not blind obedience, not dogmatism, but the link between 'practice' and 'theory'. Mao departed from the Soviet model in the 1930s because the physical condition of China made it invalid. The scientific search for truth must never lose sight of reality. Theory cannot remain mere phantasm of the mind. It has to work.

The success of the Chinese Revolution was founded upon Mao's unorthodoxy; and today's new Chinese Revolution requires new thinking which discards outmoded postulates.

China: phoenix reborn from its ashes; but the fire has seared us all, and some of us most grievously. A few scholars and artists are very bitter, because of the wasted years. Bitter also people like Sixth Brother. He was courageous, full of self-control; he never let on to me – until now – what he has really suffered. 'Ten years ago I was full of energy, at the height of my power. I wanted to learn and to innovate. But now my brain is not so good, and I feel tired . . . my memory cannot retain new things. I could have done so much. Now I feel diminished.'

But the bitterness cannot last. Diminished or not, the tired old men who come out of jail, out of May 7 schools, who are no longer 'shunted aside', men in their sixties and their seventies, are our greatest treasure, our most precious people. They have the knowledge. They must teach, must bridge the generation gap. And the very fact that they are so desperately needed, heals them, gives them a new lease of life. 'I feel reborn,' says an eighty-two-year-old painter to me. 'I shall now work until I die.' 'The secret of eternal youth is to be needed to our last dying breath,' says George Wu, who is over sixty. All fear but one thing: that their bodies might fail them before they have been able to transmit knowledge to the 'successors'. Teng Hsiaoping tells me, 'I am seventy-five . . . but I am looking forward to working for another twenty years.' In every sector of learning there is a dearth of young specialists – and so our generation, the sixty to eighty-year olds, are mobilizing themselves.

Some of the young say, 'We feel a big black hole inside our spirit. The heart has gone out of us; it is not easy to patch up this vacancy.' But the most common phrase heard at public meetings and symposia which I attend is the following: 'I am still troubled . . . "they" might return . . . and therefore I shall not come out with all I think.'

Defeatism, cynicism, fear of a return of tyranny – these are unavoidable. We, the old ones, exhort and encourage and try to reassure. It is up to us to save the 'lost generation'. There will not be another Gang of Four!

I say, 'Unless you get off the fence, and manifest your thinking, it will start again. Weakness and vacillation will certainly play into the hands of small despots waiting in the shadows to pounce.'

My friends say to me, 'You have manifested yourself. You have very clearly taken sides.'

The doubtful and hesitant are many, but courageous people, young and middle-aged and old, who come out with their opinions, are also in great numbers. Among them is the great painter Huang Yungyu, in his late forties. He endured vicious treatment but went on working, refusing to give in. 'The Four throve on our fear. Stand up to tyrants and bullies, and they recoil. Had they come to power, I would have gone into the mountains and started a guerrilla war.'

Everywhere the old and middle-aged are tremendously busy, training the young. And although there are hopeless cases, young men and women permanently crippled in mind, who do not want to work or to study and will never be recuperated, we discover, to our joy, that there are also millions of youths whom the Cultural Revolution has matured, made wise, thoughtful beyond their years. We call them the 'thinking generation'. They use their brains without fear; they no longer think in the feudal way. They reason from cause to effect, they work, and work hard. We discover much talent, intelligence, reasoning power, eagerness for knowledge. 'In ten years we may have made up our losses, if all goes well,' some of the educational experts say to me. But if one asks these youths what they believe in, they grin and say, 'We wait and see.' I think this is healthy scepticism. It is up to us to create material and spiritual improvement, so that they can believe the system works. The thinking generation must be made to participate at all levels in decision-making processes; this will create enthusiasm, responsibility. Otherwise frustration will set in.

The present Chinese leaders know that in order to succeed, the people must be with them. For this they must ensure stability and peace, food in abundance and consumer goods.* But above all they must give constitutional guarantees of rights and liberties for the individual. This is where the new breakthrough has come. 'Twenty years ago you said to Kung Peng: Democracy in twenty years,' Fourth Sister reminds me. 'Now we speak of democracy all the time.'

Industrialization, modernization, is necessarily accompanied by social changes. It is not enough simply to buy machines, put up factories, embark on crash programmes for the construction of steel and oil plants. The whole texture of thought and action, the approach to knowledge – everything must change. And the Party leaders say this openly, officially. Change is now inevitable (or so we devoutly hope).

'Essential for success in China's four modernizations is democracy.' Mao's major speech of 1962 on democracy is reprinted. This means, of course, 'socialist democracy'.

These words: democracy, law, constitutional rights, are heard in all the meetings held since 1977. They are the main themes of the assemblies of the National People's Congress, which, far from being a 'rubber-stamp body' (as Western reports used to call it), is now forceful and exceedingly vocal

*Already in Szechuan in 1978 no more rationing was needed; meat was abundant, and cheap.

as the highest body of authority in the land. At the Congress, the Party members are in the minority. 'They used to sit right in front, as if leading the meetings . . . now they sit scattered, with non-Party delegates.'* The most astounding and severe criticisms of 'privileged high cadres', of corruption and high-handedness among Party officials, have been heard at the Congress. Guarantees that the total illegality which became in the Cultural Revolution the rule of the Four should not recur are the most urgent demand. 'Stalin used legal methods to commit illegalities,' I remark to a friend who is a member of the Congress. 'A legal system alone cannot guarantee legality, justice. In Russia courts of law condemned people to death. The courts cannot become the instrument of a political Party.'

In China, where courts of law have been in abeyance (as bourgeois manifestations) during the last few years, 'mass movements' have taken the place of law. Every organization, unit, assembled its employees, its staff (called 'the masses'), and conducted its own 'judgments'. 'This judgment by the masses . . . the Four made the masses carry out their foregone conclusions; revile people they had already decided to label as counter-revolutionaries. To utilize so-called public opinion so outrageously . . . probably no other country has ever done this on such a large scale,' say my friends.

For the intelligentsia, the worst of these mass meetings (which condemned them to doing menial work such as cleaning toilets) was the humiliation, not death. Comparatively speaking, very few people died. Mao's injunction against the death sentence remained effective throughout; though of course deaths did occur.

Now all such 'mass movements' are strictly forbidden. I remember interviewing the Minister of Justice in 1956, and being told about the project for framing laws, a civil code, a penal code, a juridical code.† The then Chairman of the

*The NPC has about 4,000 members.
†See *My House Has Two Doors*.

National People's Congress, the old and revered Tung Piwu, a founder of the Communist Party of China in 1921, had said that 'mass movements must give place to a regular system of laws and courts of law.' But this was not done until over twenty years later, when at last his words are being put into practice, with the solid backing of the new Party Chairman, Hua Kuofeng, and the government.

'We have no tradition of democracy,' says Hsia Yen to me. He was the Vice-Minister of Culture who suffered so much because he had clashed with Chiang Ching over films that she had denounced. 'We had legalists and codes of law in imperial times, but a distinction was made between some men and others. The mandarin was not punished as was the common man, and the Emperor was above the law. It has always depended upon the "upright, superior man", the mandarin, to fulfil his duty towards lesser beings, to see that "justice" was administered, but the idea of equality before a common law has been foreign to us.'

Now everything has changed. 'All men are equal before the law,' repeats Peng Chen, the ex-Mayor of Peking, who has been rehabilitated. And Marshal Yeh Chienying, whose words carry enormous weight in China, says it even more explicitly: 'All citizens are equal before the law, which is not subject to the will of any leaders.' This is momentous. It means, in the final analysis, an almost independent judiciary. It certainly means that high-ranking bureaucrats are amenable to law at last.

There will be long hard battles to wage. Almost daily now, in the newspapers, ardent 'thinking' young men dedicated to truth launch attacks against the arrogance, high-handedness and the privileges of high cadres; against their corruption. They place themselves above any law; and consider that their authority must be absolute. They request – and obtain – perks in every way: houses and cars, and university entrance without examinations for their offspring. Anything like people's rights and liberties are considered by them as dangerous to their position, their status.

'As long as there is no democracy, we shall continue to have palace intrigues and palace coups,' warns Hsia Yen. Around any high bureaucrat congregate sycophants, flatterers . . . they build for him a cohort of power, a clique, echelon by echelon; it is very hard to get rid of such cliques.

But the people's demand for legal guarantees does not go unheeded. Encouraged by Teng Hsiaoping and Hua Kuofeng, and bolstered by popular opinion, lawmakers proceed to frame a series of codes of law, a system of justice which has not existed before in China. At the same time, the government orders hundreds of thousands of people to be rehabilitated. The Tienanmen incident after Chou Enlai's death becomes a landmark in the history of China, a glorious anniversary, on a par with China's famous May 4th, 1919 movement;* it becomes the capture of the Bastille in the French Revolution; it is the Boston Tea Party of the American Revolution.

The new leadership and the lawmakers and the Congress go further. By January 1st, 1980, there will be the introduction of the secret ballot at village and district assembly level. This is of momentous significance. It means that the grassroot peasant organizations (and peasants still form 85 per cent of the population) will freely elect their heads of villages and representatives, and that these need not be Party members. In factories, too, the workers will secretly elect their representatives and their administrators from among competent, qualified staff, without 'Party leadership' committees interfering. Neither will the production and management of factories be subject to constant political surveillance. The most resented practice, which grew especially during the Cultural Revolution, was the 'Party leadership' committees having to be referred to at every point, for every activity. Nothing could be done without permission. Any initiative had to pass through them, and since they were ignorant of new techniques, and their power

* See *A Mortal Flower*.

and authority resided in negativism, they would condemn any new idea as 'adventurism' or 'bourgeois'. 'It got to the point where one couldn't fart without asking Party leadership permission,' said an exasperated foreman to me. 'The Party leadership committees even gave themselves the right to refuse permission to marry to young couples,' said a girl worker, who had defied the 'leadership', had married, and not only been ostracized but treated almost as a criminal.

There have been other changes, including a thorough revision of the class origin concept. The intelligentsia are now stated to be part of the working class. There is no distinction between mental and manual labour. Both are equally valid, and 'intellectuals work very hard.' They are no longer the 'stinking ninth class', the butt of every political campaign. I do not know what this big dent in dogma will ultimately lead to.

In the villages the peasants have put up petitions pleading for the progeny of their former landlords to be treated as ordinary peasants and commune members. 'The old landlords who oppressed us are dead. To maintain "class origin" distinction is to shift the sins of the dead parents on to their innocent sons and daughters, who are hardworking people, as we are.'

Of course there is a reason for this. Villages in China are clan villages. Quite often the landlord was also a 'relative'. Thus to maintain 'class origin' created turmoil, discontent, during the Cultural Revolution.

'The people have an innate sense of justice, moderation. We must trust them,' say the Congress delegates.

In 1979 the people are greatly pleased by Chairman Hua's report on the national economy because he gives figures, not percentages; economic indicators, and with so much frankness, without hiding a single unpleasant fact. Immediately the people respond with approval and enthusiasm. I think back to Chou Enlai, who always wanted figures, not percentages, but was not authorized to quote anything in his reports but percentages on so many occasions.

Change, but also continuity. Not all these breakthroughs are new thoughts. Some were conceived, but laid aside, way back in the 1950s and 1960s. I find myself going back to my old notebooks, finding glimpses, suggestions, of what is now being attempted.

'China must follow her own road.' Of course it will be 'socialism', but adapted to China. Capitalist development is not possible, even though some methods borrowed from capitalist expertise will surely be tried. But because of the vast and informed population of China, we cannot do what India can still do: use 120 million Untouchables in a semi-feudal countryside to feed the prosperity of the cities. In China the peasantry still determines the rise and fall of dynasties, socialist or not. 'We cannot have trouble in the rural areas. Immediately the whole economy is affected,' says a vice-minister to me. 'The discontent of youth in the cities is only a minor matter. But no system in China can be stable without a contented peasantry. We must raise the living standards and the purchasing power of the peasantry swiftly. We must decentralize industry, bring it to the villages. We must continue to have informed, literate peasants.' Giving priority to the peasantry (which Mao also insisted on) means that no 'crash industrialization' programme, concentrating all investment in heavy industry, is possible. Such over-sanguine projects (mooted at first in 1977 and 1978) have had to yield to more reasonable, even if slower-paced development plans, with more investment in rural areas.

Industrialization is idealized by the Third World. But it has never provided the means of coping with unemployment. On the contrary, it produces further unemployment. Europe, in its industrial heyday of the nineteenth century, exported its surplus labour to America, to Australia, to Canada. Periodic and numerous wars in Europe took care of extra numbers; even created, temporarily, labour shortages.

But China cannot solve in the same manner the problem of twenty million young who come on to the labour market every year. 'We have no limitless, unpopulated Siberia to send people to, as did the Tsars for nearly two hundred years,' say my friends. 'We shall have to find a way to solve our own population problems within the limits of our own land.' There must be, first of all, intensive, nationwide family planning, which I have considered of prime importance for over twenty years. At last, all over China, I get accurate figures; particularly in Szechuan province, which contains 10 per cent of China's peoples, and where family planning is now undertaken very seriously. Five *yuan* a month will be given to the one-child family. Its bestowal will cease if the family acquires a second child. In Pihsien, my native town, the birth rate has dropped to 6 per 1,000 in 1978. Even so, China's population will pass the billion mark very soon, and by the year 2000 we may have 240 million couples able to procreate. Obviously we cannot merely industrialize. We must find work, productive work, and food, for all these young millions, and satisfy their rising expectations. We must, therefore, find our own road to cope with these problems.

Bureaucracy – one of the Cultural Revolution's targets – has not diminished but increased. Besides the old cadres returning, there are new cadres who have been promoted during the last ten years. Two bureaucracies, uneasily co-existing. The Party has grown from 17 million in 1966 to 35 million in 1976. How many of the new members are hidden partisans of the Four? How many are obscurantists who would like to get rid of all the old cadres? To bolster themselves, they quote Mao, in and out of context.

Anyone who has read Mao thoroughly realizes that he was a populist; that he tried hard to give the people of China more voice in their own affairs; that he tried to curb bureaucracy; that he retained the eight non-communist parties of China when some Party chiefs wanted to abolish them. These parties only represent altogether 1 per cent of the population, but, said Mao, 'They are a long-term necessity'. No other socialist country, no other head of a communist party, has kept alive and functioning – even on a minor scale – potential rivals.

Mao remains China's great liberator. Without him, the present-day rebirth could not have happened. And even if the Cultural Revolution was monstrously deviated and twisted, and brought hardship and suffering, yet it left no one in China untouched, unstirred, or unthinking. History's verdict on it is not yet; it may be kinder than expected.

Even if Mao himself, in his last years, was incapable of living up to his vision, he still remains the man whose great dreams and words wrought wonders. China cannot do without him. There will not be, because there cannot be, a 'demaoization'. Mao's place in Chinese history is unequalled.

In January 1977 old Marshal Yeh Chienying receives me. My father liked him very much; he looked after the engineers so well who were restoring the coal mines at Tatung. Yeh Chienying, with Hua Kuofeng, laid the plans for the arrest of the Four.

Marshal Yeh is eighty years old, but he is certainly not doddery, and there is instant liking between us. He talks to me as a friend, plunging right into the heart of the matter without any circumlocution. 'What do you think of the Vietnamese incursions? They've been shooting at us since late 1975. It's the Polar Bear,* no doubt, instigating it. We shan't say anything yet. We'll give them a chance.'

He tells me that Albania now disagrees with China's new stance. 'But we shall ignore them. We had to tell them we had no spare rice for them this year.' For more than two decades China has given rice, and many other things, to Albania.

Marshal Yeh speaks of the Gang of Four. But not of what

* The USSR.

his relatives suffered. By his side is his faithful secretary, who stuck to him when he was under house arrest. He says, 'We shall certainly give work to Teng Hsiaoping.' It is January; Teng will be back in July. Marshal Yeh knows, as I do, that people in China walk about the streets with little bottles full of red ink, which they hang on trees. Teng Hsiaoping's nickname is Little Bottle, and the red ink means that people think he is a true revolutionary.

'We shall be neither soft-handed nor soft-headed,' says Yeh mildly, and this means that the Four and their close allies have no chance at all. The people apprehended or punished must be important malefactors, not the small fry. Extensive random purges, self-defeating, would shatter the demoralized Party at all levels.

'We want, we need stability and unity,' says Teng Hsiaoping to me when I see him in September 1977. 'It is good that the Party Chairman is a younger man. I do not want to be Chairman or Premier. I am seventy-five and all I want to do is to be useful. We need a young Chairman, long continuity in the Party.'

I am also received by Chairman Hua. It is true that he is a man most calm, of few words, not at all like the ebullient Teng. He has great poise, and I think back to what I have been told about him: 'Noble-minded, not mean; good-mannered, and very cool-headed'.

Thus am I integrated in China's rebirth, accepted at last as I am, and everything I have done has acquired meaning, is a minute stitch in that great tapestry of living and doing wrought by the many millions of China. I am linked with them now, more than ever. But at the same time, at last, totally liberated.

CHAPTER 11

The End and the Beginning

China is thirty years old and I am over sixty. In these thirty years I have lived through her an abundance and a multiplicity of lives, emotions and passions. I have pursued my beautiful chimera with Chinese obstinacy; yet I have not ignored or cast away other gifts of living, other lands and peoples. I have friends all over the world. And if I do not write about them, that is not forgetfulness, only lack of space in this book.

Neither do I forget how much Europe and America, Australia and India, South East Asia and so many other lands gave me, enlarging my horizons, until the whole world became my home, until my roots extended and broadened to encompass the round earth. A harvest of knowledge is beyond price, and I keep on learning.

But this book is about the fixed star of my self-completion, the one I had to follow despite all hazards. In doing so, I was only following in the footsteps of my Chinese and Belgian heritage, continuing the story which was begun at the turn of the century.

My father. I have a photograph of him when he was nineteen, leaving Szechuan province to go to Europe in 1903 to study engineering. He was to return in order to build railways in his province. But when he came back in 1913 China was torn by internal wars, and until 1949 my father coped with war and destruction, and kept the railways running, patching them up, making do.

My mother. That stubborn woman I hated with such utter love; and how beneficial and stimulating this hate proved, pushing me to do all the things she did not want me to do! And now I like her, know what she gave to me, although my mind is not built as hers was. She braved all the prejudices of her day, her staid Belgian family, to fall in love with a Chinese. She came to China with him, and gave birth to eight children, and lived in the stations along the railway lines of China. Their decades together were of sorrow and pain and insecurity, of war and running away and making do; and seeing their children despised for being Eurasians. Only I had the courage (or the foolishness) to scream against the general contempt for Eurasians, 'But we are the future.' I stuck to my 'foolishness', and in this extravagance I was like her when she chose Papa, deliberately becoming pregnant to force her marriage.

But it is from Papa, from being born in China, from all my childhood and growing up there that I have this inescapable passion and obsession with China. In this I have been, all unknown to myself, a Chinese intellectual of my generation and of my time. All my reactions, everything I have done, has always been conditioned by this inner prompting of the heart, of which I am only now fully aware.

I think of three childhood scenes perhaps responsible for my obsession, since they constantly recur to me. One is of our rickshaw coolie, and his back. He pulled me and my sisters, this man, in those terrible days of Old China when men were used as beasts. He was beautiful. I think I was six years old; and my first erotic experience was seeing his back, naked in the hot summer, glistening with sweat. He was so beautiful that even today my heart is seized by the remembrance of his back, and I smell it again.

The second is of the dead babies wrapped in newspapers which I saw on my way to school in the blizzards of winter. Their purple-black faces like rotting fruit sometimes protruded from the frozen package.

The third was going to the Catholic church with Mama, hacking our way through the beggars clawing and whining, and the white stones for eyes of the blind beggar children.

These, and not intellectual conviction, explain my commitment. It is almost biological; only later would come reinforcing knowledge and understanding. But I had to live by what was imprinted in my cells, remaining averse to and suspicious of high-flown abstractions, but totally engaged to that smell and savour and warmth, that feel of the tide, blood beat, which is for me the people of China. With others, exultant ideologies may have priority, but it has never been so with me. I shoulder and make do with systems, with ideologies. I am not committed to any. Only one thing concerns me: in the great sweep of history, will this or that system have been another step forward for the Chinese people? They are the only 'side' I am on.

I often pass in Peking the hospital where as typist not quite fifteen years old I earned money in order to go to university, to study and to become a doctor. On to Yenching University, and then a scholarship to Brussels, to study medicine. But the Japanese invaded China, and this old biological stir took over: I could *not* stay in peace in Europe, studying, when there was war in China. I gave up scholarship, studies and a boy friend. I returned to China. I was twenty-one.

I married on a misunderstanding: that Pao and I would serve China together. Then I discovered what 'feudalism' meant. I lived it. For seven years I endured the illogicality, the madness of a feudal mind and its self-torturing angers and its reasoning by symbolism. For seven years Pao tried to 'remould' me. Thought remoulding was practised by the Kuomintang. His was by physical beating; striving to teach me proper humility and virtue because I had not been a virgin at marriage.

He scarred me for ever, deep down in my woman being. I never completely recovered, but today how grateful I am to him, how grateful! For his training so well enabled me to understand China in all her many ambiguities and contradictory facets. It enabled me to understand Chiang Ching, Mao's wife; and her paranoia and her pursuit of revenge. It also increased my conviction and hope that one day, one day, the Chinese people would grasp their own destiny . . .

London during the war, and again medicine. And then

again the stir, the crazy hankering, making me leave for Hong Kong. And there came to me, at last, love. Ian Morrison. He will be with me always. I knew then the great marvel and enchantment of love; it cured me, almost. And after that life was kind, and even fame came, but it never meant a great deal to me. When it came to choosing what I would do, I would always choose the loyalty of my emotions. Not for fame or money or opportunity.

And so I had to go back to China once again, only to find that there was no place for me at the time. I waited. Twenty years. And lived divided in a divided world, whose divisions I would never accept. The metaphysical distortion does not inhabit my spirit. For me good and evil are two faces of the same coin, not mutually exclusive but intimately bound.

Twenty years, and today comes my harvest, so abundant that I shall not have enough of the next twenty years to use it up. Before me a whole new generation, a China reborn. My books will one day help them greatly to know how to believe without faith; how to keep faith with oneself and serve Man's cause with a clean heart. I want to help others to write their stories; the young will need to know them. Stories of courage and loyalty and unshaken devotion. Because I have refused to see the world in white/black, good/evil terms, all worlds are mine. I have built bridges which many people will cross from one civilization and culture and mode of thinking to another. Bridges of goodwill.

Sometimes I am told that I have sacrificed 'popularity and success' by 'giving up' writing love stories and novels, writing all too serious books. But I could not do otherwise, from 1966 until today, during the Cultural Revolution. I would despise myself today had I not *also* been blocked, even though no visible compulsion existed, by something stronger than compulsion. Just as in 1938 I gave up my precious studies to return to China, so during the Cultural Revolution I could not face entertaining readers in the West while my colleagues and friends were undergoing great stress, were unable to write. I was as much a prisoner as they were of the

Cultural Revolution. And perhaps, in the end, the result will be a great burst of creativity . . .

Now it is over. I am liberated, as they are. They are writing, creating, in a frenzy, making up for the lost years. I have garnered such a harvest of love and care that twenty years will not be enough to set it down. Not for me the thin gossamer of shadows, but love, with its many faces, and the infinite diversity of the human heart in love. Not only the love of another human being. Not only that urgency between the legs so often described. All this and more. The real substance and the reality of love.

I have not missed love.

Patient and observant and watchful and silent and joyous and enduring for twenty-three years now with me. Vincent.

Vincent, who has let me work out my magnificent obsession and hunt my dream. Who has endured days and weeks and months when I saw him not, heard him not, even though he was with me. Because I thought of China. And yet all the time he was there; comforting me, his arms warm around me, cradling me. Giving all of himself to my fabulous other passion. Not because he was resigned, but because he loved me. All of me. Without trying to change me in any way. Can many women boast of having been loved like that?

Vincent. Essential as earth itself; forgotten at times as earth, lifegiving and bounteous, is forgotten . . . yet never lost.

Vincent, bringing me another world: the world of India. And all the amazement and wondrous new ways of looking at everything and all things that are India.

India. China. Together half the world's peoples.

'Vincent, how could you stand it all these years?' He looks at me; his eyebrow goes up (the left one). He fits into no niche, evades all description. He does not correspond to any of the dreary catalogue of stereotypes which men live by. Vincent just is.

Vincent loves me. It is his universe and the explanation of the universe for him. He is so sure of his love that he never questions it or worries about its existence. Love is like the sun. The sun shines. Even at night the sun is there. One has only to wait until the night is over. He waits without waiting, in the tranquillity of night.

'I would have been bored with any other woman. With you, I never know what is going to happen next. How can I ever bless God for letting you be with me?' says Vincent.

'Let's go back to the Himalayas, where we began,' I say. 'Now I really can write a love story. Because China is in the hands of her own people, at last.'

I want to write about love: the love of Heart of Ice for her husband; when they held hands gently going down that dim hotel corridor in Peking together. I want to write about my friend Yeh and his wife, and her long waits in the dark nights by the bus stop . . . seven years, every day, waiting, not knowing whether he would or would not be on the last bus . . . I want to write about so many, so many loves; about what it is like to grow young with love when one is old.

'Autumn is the best time,' says Vincent. 'We shall go to the Himalayas in autumn. Autumn is the time of the golden sun and the innocent sky.'

In another twenty years, perhaps, I shall say to Vincent, 'Do you remember when sunlight fell on the slight twigs and our ears heard the beating of a bird's wing?'

I hear it now, the beating of great wings. Perhaps it is the phoenix of my heart; but perhaps it is only the friendly sparrow flying on to my balcony, to pick at the breadcrumbs I scatter.

When calm and lovely death shall come for me, it will add to my treasure trove of love. I shall be one of a goodly company. How can I forget what the dead gave me? Chou Enlai and Chen Yi and Kung Peng . . . how strong is their whisper in my spirit: 'None of us live for ourselves alone. That is the way of the beast; the way of Man is to live for others, for posterity.'

And this is what I too have tried to do.

A selection of titles by Han Suyin available in
Panther Books

China: Autobiography, History

The Crippled Tree	£2.50	☐
A Mortal Flower	£2.50	☐
Birdless Summer	£2.50	☐
My House Has Two Doors	£2.50	☐
Phoenix Harvest	£1.95	☐

Novels

A Many-Splendoured Thing	£1.95	☐
Destination Chungking	£1.95	☐
. . . And the Rain My Drink	£1.25	☐
The Mountain is Young	£2.95	☐
Cast But One Shadow and Winter Love	60p	☐
The Four Faces	£1.25	☐

Non-Fiction

The Morning Deluge (Volume 1): Mao Tsetung and the Chinese Revolution 1893-1935	£1.75	☐
The Morning Deluge (Volume 2): Mao Tsetung and the Chinese Revolution 1935-1953	£1.75	☐
Wind in the Tower: Mao Tsetung and the Chinese Revolution 1949-1976	£1.25	☐

To order direct from the publisher just tick the titles you want
and fill in the order form.

All these books are available at your local bookshop or newsagent, or can be ordered direct from the publisher.

To order direct from the publisher just tick the titles you want and fill in the form below.

Name _____

Address _____

_____

Send to:
Panther Cash Sales
PO Box 11, Falmouth, Cornwall TR10 9EN.

Please enclose remittance to the value of the cover price plus:

UK 45p for the first book, 20p for the second book plus 14p per copy for each additional book ordered to a maximum charge of £1.63.

BFPO and Eire 45p for the first book, 20p for the second book plus 14p per copy for the next 7 books, thereafter 8p per book.

Overseas 75p for the first book and 21p for each additional book.